THE PICKERING MASTERS

THE WORKS OF DANIEL DEFOE

General Editors:
W. R. Owens and P. N. Furbank

THE NOVELS OF DANIEL DEFOE

THE NOVELS OF DANIEL DEFOE

General Editors: W. R. Owens and P. N. Furbank

Volume 5:

THE LIFE, ADVENTURES, AND PYRACIES, OF THE FAMOUS CAPTAIN SINGLETON (1720)

Edited by
P. N. Furbank

LONDON
PICKERING & CHATTO
2008

Published by Pickering & Chatto (Publishers) Limited
21 Bloomsbury Way, London, WC1A 2TH

Old Post Road, Brookfield, Vermont 05036, USA
www.pickeringchatto.com

BRITISH LIBRARY CATALOGUING IN PUBLICATION DATA

Defoe, Daniel, 1661?–1731
The novels of Daniel Defoe
Part 1, vols. 1–5. – (The works of Daniel Defoe) (The Pickering masters)
1. Defoe, Daniel, 1661?–1731 – Criticism and interpretation 2. Adventure stories, English 3.
Adventure stories, English – History and criticism
I. Title II. Owens, W. R. III. Furbank, Philip Nicholas
823.5[F]

ISBN-13: 9781851967483

Typeset by P&C

Printed in Great Britain by the MPG Books Group

CONTENTS

INTRODUCTION

The title, *The Life, Adventures, and Pyracies, of the famous Captain Singleton*, gives us a hint as to Defoe's conception of a 'criminal' novel: that is to say, that it should trace the steps by which the name of a wrongdoer became celebrated and a household word. It is so with the 'famous' Moll Flanders, whose fellow-thieves give her this name, which she makes 'as famous as any thief of my sort ever had been at *Newgate*, and in the Old Bayly';[1] and likewise *The Fortunate Mistress* is the history of a courtesan who (having been given the fashionable nickname of 'Roxana'), becomes celebrated 'all over the Court End of Town'.[2] As for the 'famous' Captain Singleton, he eventually makes the world so hot for himself, while becoming an immensely rich pirate, that he does not believe it possible ever to return to England, and only in the end does so on the understanding that he and his partner in crime shall keep their identity entirely secret: shall dress in 'Grecian' robes and never speak a word of English in public.

It is another convention of Defoe's, in the first few pages of a novel, to furnish the hero or heroine with a dominant character trait, on which much of the plot will depend. With Crusoe it is restlesness; with Moll Flanders a determination to rise in the world; with Roxana a species of obduracy and a passion for independence. In *Captain Singleton*, as early as the fourth page, we are given a hint of the trait that will dog Bob Singleton nearly to the end. It is indifference, *anomie*, an absence of hope or fear. As a boy in his early teens, returning with his kindly master from a voyage to Newfoundland, their ship is captured by an Algerine rover, and he sees his master 'very barbarously used', but, he tells us, he is 'not much concerned' (or at least not until the Turks seize him also and submit him to *bastinado*).[3] The

---

1 *The Fortunes and Misfortunes of the Famous Moll Flanders* (London, 1721), p. 323.

2 *The Fortunate Mistress* (London, 1724), p. 215.

3 *Captain Singleton* (1720), below, pp. 20–1. All further references are to this edition and are given in parentheses in the text.

1

English ship is rescued by two Portuguese men-of-war, but again he is not 'suitably sensible of my deliverance' (p. 21). His master dying in Lisbon from his wounds, Bob Singleton – having no home to return to and no friend in the world except the ship's dog – comes near to starving, until an old Portugese pilot takes him under his care. They join a Portuguese ship *en route* for Goa, and it begins to dawn on Bob's utterly ignorant mind that he might as well learn something, and what he is quickest to learn is to thieve and to be a bad sailor. 'I think I may say', he remarks uncharitably, 'they [the Portuguese] are the best Masters for Teaching both these, of any Nation in the World' (p. 22). Indeed, he is 'as ripe for any Villainy as a young Fellow that had no solid Thought ever placed in his Mind could be supposed to be' (p. 27). Being maltreated by his protector, the old pilot, he plans to murder him, and only fails to because, on their arrival in Madagascar, there is an abortive mutiny, which he joins, and for which he expects to be hanged. But again, he says, 'I do not remember any great Concern I was under about it' (p. 26). In fact, what he calls his 'stupidity' proves to be an advantage to him in these dire circumstances, 'for it left my Thoughts free to act upon Means of Escape and Deliverance in my Distress, however great it might be; whereas my Companions in the Misery were so sunk by their Fear and Grief that they abandoned themselves to the Misery of their condition' (p. 27).

He and his mutinous companions are not in fact hanged but are left stranded in Madagascar, and it is not long before the clear-headed and motiveless Singleton emerges as their leader. The Malagasies appear brutish and unfriendly, and the party determine to escape. But how, they ask themselves; and to where? To build a seagoing ship seems to them to be beyond their resources. At most they can build a canoe, but it is hopeless to think of embarking in such a craft for the distant coasts of India or Africa. At this point Singleton, who so far has not spoken in the debate, says he agrees, yet none the less they ought to build a canoe. The rest are puzzled, but soon his reasoning is made clear. Their business is to cruise along the coast of the island in their little boat and seize upon the first vessel that is better than their own, 'and so from that to another, till perhaps we might at last get a good Ship to carry us whither ever we pleased to go' (p. 37). The suspicions of the elderly gunner, who has already had his eyes upon the young Singleton, are confirmed. Singleton, he tells him, has 'commenced Pyrate very young', and he needs to 'have a Care of the Gallows'. Nevertheless the Portuguese, who nickname him 'Captain' Bob, act upon his plan, it being well suited to his ingrained indifference. 'For we were upon a Voyage and no Voyage, we were bound *some* where and *no* where; for tho' we knew what we intended to do, we did really not know what we were doing' (p. 42). As for himself, he told his companions, 'truly I was on no Side, it was not one Farthing Matter to me ... whether we went or stayed, I had no home, and all the World was alike to me' (p. 45).

It is at this point of the novel that the emphasis changes, for the moment, from Singleton and criminality to the wonders and terrors of an unknown continent. For with the aid of materials from a wrecked Dutch ship the crew at last contrive to build a boat, in which they cross the sea to Africa, and there they take 'one of the rashest and wildest, and most desperate Resolutions that ever was taken by man' (p. 54): that is, to travel overland right across the continent, from their landing place in Mozambique to Angola or the Guinea coast.

Knowledge of Africa, apart from the coastal settlements, was very meagre in Defoe's day, and he deliberately chose for his travellers a route which had never been explored and about which his imagination could have free play. It was, on the other hand, an age very rich in printed 'voyages' and travel journals, a species of literature Defoe was addicted to and which he would imitate. A work like the immensely popular *New Voyage round the World* (4 vols, 1697–1709) by the buccaneer William Dampier supplied him with, not so much direct information, as an anthology of the kind of event – nautical and navigational incidents, transactions with natives, piracies, mutinies, storms and shipwecks – with which he might fill his own narrative. The influence of Dampier is pervasive in *Captain Singleton*, and so, so far as Singleton's early adventures in Madagascar are concerned, is that of the *Voyages and Travels of J. Albert de Mandelslo* (1662) and the *New Voyage of François Leguat* (1707) by Maximilian Misson. Defoe, in his account of Singleton and his companions constructing a sloop, closely follows Misson's account of a similar incident. At one point – as may be seen by comparison with p. 49 of Defoe's novel – the likeness is almost word-for-word. 'This enterpize appear'd very difficult', says Misson's protagonist, Leguat; 'we had ... few tools; we had neither pitch nor tar, nor cordage, nor anchor, nor compass, nor a hundred and other necessaries – and all eight of us without serving any apprenticeship, became carpenters, smiths, rope-makers ... and generally everything that was necessary for us to be ... necessity was a law to us, it supply'd all our defects'.[4]

In regard to geography, Defoe made what use he could of existing maps, vague and inaccurate as they were. As A.W. Secord points out in his *Studies in the Narrative Method of Defoe*, the third of the great lakes described by

4 See Maximilian Misson, *New Voyage of François Leguat* (London, 1707), p. 106.

Singleton on p. 95 has no basis in reality, but it corresponds closely to a map of the world in Dampier's *New Voyage*; and the course of the Niger, down which Singleton imagines himself and his party floating to Cape Verde (p. 100), 'though in precise accord with that of the maps of the day, was wrong in every particular'.[5] Nevertheless certain scholars of the late Victorian period, by which time Stanley and Livingstone had done their great feats of exploration, fancied that Defoe might have had special sources of information – had perhaps talked to, or seen the notes of, actual travellers. William Minto, one of these scholars, also persuaded himself that Defoe had anticipated certain modern discoveries by his great powers of intuition – for instance that, unlike the map-makers of his time, he had formed by guesswork a right idea of the course of the Congo; but this proves to have been a muddle.[6]

Imaginatively speaking, the leading feature of Defoe's vision of Africa is its emptiness. It is a place of vast deserts and huge lakes, only very sparsely inhabited by humans: as it were, an accursed region. The travellers, in their wanderings, follow the shore of a lake for twenty-three days, believing it to be the sea, and meeting no humans, though encountering a hideous and ferocious snake or serpent. Singleton's companions insist that it is the Devil – 'only that we did not know what Business Satan could have there, where there were no people' (p. 97). 'It was very remarkable', says Singleton, later, 'that we had now travelled 1000 Miles without meeting with any People, in the Heart of the whole Continent of *Africa*, where to be sure never Man set his Foot since the Sons of *Noah* spread themselves over the Face of the whole Earth' (p. 97). There is for him a kind of affinity between the vast unpeopled space and vistas of huge tracts of time. The sheer enormous extent of the elephants' burial ground which Singleton and his party come upon near the first great lake, is visible proof of its antiquity, and the undecaying tusks and bones suggest eternity. 'They may lye there for ought I know', says Singleton, 'to the End of Time' (p. 83.)

One of the most dramatic episodes of Singleton's African journey is the encounter, in the heart of Africa, with a white man – stark naked, his skin blackened and blistered by the sun, and his beard covering him to his midriff – plainly having 'gone native'. He had been a factor for the English Guinea Company at Sierra Leone, but had left the company after a quarrel, joining what were known as the 'separate traders', and eventually had been captured by natives, reaching this remote village. The local 'petty king'

5 See A. W. Secord, *Studies in the Narrative Method of Defoe* (Urbana, Illinois, 1924), p. 133.

6 The muddle is explained by Secord, *Studies in the Narrative Method*, pp. 134–7.

had made him welcome, though as a prisoner, and he had expected to end his days there. Overwhelmed with gratitude to Singleton and his friends for so astonishingly rescuing him and restoring him to civilised ways, he becomes obsessed with a desire to make their fortune and to help them exploit the gold (for this is gold country) which had been so useless to him in his exile. Singleton reluctantly agrees but, characteristically, with gloom. He thinks he has enough money already, 'and all the Thoughts I had about disposing of it, if I came to Europe, was only how to spend it as fast as I could, buy me some Clothes, and go to Sea again, to be a Drudge for more' (p. 117). At last, laden with gold dust and ivory, the party reaches a Dutch factory (i.e. trading settlement) on the Guinea coast, and Singleton, with two native servants, secures a passage to England. By contrast, the Englishman (it has the force of a parable) lingers in Africa in order to send a thousand pounds to England by way of Holland and dies of grief when the ship is captured by the French.

Defoe's naked Englishman was, in fact, based on a real-life figure, John Freeman, sometime Manager of the Royal African Company at Sherbro. He had been dismissed for malpractice and, after attempting and failing to clear his name, had returned to Sierra Leone in 1707 as a separate trader and had been kidnapped and made prisoner by natives in much the same way as his fictional counterpart. Defoe had a long-standing connection with the Royal African Company, giving it much support in his *Review* in its financial troubles and its struggle with the separate traders.[7] He would thus have known of the Freeman saga, and very possibly had seen some of the Company correspondence about it. The details of Freeman's story are rather fascinating, though only indirectly relevant to Defoe's novel, and they are given added interest by the fact that the account in the novel is supplemented by a passage in a massive *Atlas Maritimus & Commercialis* published in 1728, in which the episode is related from the point of view, not of Singleton and his party, but of Freeman himself. It is not certain whether this came from Defoe's pen, or what precise role, if any, he had in the compiling of the *Atlas*,[8] but I have thought it worth reprinting the passage, and telling more of Freeman's story, in an Appendix (below, pp. 227–31).

* * * * * *

Singleton's vision of how he would behave and would handle his riches on his arrival in England (a country which he can hardly call his 'home')

7   See, for instance, the *Review* for 17, 22 and 24 February 1709.
8   See the discussion in P. N. Furbank and W. R. Owens, *A Critical Bibliography of Daniel Defoe* (London, 1998), pp. 276–9.

proves dismally prophetic. He is cheated of much of his wealth by a public-house keeper in Rotherhithe; his money buys him friends (his 'Spoilers' as he calls them), who encourage him to spend it on 'Folly and Wickedness' (p. 121), and they quickly desert him when it runs out. It is with relief that he resumes his sailing life, the only kind of life that he understands. Moreover he now, as he realises, has a profession: he is a born pirate. When, during a stay at the 'Groyn' (Corunna), a fellow-sailor suggests his joining a mutiny, he is overjoyed. 'I ... was now in my Element, and never undertook any Thing in my Life with more particular Satisfaction' (p. 122).

Captain Singleton is set in the last decade or so of the seventeenth century and the first years of the eighteenth (though Defoe's dating is rather vague and not entirely consistent), and this was a period of considerable pirate activity – in the Caribbean, the South Seas as well as the Indian Ocean – and of growing anxiety about it on the part of the English government. The scare about piracy centred at the time on the semi-legendary exploits of the captain Henry Avery and on the much-publicised trial in London in 1695 of members of his crew for the seizing of the Grand Mogul's treasure ship off the coast of India. The exploit caused the East India Company to ask for a vessel of war to be sent to those seas to destroy these and other such marauders.

It has to be remembered, however, that in theory at least piracy was essentially distinct from privateering, the system by which vessels were given 'letters of marque' by the government, entitling them to attack enemy shipping and to keep a large portion of the proceeds. During much of the seventeenth century English privateers, in their attacks on Spanish merchant vessels and galleons, were warmly regarded as patriots. Privateering was legitimised by warfare, and with the coming of the War of the Spanish Succession in 1702 there was, for the moment, a great increase in privateering, giving employment to out-of-work sailors (not only on the English side but on the French side), and piracy proper declined in proportion. The signing of the Treaty of Utrecht in 1713, bringing the war to an end, however, changed matters radically and ushered in what Manuel Schonhorn has called 'the greatest decade of pirate activity in modern history'.[9] This was the era of Captain Teach (alias 'Black-Beard'), the gentleman-pirate Major Stede Bonnet and Captain Bartholomew Roberts, who by official count took almost 400 vessels and whose death and the trial

9 See the excellent Preface to his edition of *A General History of the Pyrates* (New York, 1999), p. xxi. (W. R. Owens and the present editor have, however, argued in *The Canonisation of Daniel Defoe* (New Haven, Connecticut, and London, 1988), pp. 100–6, that there is no basis for attributing the *General History* to Defoe.)

of whose crew in 1722 would mark the end of piracy's 'golden age'. Thus Defoe's *Captain Singleton* was written and published at a moment of crisis.

The leader of the mutinous gang Singleton is invited to join while at Corunna (see p. 121) is a certain Captain Wilmot. Wilmot takes possession of the ship of which he is a officer, setting off on a piratical career, and he and his gang soon acquire additional ships as prizes. This enables Singleton and his friend Harris, by agreement with Wilmot, to go cruising on their own account in the Caribbean, taking English or Dutch ships if they come upon them, but chiefly attacking Spanish vessels, for these generally have money on board, 'which was what we best knew what to do with' (p. 124). On a sloop bound from Pennsylvania to Barbados they capture a Quaker surgeon named William Walters, a 'very merry Fellow' (p. 125); he is happy to join them on condition that they stage a mock struggle and certify that he was taken away by force.

Defoe evidently felt well disposed towards Quakers, declaring it to be uncharitable not to allow them to be Christians, 'and many of them better Christians than those that pretend to condemn them'.[10] He praises their decent seemliness and good sense, and their willingness to stand by their principles. One thinks of Roxana's Quaker friend, with her steadfast loyalty, benevolence and tolerance, and of the obsession with truth that drives the Quaker in *The Secret History of the Secret History of the White Staff* (1715) to seek out the (supposedly dying) Defoe, to cross-examine him about the authorship of the *Secret History of the White Staff*.[11] A 'Quaker' persona is also used to great effect in several of Defoe's pamphlet satires: for instance *A Declaration of Truth to Benjamin Hoadly* (1717), in which the 'Quaker' spokesman praises the latitudinarian Bishop of Bangor for so clearly bearing witness to Quaker doctrines, and teasingly urges him (abandoning his episcopal lawn sleeves) to take the obvious remaining step. But Defoe's most elaborate study of Quakerdom is William Walters. He is a sort of Quaker casuist (and, when necessary, equivocator) with a complicated set of ethical principles, only gradually revealed. His personality will dominate the later pages of the novel.

Suffering damage in a storm, Singleton and Harris put in to Trinidad to undertake repairs, and then they quit the Caribbean for the coast of Brazil. Espying a Portuguese fleet in the Bay of All Saints, they prudently retire, but next day they come upon a solitary vessel and pursue it till nightfall. Here we are given an example of William Walters's ironic shrewdness. He

10 *Review*, 13 December 1705.

11 See *The Secret History of the Secret History of the White Staff* (1715), in *Political and Economic Writings of Daniel Defoe* (London, 2000), Vol. 2, ed. J. A. Downie, pp. 295–314.

asks Singleton why they are runnng away from their supposed prey. 'I am greatly in hopes, Friend, *says the dry gibing Creature*, Thou wilt turn Quaker, for I see thou art not for Fighting' (p. 128). Singleton asks Walters, with an oath, what he means. He means, William explains, that their quarry, which is sailing due east, cannot possibly really be aiming for Africa and will double back under cover of darkness. Accordingly the English change course and are enabled to take the Portuguese ship by surprise almost within the habour.

What is amusing is that at this point Defoe has visibly determined to show off his mastery of nautical jargon:[12]

> Accordingly, we went about ship, got our Larboard Tacks on board, set the Top-gallant Sails, and crowded for the Bay of *All-Saints*, where we came to an Anchor, early in the Morning just out of Gun Shot of the Forts; we furl'd our Sails with Rope-Yarns, that we might haul home the Sheets without going up to loose them, and lowering our Main and Fore-Yards, looked just as if we had lain there a good while.
>
> In two Hours after, we saw our Game, standing in for the Bay with all the Sail she could make, and she came innocently into our very Mouths, for we lay still, till we saw her almost within Gun Shot; when our Fore Mast Geers being stretched fore and aft, we first run up our Yards and then hauled home the Top-Sail Sheets; the Rope-Yarns that furled them giving Way of themselves, the Sails were set in a few Minutes; at the same time slipping our Cable, we came upon her before she could get under Way upon 'tother Tack. (pp. 126–7)

There seems indeed, as this might suggest, to have been a vogue for blue-water narratives at this time, both real-life and fictional. *Captain Singleton* was serialised in *The Post-master, or, The Loyal Mercury* (an Exeter weekly, conducted by Andrew Brice) from 4 November 1720 onwards. It interrupted an earlier narrative, featuring a group of mariners shipwrecked in the vicinity of Java and desperately struggling to find land before dying of thirst and starvation. Printing such narratives appears to have been a recent innovation, at least in the *Post-master*, for in the issue for 5 September 1720 a correspondent writes that, being a constant reader, he had been at first 'a little displeased' at 'what I thought *Vanity* in you, namely your presuming to supply the Deficiency of *News* with Matters of a more diverting Nature', but he had been won round and was 'well pleas'd with your Sea-Journal'.

---

12 Swift did something similar, more obviously with comic intent, in Book 2 of *Gulliver's Travels*, in which he copied out, with very little alteration, a passage from Samuel Sturmy's *Mariner's Magazine*: 'Finding it was like to overblow, we took in our Sprit-sail, and stood by to hand the Foresail', etc.

Indeed he would like readers to entertain their fellows ('like as in a merry Conversation at Christmas') with further tales, and he transcribes a brief example by 'a Native of this Parish'. It describes the efforts of some Englishmen, made prisoner by Algerine rovers, to escape by secretly constructing a boat. The supplanting of the original 'Sea-Journal' by *Captain Singleton* in turn provoked a plaintive letter from a reader, lamenting the loss of his weekly enjoyment.

> Sir,
>
> Tho' many of the little Narratives, &c. which you have obliged us with have been very pleasing yet none were so diverting as your Sea-Journal to me, and (as far as I can learn) to most of your other Customers in this Town. For my part, I were so taken with the very remarkable and odd occurrences thereof, that I past all the Week but Saturday with a tedious Impatience.

It is to be noticed that the *Post-master* refers to *Captain Singleton* not as a 'romance' or 'novel' but as a 'Treatise', and this is no doubt in response to Defoe's circumstantial style. It could indeed be that this new enthusiasm for sea stories is simply a legacy of *Robinson Crusoe*, published the previous year, but the point could do with further exploring.

Singleton and his companions decide not to meddle any further with the Portuguese fleet, and they make their way down the coast to the mouth of the Janeiro. But news of their exploits has run ahead of them, and there are men-of-war waiting for them, one of them ready to slip its cable. By morning, with this ship hard on their heels, it is plain that they must fight. In which case, says the 'dry Wretch' Walters (p. 130), what is the point of running any further? Why not fight here and now?

It proves a ferocious engagement, in which William is to be seen, the shot flying all round his head, coolly giving the sailors a dram from his pocket flask, 'in as perfect Tranquillity as to Danger, as if he had been over a Bowl of Punch' (p. 131). It becomes plain that, though as a Quaker he cannot engage in fighting, he has no absolute moral objection (though some practical ones) to fighting in itself. The Portuguese ship is the more heavily armed of the two, but Singleton's men have put most of its guns out of action, and William asks Singleton why they do not board it, '*the Door being open for thee*' (p. 131). They do so, causing much carnage, and at last the Portuguese are forced to cry for quarter. For Captain Wilmot, who is lying ill in his cabin, the sound is such a joyful surprise that his fever abates the same night.

Wilmot wants to go in pursuit of the second man-of-war, but William asks Singleton what his, and his companions', business is. 'Is it not to get Money?' And would they rather have 'Money without Fighting, or Fighting without Money?' The first, says Singleton. 'Why then', says William, 'what great Gain hast thou made of the Prize thou hast taken now, tho' it has cost the Lives of thirteen of thy Men, besides some hurt?' (p. 133). They would gain twice the booty in a merchant ship, with a quarter of the fighting.

So they go further down the coast to the River Plate and, while 'hankering' about there (p. 133), they have a momentous encounter. They catch sight of a ship showing no flag and in the most desperate plight, its top-mast broken and its mizen topsail sprawling over the quarterdeck like an awning. They can see no-one on deck and surmise that the ship has been deserted, but on approaching they hear noises and glimpse figures passing by the portholes. When they attempt to board her, a crowd of negroes pours onto the deck, and the English, retreating, prepare to bombard her; but William tells them in Quaker laguage they may take her 'without making use of those things call'd Guns' (p. 135). He has guessed, rightly, that it is a slave ship and that the negroes have murdered their white gaolers, but, understanding nothing whatever about sails or sailing, they have since then simply been adrift. Singleton's men want to cut the 'black Devils' to pieces, but William earnestly persuades them that the rebellion and murder was only what they themselves would have done in the same circumstances. The negroes had had 'really the highest Injustice done them, to be sold for Slaves without their Consent' (p. 135).

The two parties cannot, at first, understand a word that the other says, and the second lieutenant, absurdly, is keen to torture them to make them 'confess'. But at last their story emerges. A white man had abused the wife and daughter of one of them and this had driven them all mad with rage. Their ill-used companion had contrived to knock the white man's brains out, and he had stolen from the body the keys to the other slaves' handcuffs. A massacre had ensued. All the whites had been murdered or driven to escape in boats, and the slaves had thrown all the guns and shot they could find into the sea, in case otherwise these mysterious objects, even without their owners, could kill them.

The negroes had first imagined, with terror, that Singleton and his crew had been survivors of their original captors, returned to wreak vengeance. On this they are reassured; but it remains a problem what Singleton and his men, without danger to themselves, are to do with them. At last William comes up with a typically pragmatic (and in the circumstances not altogether inhumane) solution. He takes them off aboard a sloop and sells them, by private bargain, to local planters.

It has been a long-standing ambition of Singleton's to return to Madagascar, the notorious pirate haunt with which he felt his destiny entwined;

and he convinces his companions that this is where they might best ply their trade, preying on the rich argosies of the Mogul empire. On the way there they pause at the Cape, where their crew is enlarged by a party of English mutineers. They spend some fruitless months cruising in the Persian Gulf, but at last, off the coast of Africa, they capture a Mogul vessel, a very rich prize. It seems time for them to rejoin Wilmot, who is in a separate vessel and will be waiting for them at a rendezvous in Madagascar; but while they are still at anchor off the Madagascaran coast, William, who has had a dream about finding a mine of gold, gets Singleton's reluctant permission to go on shore, with a small troop; and he does indeed, in a sense, find gold. For he and his party come upon Wilmot's ship, which has been wrecked, and then a camp set up by the survivors. They had been cruising in the company of the famous pirate Captain Avery, who had also eventually lost his ship; but they show William their vast stock of ill-gotten treasure – which, however, is 'a Trifle to what Captain *Avery* had wherever he was gone' (p. 152).

It becomes a question what the pirates' next step should be. Captain Avery envisages their building a little fortified city in the island, from which they could pursue their trade and bid defiance to the world. But Singleton argues that if they did so, all the nations of the world would combine to root them out.[13] Their only hope of a settled life would be to give up pirating and buy a tract of land up country – on a navigable river but safe from hostile shipping – and become farmers. Wilmot, who has secret plans for getting back to England, once he feels rich enough, supports Avery's line, and he and Singleton have a furious quarrel. As a result the two captains, and their followers, agree to go their different ways.

Singleton now seizes the chance to fulfil a long-cherished plan: to 'fall in amongst the *Dutch* Spice Islands, and see what Mischief I could do there' (p. 160). He and his men are in quest of nutmegs and cloves and relieve a number of vessels – Chinese, Japanese and Dutch – of their cargo without resorting to violence. Where occasion offers, they even trade as respectable merchants. The crews of their two ships (a great carrack and a sloop) begin to be weary of success and to think it time to turn homeward

But a new subject now comes to the fore, Singleton's conscience; and the novel, which has been rather drifting, comes together again at this point.

13 There is a striking discussion of the problem of the supposed pirate kingdom in Madagascar in Defoe's *Review* for 18 October 1707. He argues in it that if rumour is correct and the pirates there are willing to pay vast sums for a pardon, the offer should be listened to very seriously. For if they were to form a pirate nation or state, at war with the world, what would become of European trade? But, failing a peaceful negotiation of this kind, they must at all costs be 'rooted out of that Place'.

While they are cruising in the vicinity of Banda they experience a quite apocalyptic flash of lightning and a few moments later 'the terriblest Clap of Thunder ... that was ever heard by Mortals' (p. 163). It fills Singleton with horror, as a divine judgement aimed at him personally. 'My Soul was all Amazement and Surprize; I thought my self just sinking into Eternity.' Yet he does not feel any of the 'moving, softning Token of a sincere Penitent'. He is 'afflicted at the Punishment, but not at the Crime' (p. 163). Thus the effect on him does not last.

But William by now is keeping a watchful eye on him, and one day he tells Singleton he would like to have a serious talk. William asks him if he has ever thought of giving up the pirate life, 'For most people leave off Trading when they are satisfied with getting, and are rich enough; for no body trades for the sake of Trading, much less do any Men rob for the sake of Thieving' (p. 209). So poor William is hankering after home, Singleton comments teasingly; and this brings on a conversation about home, which takes a turn that William has not foreseen. For Singleton's answer is as pathetic as it is realistic. 'Why, Man, I am at Home, here is my Habitation, I never had any other in my Life time; I was a kind of Charity School-Boy, so that I can have no Desire of going any where for being rich or poor, for I have no where to go' (p. 209). Is he not an Englishman, asks William. 'Yes ... I think so', says Singleton, 'you see I speak *English*; but I came out of *England* a Child, and never was in it but once since I was a Man, and then I was cheated and imposed upon, and used so ill, that I care not if I ever see it more'. But has he no friends or relations or anyone he has a kindness for there? No, not more than he has in the court of the great Mogul, says Singleton. And does he feel no fondness for the country where he was born? 'Not I, any more than for the Island of *Madagascar*, nor so much neither, for that has been a fortunate Island to me more than once, as thou knowest' (p. 209). William is for the moment nonplussed.

Nevertheless, says Singleton, he would like to hear what William was going to propose; for it is true, he does not love the pirate life so much as never to give it up, if William can convince him there is anything beyond it. Certainly there is something beyond it, says William, with unaccustomed solemnity. 'You mean *Death*, I warrant you,' says Singleton truculently, deliberately misunderstanding him; and he jokes on recklessly about death, until William's tone begins to touch his heart. By this time William is in tears. He tells Singleton he is not talking about death but repentance. 'Why', says Singleton cynically, 'did you ever know a Pirate repent?' Once, at the gallows, returns William quietly. So Singleton asks him how they could manage to give up their pirate life: 'I'll begin there with you with all my Heart'. William weeps for joy at this, too overcome to speak, and Singleton, overwhelmed by his long-standing admiration for William and for his good judgement, puts himself unreservedly in his hands. 'As I have commanded you all along, from the Time I took you on Board, so you shall command me from this Hour; and every thing you direct me, I'll do' (p. 211).

William's plan involves their making a new expedition into the Persian Gulf, under cover of which they would secretly put their own share of the common spoils into safe hands, against the time when they can break with their fellow-pirates. William makes one such trip alone, in the sloop, and then Singleton – who has hidden his private treasure among the bales of merchandise – comes with him on a second one, on which, having landed the remainder of their goods and valuables, they play an unscrupulous trick on their companions – fooling them, by means of a forged letter, into deserting them for their own safety.

We come now to the second stage of Singleton's conversion. He and William are in Basra, masquerading as Persian merchants, and Singleton, made no more comfortable by their disloyalty to their companions, falls into profound self-hatred and thoughts of suicide. William, returning to his usual gibing and ironic manner, handles him with much skill and delicacy. Hearing Singleton say that he wants to shoot himself, he asks what good he thinks it will do him. 'Why', says Singleton, ''twill put an End to a miserable Life'. But will the next life be any better, asks William? No, Singleton has to admit; indeed, much worse. But there is no bearing life as it is: he is 'past Remedy'. How do you know that, says William. Singleton says he is convinced of it. Well, says William, but 'you are not sure, so you will shoot yourself to make it certain?' (p. 218). Anyway, says William, Singleton had better give him the pistol, since he may need to do the shooting for him. For Singleton has such bad dreams that he cries out in his sleep, accusing himself of being a thief and a murderer, and if anyone heard and understood him it would be the end for them both.

The indifference which up to now has always dogged Singleton's career has finally been pierced by terror of divine vengeance, and also by the discovery of friendship. But there remains a considerable relic of it in his inability to enjoy his riches. 'As to the Wealth I had, which was immeasurably great, it was like Dirt under my Feet; I had no Value for it, no Peace in the Possession of it, no great Concern about me for the leaving of it' (p. 216). For this is a man who, partly perhaps from natural bent, but partly also from sheer deprivation, has never formed a rational theory of enjoyment. He has been a pirate not out of greed or lust for cruelty but simply because it was what he best knew how to do.

He grows obsessed with the dilemma he and William are faced with. They want to reform, but how can there be reform without restitution? Yet on the other hand, how could they hope to restore what they have stolen to its rightful owners? It takes all of William's pragmatism and persuasive art to settle Singleton's mind. (It is plain enough why Singleton should have grown dependent on William – who is one of Defoe's most brilliant character creations. It is less clear what makes him so attached to Singleton, though the fact itself is easy to accept.)

Defoe is clearly finishing *Captain Singleton* under pressure. The labour-saving device of representing the pirates' experience in Ceylon by extracts from someone else's book, Robert Knox's *Historical Relation*, is awkward and inaesthetic. Again – another sign that Defoe is improvising hastily – he brings in matters that, so he says, he may, but equally well may not, get round to (and in fact does not).[14]

Let us notice, too, that Singleton is explicitly censoring his own narrative, drawing a veil over the worst excesses of his, or his companion's, behaviour. For example:

> Captain *Wilmot* was indeed more particularly cruel when he took any *English* Vessel, that they might not too soon have advice of him in *England,* and so the Men of War have Orders to look out for him. But this Part I bury in Silence for the present. (p. 124)

One might think the motives for this censorship could be patriotism, but Singleton, as he tells William, is not a patriot, at least so far as England is concerned. Thus one supposes it must be for personal security. For it is important to Defoe's novel, as with all first-person narratives, that the author is, in the nature of things, still alive. As the novel presents it, Singleton ends his career in limbo, still utterly perplexed about restitution. He makes William linger with him for two years in Venice, 'in the greatest Hesitation imaginable, irresolute and unfixed to the last Degree' (p. 224); and to have opted for England at last and have landed his enormous cargo in a English port hardly seems to get him any further. For given that one of the rules he has laid down to William about their return is that no stranger shall be allowed to hear them speak English, how on earth can he hope to put his cargo to use or profit?

But here, opportunely, a piece of artistic logic comes to the author's aid. For among Singleton's many potential enemies the greatest and most incal-

---

14 Singleton says, for example (p. 220), that the story of the 'miraculous Opportunity' he has of doing justice to a family he had robbed 'may be worth reading, if I have Room for it in this Account'.

culable of all is the reader, i.e. ourselves. Who knows what inquisitive or legally-minded person may be interesting himself or herself in this confessed criminal, up to now unpunished? Thus, so far as the reader is concerned, Singleton's new life must remain vague and a limbo. Pirate lore reinforces this. For rumour has it that the report of Captain Avery's death was false and the great Avery himself could still be lurking somewhere on earth.

THE

LIFE,

ADVENTURES,

AND

PYRACIES,

Of the Famous
Captain SINGLETON:

Containing an ACCOUNT of his being set on Shore in the Island
of *Madagascar*, his Settlement there, with a Description of
the Place and Inhabitants: Of his Passage from thence, in a
Paraguay,[1] to the main Land of *Africa*, with an Account of
the Customs and Manners of the People: His great Deliver-
ances from the barbarous Natives and wild Beasts: Of his
meeting with an *Englishman*, a Citizen of *London*, among
the *Indians*, the great Riches he acquired, and his Voyage
Home to *England:* As also Captain *Singleton*'s Return to Sea,
with an Account of his many Adventures and Pyracies with
the famous Captain *Avery* and others.

LONDON: Printed for *J. Brotherton*, at the *Black Bull* in *Cornhill*, *J. Graves* in
St. James's Street, A. *Dodd*, at the *Peacock* without *Temple bar*, and *T.*
Warner, at the *Black Boy* in *Pater-Noster-Row.* 1720.

THE
ADVENTURES
AND
PYRACIES, *&c.*

As it is usual for great Persons whose Lives have been remarkable, and whose Actions deserve Recording to Posterity, to insist much upon their Originals, give full Accounts of their Families, and the Histories of their Ancestors: So, that I may be methodical, I shall do the same, tho' I can look but a very little Way into my Pedigree as you will see presently.

If I may believe the Woman, whom I was taught to call Mother, I was a little Boy, of about two Years old, very well dress'd, had a Nursery Maid to tend me, who took me out on a fine Summer's Evening into the Fields towards *Islington*, as she pretended, to give the Child some Air, a little Girl being with her of Twelve or Fourteen Years old, that lived in the Neighbourhood. The Maid, whether by Appointment or otherwise, meets with a Fellow, her Sweet-heart, as I suppose; he carries her into a Publick-House, to give her a Pot and a Cake; and while they were toying in the House, the Girl plays about with me in her Hand in the Garden, and at the Door, sometimes in Sight, sometimes out of Sight, thinking no Harm.

At this Juncture comes by one of those Sort of People, who, it seems, made it their Business to Spirit away little Children. This was a Hellish Trade in those Days, and chiefly practised where they found little Children very well drest, or for bigger Children, to sell them to the Plantations.

The Woman pretending to take me up in her Arms and kiss me, and play with me, draws the Girl a good Way from the House, till at last she makes a fine Story to the Girl, and bids her go back to the Maid, and tell her where she was with the Child; that a Gentlewoman had taken a Fancy to the Child, and was kissing of it, but she should not be frighted, or to that Purpose; for they were but just there; and so while the Girl went, she carries me quite away.

From this time it seems I was disposed of to a Beggar-Woman that wanted a pretty little Child to set out her Case, and after that to a Gypsey, under whose Government I continued till I was about Six Years old; and this Woman, tho' I was continually dragged about with her, from one Part of the Country to another, yet never let me want for any thing, and I called her Mother; tho' she told me at last, she was not my Mother, but that she bought me for Twelve Shillings of another Woman, who told her how she came by me, and told her that my Name was *Bob Singleton*, not *Robert*, but plain *Bob*; for it seems they never knew by what Name I was Christen'd.

It is in vain to reflect here, what a terrible Fright the careless Hussy was in, that lost me; what Treatment she received from my justly enraged Father and Mother, and the Horror these must be in at the Thoughts of their Child being thus carry'd away; for as I never knew any thing of the Matter, but just what I have related, nor who my Father and Mother were; so it would make but a needless Digression to talk of it here.

My good *Gypsey Mother*, for some of her worthy Actions *no doubt*, happened in Process of Time to be hang'd; and as this fell out something too soon for me to be perfected in the Strolling Trade,[2] the Parish where I was left, which for my Life I can't remember, took some Care of me to be sure; for the first thing I can remember of my self afterwards, was, that I went to a Parish-School, and the Minister of the Parish used to talk to me to be a good Boy; and that tho' I was but a poor Boy, if I minded my Book,[3] and served God, I might make a good Man.

I believe I was frequently removed from one Town to another, perhaps as the Parishes disputed my supposed Mother's last Settlement. Whether I was so shifted by Passes,[4] or otherwise, I know not; but the Town where I last was kept, whatever its Name was, must be not far off from the Sea Side; for a Master of a Ship who took a Fancy to me, was the first that brought me to a Place not far from *Southampton*, which I afterwards knew to be *Busselton*,[5] and there I tended the Carpenters, and such People as were employ'd in Building a Ship for him; and when it was done, tho' I was not above Twelve Years old, he carried me to Sea with him, on a Voyage to *Newfoundland*.

I lived well enough, and pleased my Master so well, that he called me his own Boy; and I would have called him Father, but he would not allow it, for he had Children of his own. I went three or four Voyages with him, and grew a great sturdy Boy, when coming Home again from the Banks of *Newfoundland*, we were taken by an *Algerine* Rover, or Man of War; which, if my Account stands right, was about the Year 1695, for you may be sure I kept no Journal.

I was not much concerned at the Disaster, tho' I saw my Master, after having been wounded by a Splinter in the Head during the Engagement, very barbarously used by the *Turks*;[6] *I say*, I was not much concerned, till upon some unlucky thing I said, which, as I remember, was about abusing my Master, they took me and beat me most unmercifully with a flat Stick on the Soles of my Feer, so that I could neither go or stand for several Days together.

But my good Fortune was my Friend upon this Occasion; for as they were sailing away with our Ship in Tow as a Prize, steering for the Streights, and in Sight of the Bay of *Cadiz*, the *Turkish* Rover was attack'd by two great *Portuguese* Men of War, and taken and carried into *Lisbon*.

As I was not much concerned at my Captivity, not indeed understanding the Consequences of it, if it had continued; so I was not suitably sensible of my Deliverance: Nor indeed was it so much a Deliverance to me, as it would otherwise ha' been; for my Master, who was the only Friend I had in the World, died at *Lisbon* of his Wounds; and I being then almost reduced to my primitive State, *viz.* of Starving, had this Addition to it, that it was in a foreign Country too, where I knew no body, and could not speak a Word of their Language. However, I fared better here than I had Reason to expect; for when all the rest of our Men had their Liberty to go where they would, I that knew not whither to go, staid in the Ship for several Days, till at length one of the Lieutenants seeing me, enquired what that young *English* Dog did there, and why they did not turn him on Shore?

I heard him, and partly understood what he meant, tho' not what he said, and began then to be in a terrible Fright; for I knew not where to get a Bit of Bread; when the Pilot of the Ship, an old Seaman, seeing me look very dull,[7] came to me, and speaking broken *English* to me, told me, I must be gone. Whither must I go (said I?) Where you will, (said he), Home to your own Country, if you will. How must I go thither (said I?) Why have you no Friend (said he?) No, (said I) not in the World, but that Dog, pointing to the Ship's Dog, (who having stole a Piece of Meat just before, had brought it close by me, and I had taken it from him, and eat it) for he has been a good Friend, and brought me my Dinner.

Well, well, says he, *you must have your Dinner; Will you go with me? Yes*, says I, *with all my Heart*. In short, the old Pilot took me Home with him, and used me tolerably well, tho' I fared hard enough; and I lived with him about two Years, during which time he was solliciting his Business, and at length got to be Master or Pilot under *Don Garcia de Pimentesia de Carravallas*, Captain of a *Portuguese* Gallion,[8] or Carrack,[9] which was bound to *Goa* in the *East-Indies*; and immediately having gotten his Commission, put me on Board to look after his Cabbin, in which he had stored himself with Abundance of Liquors, Succades,[10] Sugar, Spices, and other things for his Accommodation in the Voyage, and laid in afterwards a considerable

Quantity of *European* Goods, fine Lace, and Linnen; and also Bays,[11] Wool-
len, Cloath, Stuffs, *&c.* under the Pretence of his Clothes.

I was too young in the Trade to keep any Journal of this Voyage, tho' my
Master, who was for a *Portuguese* a pretty good Artist,[12] prompted me to it:
But my not understanding the Language, was one Hindrance; at least, it
served me for an Excuse. However, after some time I began to look into his
Charts and Books; and as I could write a tolerable Hand, understood some
Latin, and began to have a Smattering of the *Portuguese* Tongue; so I began
to get a little superficial Knowledge of Navigation, but not such as was
likely to be sufficient to carry me thro' a Life of Adventure, as mine was to
be. *In short,* I learnt several material Things in this Voyage among the *Portuguese:* I learnt particularly to be an errant Thief and a bad Sailor; and I
think I may say they are the best Masters for Teaching both these, of any
Nation in the World.

We made our Way for the *East-Indies,* by the Coast of *Brasil;* not that it
is in the Course of Sailing the Way thither; but our Captain, either on his
own Account, or by the Direction of the Merchants, went thither first,
where at *All Saints Bay,* or as they call it in *Portugal,* the *Rio de Todos los San-
tos,* we delivered near an Hundred Ton of Goods, and took in a considerable
Quantity of Gold, with some Chests of Sugar, and Seventy or Eighty great
Rolls of Tobacco, every Roll weighing at least 100 Weight.

Here being lodged on Shore by my Master's Order, I had the Charge of
the Captain's Business, he having seen me very diligent for my own Master; and in Requital for his mistaken Confidence, I found Means to secure,
that is to say, to steal about twenty Moydores[13] out of the Gold that was
Shipt on Board by the Merchants, and this was my first Adventure.[14]

We had a tolerable Voyage from hence to the Cape *de bona Speranza;*[15]
and I was reputed as a mighty diligent Servant to my Master, and very
faithful (I was diligent indeed, but I was very far from honest; however,
they thought me honest, which by the Way, was their very great Mistake)
upon this very Mistake, the Captain took a particular Liking to me, and
employ'd me frequently on his own Occasions; and on the other Hand, in
Recompence for my Officious Diligence, I received several particular
Favours from him; particularly, I was by the Captain's Command, made a
kind of a Steward under the Ship's Steward, for such Provisions as the Captain demanded for his own Table. He had another Steward for his private
Stores besides, but my Office concerned only what the Captain called for of
the Ship's Stores, for his private Use.

However, by this Means I had Opportunity particularly to take Care of
my Master's Man, and to furnish my self with sufficient Provisions to make
me live much better than the other People in the Ship; for the Captain sel-

dom ordered any thing out of the Ship's Stores, as above, but I snipt some of it for my own Share. We arrived at *Goa* in the *East-Indies*, in about seven Months, from *Lisbon*, and remained there eight more; during which Time I had indeed nothing to do, my Master being generally on Shore, but to learn every thing that is wicked among the *Portuguese*, a Nation the most perfidious and the most debauch'd, the most insolent and cruel, of any that pretend to call themselves Christians, in the World.

Thieving, Lying, Swearing, Forswearing, joined to the most abominable Lewdness, was the stated Practice of the Ship's Crew; *adding to it*, that with the most unsufferable Boasts of their new Courage, they were generally speaking the most compleat Cowards that I ever met with; and the Consequence of their Cowardice was evident upon many Occasions. However, there was here and there one among them that was not so bad as the rest; and as my Lot fell among them, it made me have the most contemptible Thoughts of the rest, as indeed they deserved.

I was exactly fitted for their Society indeed; for I had no Sense of Virtue or Religion upon me. I had never heard much of either, except what a good old Parson had said to me when I was a Child of about Eight or Nine Years old; nay, I was preparing, and growing up apace, to be as wicked as any Body could be, or perhaps ever was. Fate certainly thus directed my Beginning, knowing that I had Work which I had to do in the World, which nothing but one hardened against all Sense of Honesty or Religion, could go thro'; and yet even in this State of Original Wickedness, I entertained such a settled Abhorrence of the abandon'd Vileness of the *Portuguese*, that I could not but hate them most heartily from the Beginning, and all my Life afterwards. They were so brutishly wicked, so base and perfidious, not only to Strangers, but to one another; so meanly submissive when subjected; so insolent, or barbarous and tyrannical when superiour, that I thought there was something in them that shock'd my very Nature. Add to this, that 'tis natural to an *Englishman* to hate a Coward, it all joined together to make the Devil and a *Portuguese* equally my Aversion.

However, according to the *English* Proverb, *He that is Shipp'd with the Devil must sail with the Devil*; I was among them, and I manag'd my self as well as I could. My Master had consented that I should assist the Captain in the Office as above; but as I understood afterwards, that the Captain allowed my Master Half a Moydore a Month for my Service, and that he had my Name upon the Ship's Books also, I expected that when the Ship came to be paid four Months Wages at the *Indies*, as they it seems always do, my Master would let me have something for my self.

But I was wrong in my Man, for he was none of that Kind: He had taken me up as in Distress, and his Business was to keep me so, and make his Market of me as well as he could; which I began to think of after a different Manner than I did at first; for at first I thought he had entertained me in meer Charity, upon seeing my distrest Circumstances, but did not doubt, but when he put me on Board the Ship, I should have some Wages for my Service.

But he thought, it seems, quite otherwise; and when I procured one to speak to him about it when the Ship was paid at *Goa*, he flew into the greatest Rage imaginable, and called me *English* Dog, young Heretick, and threaten'd to put me into the Inquisition. Indeed of all the Names the Four and Twenty Letters could make up, he should not have called me Heretick; for as I knew nothing about Religion, neither *Protestant* from *Papist*, or either of them from a *Mahometan*, I could never be a Heretick. However, it pass'd but a little,[16] but as young as I was, I had been carried into the Inquisition; and there, if they had ask'd me, if I was a *Protestant* or a *Catholick*, I should have said Yes to that which came first. If it had been the *Protestant* they had ask'd first, it had certainly made a Martyr of me for I did not know what.

But the very Priest they carried with them, or Chaplain of the Ship, as we call him, saved me; for seeing me a Boy entirely ignorant of Religion, and ready to do or say any thing they bid me, he ask'd me some Questions about it, which he found I answered so very simply,[17] that he took it upon him to tell them, he would answer for my being a good Catholick; and he hoped he should be the Means of saving my Soul; and he pleased himself, that it was to be a Work of Merit to him; so he made me as good a *Papist* as any of them in about a Week's Time.

I then told him my Case about my Master how, it is true, he had taken me up in a miserable Case, on Board a Man of War at *Lisbon*; and I was indebted to him for bringing me on Board this Ship; that if I had been left at *Lisbon*, I might have starv'd, and the like: And therefore I was willing to serve him; but that I hop'd he would give me some little Consideration for my Service, or let me know how long he expected I should serve him for nothing.

It was all one; neither the Priest or any one else could prevail with him, but that I was not his Servant but his Slave; that he took me in the *Algerine*; and that I was a *Turk*, only pretended to be an *English* Boy, to get my Liberty, and he would carry me to the Inquisition as a *Turk*.

This frighted me out of my Wits; for I had no body to vouch for me what I was, or from whence I came; but the good *Padre Antonio*, for that was his Name, cleared me of that Part by a Way I did not understand: For he came to me one Morning with two Sailors, and told me they must search me, to bear Witness that I was not a *Turk*. I was amazed at them, and frighted; and did not understand them; nor could I imagine what they intended to do to me. However, stripping me, they were soon satisfy'd;[18] and Father *Anthony* bad me be easy, for they could all Witness that I was no *Turk*. So I escaped that Part of my Master's Cruelty.

And now I resolved from that time to run away from him if I could; but there was no doing of it there; for there were not Ships of any Nation in the World in that Port, except two or three; *Persian* Vessels from *Ormus*;[19] so that if I had offer'd to go away from him, he would have had me seized on Shore, and brought on Board by Force. So that I had no Remedy but Patience, and this he brought to an End too as soon as he could; for after this he began to use me ill, and not only to straiten my Provisions, but to beat and torture me in a barbarous Manner for every Trifle; so that in a Word my Life began to be very miserable.

The Violence of this Usage of me, and the Impossibility of my Escape from his Hands, set my Head a-working upon all Sorts of Mischief; and in particular, I resolved, after studying all other Ways to deliver my self, and finding all ineffectual; I say, I resolved to murther him. With this Hellish Resolution in my Head, I spent whole Nights and Days contriving how to put it in Execution, the Devil prompting me very warmly to the Fact. I was indeed entirely at a Loss for the Means; for I had neither Gun or Sword, nor any Weapon to assault him with. Poison I had my Thoughts much upon, but knew not where to get any; or if I might have got it, I did not know the Country Word for it, or by what Name to ask for it.

In this Manner I quitted the Fact intentionally a Hundred and a Hundred Times; but Providence, either for his sake, or for mine, always frustrated my Designs, and I could never bring it to pass; so I was obliged to continue in his Chains[20] till the Ship, having taken in her Loading, set Sail for *Portugal*.

I can say nothing here to the Manner of our Voyage; for as I said, I kept no Journal; but this I can give an Account of, that having been once as high as the *Cape of Good Hope*, as we call it; or *Cabo de bona Speranza*, as they call it, we were driven back again by a violent Storm from the W.S.W. which held us six Days and Nights, a great Way to the Eastward; and after that standing afore the Wind for several Days more, we at last came to an Anchor on the Coast of *Madagascar*.

The Storm had been so violent, that the Ship had received a great deal of Damage, and it required some time to repair her; so standing in nearer the Shore, the Pilot, *My Master*, brought the Ship into a very good Harbour, where we rid in Twenty six Fathom Water, about Half a Mile from the Shore.

While the Ship rode here, there happen'd a most desperate Mutiny among the Men, upon Account of some Deficiency in their Allowance, which came to that Height, that they threaten'd the Captain to set him on Shore, and go back with the Ship to *Goa*. I wish'd they would, with all my Heart, for I was full of Mischief in my Head, and ready enough to do any. So, tho' I was but a Boy, as they called me, yet I prompted the Mischief all I could, and embarked in it so openly, that I escap'd very little being hang'd in the first and most early Part of my Life; for the Captain had some Notice, that there was a Design laid by some of the Company to murther him; and having partly by Money and Promises, and partly by Threatning and Torture, brought two Fellows to confess the Particulars, and the Names of the Persons concerned, they were presently apprehended, till one accusing another, no less than sixteen Men were seized, and put into Irons, whereof I was one.

The Captain, who was made desperate by his Danger, resolving to clear the Ship of his Enemies, try'd us all, and we were all condemned to die. The Manner of his Process I was too young to take Notice of; but the Purser and one of the Gunners were hang'd immediately, and I expected it with the rest. I do not remember any great Concern I was under about it, only that I cry'd very much; for I knew little then of this World, and nothing at all of the next.

However, the Captain contented himself with executing these two; and some of the rest, upon their humble Submission, and Promise of future good Behaviour, were pardoned; but five were ordered to be set on Shore on the Island, and left there, of which I was one. My Master used all his Interest with the Captain to have me excused, but could not obtain it; for somebody having told him that I was one of them, who was singled out to have killed him, when my Master desired I might not be set on Shore, the Captain told him, I should stay on Board if he desired it, but then I should be hang'd; so he might chuse for me which he thought best: The Captain, it seems, was particularly provok'd at my being concerned in the Treachery, because of his having been so kind to me, and of his having singled me out to serve him, as I have said above; and this perhaps obliged him to give my Master such a rough Choice, either to set me on Shore, or to have me hang'd on Board: And had my Master indeed known what good Will I had for him, he would not ha' been long in Chusing for me; for I had certainly determined to do him a Mischief the first Opportunity I had had for it. This was therefore a good Providence for me, to keep me from dipping my Hands in Blood, and it made me more tender afterwards in Matters of Blood, than I believe I should otherwise have been. But as to my being one of them that was to kill the Captain, that I was wrong'd in, for I was not the Person; but it was really one of them that were pardoned, he having the good Luck not to have that Part discovered.

I was now to enter upon a Part[21] of independent Life, a thing I was indeed very ill prepared to manage; for I was perfectly loose and dissolute in my Behaviour, bold and wicked while I was under Government, and now perfectly unfit to be trusted with Liberty; for I was as ripe for any Villainy, as a young Fellow that had no solid Thought ever placed in his Mind could be supposed to be. Education, as you have heard, I had none; and all the little Scenes of Life I had pass'd thro', had been full of Dangers and desperate Circumstances; but I was either so young, or so stupid, that I escaped the Grief and Anxiety of them, for want of having a Sense of their Tendency and Consequences.

This thoughtless, unconcern'd Temper had one Felicity indeed in it; that it made me daring and ready for doing any Mischief, and kept off the Sorrow which otherwise ought to have attended me when I fell into any Mischief; that this Stupidity was instead of a Happiness to me, for it left my Thoughts free to act upon Means of Escape and Deliverance in my Distress, however great it might be; whereas my Companions in the Misery, were so sunk by their Fear and Grief, that they abandoned themselves to the Misery of their Condition, and gave over all Thought but of their perishing and starving, being devoured by wild Beasts, murthered, and perhaps eaten by *Cannibals, and the like.*

I was but a young Fellow about 17 or 18; but hearing what was to be my Fate, I received it with no Appearance of Discouragement; but I asked what my Master said to it, and being told that he had used his utmost Interest to save me, but the Captain had answered I should either go on Shore or be hanged on Board, which he pleased; I then gave over all Hope of being received again: I was not very thankful in my Thoughts to my Master for his solliciting the Captain for me, because I knew that what he did was not in Kindness to me, so much as in Kindness to himself; I mean to preserve the Wages which he got for me, which amounted to above six Dollars[22] a Month, including what the Captain allowed him for my particular Service to him.

When I understood that my Master was so apparently kind, I asked if I might not be admitted to speak with him, and they told me I might, if my Master would come down to me, but I could not be allowed to come up to him; so then I desired my Master might be spoke to to come to me, and he accordingly came to me; I fell on my Knees to him, and begg'd he would forgive me what I had done to displease him; and indeed the Resolution I had taken to murther him, lay with some Horrour upon my Mind just at that Time, so that I was once just a-going to confess it, and beg him to forgive me, but I kept it in: He told me he had done all he could to obtain my Pardon of the Captain, but could not; and he knew no Way for me but to have Patience, and submit to my Fate; and if they came to speak with any Ship of their Nation at the Cape, he would endeavour to have them stand in,[23] and fetch us off again if we might be found.

Then I begg'd I might have my Clothes on Shore with me. He told me he was afraid I should have little Need of Clothes, for he did not see how we could long subsist on the Island, and that he had been told that the Inhabitants were *Cannibals* or *Men-eaters* (tho' he had no Reason for that Suggestion) and we should not be able to live among them. I told him I was not so afraid of that, as I was of starving for want of Victuals; and as for the Inhabitants being *Cannibals*, I believed we should be more likely to eat them, than they us, if we could but get at them: But I was mightily concerned, I said, we should have no Weapons with us to defend our selves, and I begg'd nothing now, but that he would give me a Gun and a Sword, with a little Powder and Shot.

He smiled and said, they would signify nothing to us, for it was impossible for us to pretend to preserve our Lives among such a populous and desperate Nation as the People of the Island were. I told him, that however it would do us this Good, for we should not be devoured or destroy'd immediately; so I begged hard for the Gun. At last he told me, he did not know whether the Captain would give him Leave to give me a Gun, and if not, he durst not do it; but he promised to use his Interest to obtain it for me, which he did, and the next Day he sent me a Gun, with some Ammunition, but told me, the Captain would not suffer the Ammunition to be given us, till we were set all on Shore, and till he was just going to set Sail. He also sent me the few Clothes I had in the Ship, which indeed were not many.

Two Days after this we were all carried on Shore together; the rest of my Fellow-Criminals hearing I had a Gun, and some Powder and Shot, sollicited for Liberty to carry the like with them, which was also granted them; and thus we were set on Shore to shift for our selves.

At our first coming into the Island, we were terrified exceedingly with the Sight of the barbarous People; whose Figure was made more terrible to us than really it was, by the Report we had of them from the Seamen; but when we came to converse with them a while, we found they were not *Cannibals*, as was reported, or such as would fall immediately upon us and eat us up; but they came and sat down by us, and wondered much at our Clothes and Arms, and made Signs to give us some Victuals, such as they had, which was only Roots and Plants dug out of the Ground, for the present, but they brought us Fowls and Flesh afterwards in good Plenty.

This encouraged the other four Men that were with me very much, for they were quite dejected before; but now they began to be very familiar with them, and made Signs, that if they would use us kindly, we would stay and live with them; which they seemed glad of, tho' they knew little of the Necessity we were under to do so, or how much we were afraid of them.

However, upon other Thoughts, we resolved that we would only stay in that Part so long as the Ship rid in the Bay, and then making them believe we were gone with the Ship, we would go and place our selves, if possible, where there were no Inhabitants to be seen, and so live as we could, or perhaps watch for a Ship that might be driven upon the Coast, as we were.

The Ship continued a Fortnight in the Road[24] repairing some Damage which had been done her in the late Storm, and taking in Wood and Water; and during this time the Boat coming often on Shore, the Men brought us several Refreshments, and the Natives believing we only belong'd to the Ship, were civil enough. We lived in a kind of a Tent on the Shore, or rather a Hut, which we made with the Boughs of Trees, and sometimes in the Night retired to a Wood a little out of their Way, to let them think we were gone on board the Ship. However, we found them barbarous, treacherous, and villainous enough in their Nature, only civil for Fear, and therefore concluded we should soon fall into their Hands when the Ship was gone.

The Sense of this wrought upon my Fellow-Sufferers even to Distraction; and one of them, being a Carpenter, in his mad Fit, swam off to the Ship in the Night, tho' she lay then a League to Sea, and made such pitiful Moan to be taken in, that the Captain was prevailed with at last to take him in, tho' they let him lye swimming three Hours in the Water before he consented to it.

Upon this, and his humble Submission, the Captain received him, and, in a word, the Importunity of this Man (who for some time petition'd to be taken in, tho' they hanged him[25] as soon as they had him) was such as could not be resisted; for, after he had swam so long about the Ship, he was not able to have reached the Shore again; and the Captain saw evidently that the Man must be taken on Board, or suffered to drown, and the whole Ship's Company offering to be bound for him for his good Behaviour, the Captain at last yielded, and he was taken up, but almost dead with his being so long in the Water.

When this Man was got in, he never left Importuning the Captain and all the rest of the Officers in Behalf of us that were behind, but to the very last Day the Captain was inexorable; when, at the time their Preparations were making to sail, and Orders given to hoist the Boats into the Ship, all the Seamen in a Body came up to the Rail of the Quarter-Deck, where the

Captain was walking with some of his Officers, and appointing the Boat-swain to speak for them, he went up, and falling on his Knees to the Captain, begged of him in the humblest manner possible, to receive the four Men on Board again, offering to answer for their Fidelity, or to have them kept in Chains till they came to *Lisbon*, and there to be delivered up to Justice, rather than, as they said, to have them left to be murthered by Savages, or devoured by wild Beasts. It was a great while e'er the Captain took any Notice of them, but when he did he ordered the Boatswain to be seized, and threatned to bring him to the Capstern[26] for speaking for them.

Upon this Severity, one of the Seamen, bolder than the rest, but still with all possible Respect to the Captain, besought his Honour, as he called him, that he would give Leave to some more of them to go on Shore, and die with their Companions, or, if possible, to assist them to resist the Bar-barians. The Captain, rather provoked than cowd with this, came to the Barricado[27] of the Quarter-Deck, and speaking very prudently to the Men, (for, had he spoken roughly, two Thirds of them would have left the Ship, if not all of them) he told them, it was for their Safety as well as his own, that he had been obliged to that Severity; that Mutiny on board a Ship was the same thing as Treason in the King's Palace, and he could not answer it to his Owners and Employers to trust the Ship and Goods Committed to his Charge, with Men who had entertained Thoughts of the worst and black-est Nature; that he wished heartily that it had been any where else that they had been set on Shore, where they might have been in less Hazard from the Savages; that if he had designed they should be destroyed, he could as well have executed them on board as the other two; that he wished it had been in some other Part of the World, where he might have delivered them up to the Civil Justice, or might have left them among Christians; but that it was better their Lives were put in Hazard, than his Life, and the Safety of the Ship; and that tho' he did not know that he had deserved so ill of any of them, as that they should leave the Ship, rather than do their Duty; yet if any of them were resolved to do so unless he would consent to take a Gang of Traytors on board, who, as he had proved before them all, had conspired to murther him, he would not hinder them, nor, for the present, would he resent their Importunity; but if there was no body left in the Ship but himself, he would never consent to take them on board.

This Discourse was delivered so well, was in it self so reasonable, was managed with so much Temper, yet so boldly concluded with a Negative, that the greatest Part of the Men were satisfied for the present: However, as it put the Men into Juncto's and Cabals,[28] and they were not composed for some Hours; the Wind also slackening towards Night, the Captain ordered not to weigh till next Morning.

The same Night 23 of the Men, among whom was the Gunner's Mate, the Surgeon's Assistant, and two Carpenters, applying to the Chief Mate, told him, that as the Captain had given them Leave to go on Shore to their Comerades, they begged, that he would speak to the Captain not to take it ill that they were desirous to go and die with their Companions; and that they thought they could do no less in such an Extremity, than go to them; because if there was any way to save their Lives, it was by adding to their Numbers, and making them strong enough to assist one another in defending themselves against the Savages, till perhaps they might one time or other find Means to make their Escape, and get to their own Country again.

The Mate told them in so many Words, that he durst not speak to the Captain upon any such Design, and was very sorry they had no more Respect for him, than to desire him to go of such an Errand; but if they were resolved upon such an Enterprize, he would advise them to take the Long-Boat in the Morning betimes, and go off, seeing the Captain had given them Leave, and leave a civil Letter behind them to the Captain, and to desire him to send his Men on Shore for the Boat, which should be delivered very honestly, and he promised to keep their Counsel so long.

Accordingly an Hour before Day, those 23 Men, with every Man a Fire-lock[29] and Cutlass, with some Pistols, three Halbards or Half-Pikes, and good Store of Powder and Ball, without any Provision but about Half an Hundred of Bread, but with all their Chests and Clothes, Tools, Instruments, Books, &c. embarked themselves so silently, that the Captain got no Notice of it till they were gotten half the Way on Shore.

As soon as the Captain heard of it, he called for the Gunner's Mate, *the Chief Gunner being at that time sick in his Cabbin*, and ordered to fire at them; but, to his great Mortification, the Gunner's Mate was one of the Number, and was gone with them; and indeed it was by his Means they got so many Arms, and so much Ammunition. When the Captain found how it was, and that there was no Help for it, he began to be a little appeased, made light of it, and called up the Men, spoke kindly to them, and told them he was very well satisfied in the Fidelity and Ability of those that were now left; and that he would give to them, for their Encouragement, to be divided among them, the Wages which was due to the Men that were gone; and that it was a great Satisfaction to him that the Ship was freed from such a mutinous Rabble, who had not the least Reason for their Discontent.

The Men seemed very well satisfied, and particularly the Promise of the Wages of those that were gone, went a great way with them. After this the Letter which was left by the Men was given to the Captain, by his Boy, with whom, it seems, the Men had left it. The Letter was much to the same Purpose of what they had said to the Mate, and which he declined to say for them; only that at the End of their Letter they told the Captain, that as they had no dishonest Design, so they had taken nothing away with them which was not their own, except some Arms and Ammunition, such as were absolutely necessary to them, as well for their Defence against the Savages, as to kill Fowls or Beasts for their Food, that they might not perish; and as there were considerable Sums due to them for Wages, they hoped he would allow the Arms and Ammunition upon their Accounts. They told him, that as to the Ship's Long-Boat which they had taken to bring them on Shore, they knew it was necessary to him, and they were very willing to restore it to him; and if he pleased to send for it, it should be very honestly delivered to his Men, and not the least Injury offered to any of those who came for it, nor the least Perswasion or Invitation made use of to any of them to stay with them; and at the Bottom of the Letter they very humbly besought him, that for their Defence, and for the Safety of their Lives he would be pleased to send them a Barrel of Powder, and some Ammunition, and give them Leave to keep the Mast and Sail of the Boat, that if it was possible for them to make themselves a Boat of any kind, they might shift off to Sea to save themselves in such Part of the World as their Fate should direct them to.

Upon this the Captain, who had won much upon the rest of his Men by what he had said to them, and was very easy as to the General Peace; (for it was very true, that the most mutinous of the Men were gone) came out to the Quarter-Deck, and calling the Men together, let them know the Substance of the Letter; and told the Men, that however they had not deserved such Civility from him, yet he was not willing to expose them more than they were willing to expose themselves, he was inclined to send them some Ammunition; and as they had desired but one Barrel of Powder, he would send them two Barrels, and Shot, or Lead, and Moulds to make Shot in proportion: and, to let them see that he was civiller to them than they deserved, he ordered a Cask of Arrack,[30] and a great Bag of Bread to be sent them for Subsistence, till they should be able to furnish themselves.

The rest of the Men applauded the Captain's Generosity, and every one of them sent us some thing or other; and about three in the Afternoon the Pinnace[31] came on Shore, and brought us all these things, which we were very glad of, and returned the Long-Boat accordingly; and as to the Men that came with the Pinnace, as the Captain had singled out such Men as he knew would not come over to us, so they had positive Orders not to bring any one of us on board again, upon Pain of Death; and indeed both were so true to our Points, that we neither asked them to stay, nor they us to go.

We were now a good Troop, being in all 27 Men, very well armed and provided with every thing but Victuals; we had two Carpenters among us, a Gunner, and, which was worth all the rest, a Surgeon or Doctor, that is to say, he was an Assistant to a Surgeon at *Goa*, and was entertained as Supernumerary with us: The Carpenters had brought all their Tools, the Doctor all his Instruments and Medicines, and indeed we had a great deal of Baggage, that is to say, in the whole, for *some of us* had little more than the Clothes on our Backs, of whom I was one; but I had one thing which none of them had *viz.* I had the 22 Moydores of Gold, which I stole at the *Brasils*, and two Pieces of Eight. The two Peices of Eight I shewed, and one Moydore, but no more; and none of them ever suspected that I had any more Money in the World, having been known to be only a poor Boy taken up in Charity, as you have heard, and used like a Slave, and in the worst Manner of a Slave, by my cruel Master the Pilot.

It will be easy to imagine we four, that were left at first, were joyful, nay, even surprized with Joy, at the coming of the rest, tho at first we were frighted, and thought they came to fetch us back to hang us; but they took ways quickly to satisfy us that they were in the same Condition with us, only with this additional Circumstance, that theirs was voluntarily, and ours by Force.

The first Piece of News they told us after the short History of their coming away, was that our Companion was on board, but how he got thither we could not imagine; for he had given us the Slip, and we never imagined he could swim so well as to venture off to the Ship, which lay at so great a Distance; nay, we did not so much as know that he could swim at all, and not thinking any thing of what really happen'd, we thought that he must have wandered into the Woods, and was devoured, or was fallen into the Hands of the Natives and was murthered; and these Thoughts filled us with Fears enough, and of several kinds, about its being some time or other our Lot to fall into their Hands also.

But hearing how he had with much Difficulty been received on board the Ship again, and pardon'd, we were much better satisfied than before.

Being now, as I have said, a considerable Number of us, and in Condition to defend our selves, the first thing we did was to give every one his Hand, that we would not separate from one another upon any Occasion whatsoever, but that we would live and die together; that we would kill no Food, but that we would distribute it in publick; and that we would be in all things guided by the Majority, and not insist upon our own Resolutions in any thing, if the Majority were against it; that we would appoint a Captain among us to be our Governour or Leader during Pleasure; that while he was in Office, we would obey him without Reserve, on Pain of Death; and that every one should take Turn, but the Captain was not to act in any particular thing without Advice of the rest, and by the Majority.

Having established these Rules, we resolved to enter into some Measures for our Food, and for conversing with the Inhabitants or Natives of the Island, for our Supply; as for Food, they were at first very useful to us, but we soon grew weary of them, being an ignorant, ravenous, brutish sort of People, even worse than the Natives of any other Country that we had seen; and we soon found that the principal Part of our Subsistance was to be had by our Guns, shooting of Deer and other Creatures, and Fowls of all other Sorts, of which there is Abundance.

We found the Natives did not disturb or concern themselves much about us; nor did they enquire, or perhaps know whether we stay'd among them or not, much less that our Ship was gone quite away, and had cast us off, as was our Case; for the next Morning after we had sent back the Long-Boat, the Ship stood away to the South-East, and in four Hours time was out of our Sight.

The next Day two of us went out into the Country one Way, and two another, to see what kind of a Land we were in; and we soon found the Country was very pleasant and fruitful, and a convenient Place enough to live in; but as before, inhabited by a Parcel of Creatures scarce human, or capable of being made sociable on any Account Whatsoever.

We found the Place full of Cattle and Provisions; but whether we might venture to take them where we could find them, or not, we did not know; and tho' we were under a Necessity to get Provisions, yet we were loath to bring down a whole Nation of Devils upon us at once, and therefore some of our Company agreed to try to speak with some of the Country, if we could, that we might see what Course was to be taken with them. Eleven of our Men went of this Errand, well armed, and furnished for Defence. They brought Word, that they had seen some of the Natives, who appeared very civil to them, but very shy and afraid, seeing their Guns; for it was easy to perceive, that the Natives knew what their Guns were, and what Use they were of.

They made Signs to the Natives for some Food, and they went and fetched several Herbs and Roots, and some Milk; but it was evident they did not design to give it away, but to sell, making Signs to know what our Men would give them.

Our Men were perplexed at this, for they had nothing to Barter; however, one of the Men pulled out a Knife and shewed them, and they were so fond of it, that they were ready to go together by the Ears[32] for the Knife: The Seaman seeing that, was willing to make a good Market of his Knife, and keeping them chaffering[33] about it a good while, some offered him Roots, and others Milk; at last one offered him a Goat for it, which he took. Then another of our Men shewed them another Knife, but they had nothing good enough for that; whereupon one of them made Signs that he would go and fetch something; so our Men stay'd three Hours for their Return, when they came back and brought him a small sized, thick, short Cow, very fat, and good Meat, and gave him for his Knife.

This was a good Market, but our Misfortune was we had no Merchandize; for our Knives were as needful to us as to them, and but that we were in Distress for Food, and must of Necessity have some, these Men would not have parted with their Knives.

However, in a little time more we found that the Woods were full of living Creatures which we might kill for our Food, and that without giving Offence to them; so that our Men went daily out a Hunting, and never failed to kill something or other; for as to the Natives, we had no Goods to Barter; and for Money, all the Stock among us would not have subsisted us long; however, we called a general Council to see what Money we had, and to bring it all together, that it might go as far as possible; and when it came to my Turn, I pulled out a Moydore and the two Dollars I spoke of before.

This Moydore I ventured to shew, that they might not despise me too much for adding too little to the Store, and that they might not pretend to search me; and they were very civil to me upon the Presumption that I had been so faithful to them as not to conceal any thing from them.

But our Money did us little Service, for the People neither knew the Value or the Use of it, nor could they justly rate the Gold in Proportion with the Silver; so that all our Money, which was not much when it was all put together, would go but a little way with us, that is to say, to buy us Provisions.

Our next Consideration was to get away from this cursed Place, and whether[34] to go; when my Opinion came to be asked, I told them I would leave that all to them, and I told them I had rather they would let me go into the Woods to get them some Provisions, than consult with me, for I would agree to whatever they did; but they would not agree to that, for they would not consent that any of us should go into the Woods alone; for tho' we had yet seen no Lions or Tygers in the Woods, we were assured there were many in the Island, besides other Creatures as dangerous, and, perhaps worse, as we afterwards found by our own Experience.

We had many Adventures in the Woods for our Provisions, and often met with wild and terrible Beasts, which we could not call by their Names, but as they were like us seeking their Prey, but were themselves good for nothing, so we disturbed them as little as possible.

Our Consultations concerning our Escape from this Place, which as I have said, we were now upon, ended in this only, that as we had two Carpenters among us, and that they had Tools almost of all Sorts with them, we should try to build us a Boat to go off to Sea with, and that then perhaps we might find our way back to *Goa*, or land on some more proper Place to make our Escape. The Counsels of this Assembly were not of great Moment, yet as they seem to be introductory of many more remarkable Adventures which happened under my Conduct hereabouts many Years after, I think this Miniature of my future Enterprizes may not be unpleasant to relate.

To the Building of a Boat I made no Objection, and away they went to work immediately; but as they went on, great Difficulties occurred, such as want of Saws to cut out Plank; Nails, Bolts, and Spikes, to fasten the Timbers, Hemp, Pitch and Tar, to Caulk and Pay[35] her Seams, *and the like*: At length one of the Company proposed, that instead of building a Bark or Sloop, or Shalloup,[36] or whatever they would call it, which they found was so difficult, they should rather make a large *Periagua*, or Canoe, which might be done with great Ease.

It was presently objected, that we could never make a Canoe large enough to pass the great Ocean, which we were to go over, to get to the Coast of *Malabar*,[37] that it not only would not bear the Sea, but it would never bear the Burthen; for we were not only Twenty seven Men of us, but had a great deal of Luggage with us, and must, for our Provision, take in a great deal more.

I never proposed to speak in their General Consultations before; but finding they were at some Loss about what kind of Vessel they should make, and how to make it; and what would be fit for our Use, and what not; I told them I found they were at a full Stop in their Counsels of every kind; that it was true we could never pretend to go over to *Goa*, or the Coast of *Malabar* in a Canoe, which tho' we could all get into it, and that it would bear the Sea well enough, yet would not hold our Provisions, and especially we could not put fresh Water enough into it for the Voyage; and to make such an Adventure would be nothing but meer running into certain Destruction, and yet that nevertheless I was for making a Canoe.

They answered, that they understood all I had said before well enough, but what I meant by telling them first how dangerous and impossible it was to make our Escape in a Canoe, and yet then to advise making a Canoe, that they could not understand.

To this I answer'd that I conceiv'd our Business was not to attempt our Escape in a Canoe but that as there were other Vessels at Sea besides our Ship, and that there were few Nations that lived on the Sea-Shore that were so barbarous, but that they went to Sea in some Boats or other, our Business was to cruise along the Coast of the Island, which was very long, and to seize upon the first we could get that was better than our own, and so from that to another, till perhaps we might at last get a good Ship to carry us whither ever we pleased to go.

Excellent Advice, says one of them, admirable Advice, says another. Yes, yes, says the third, which was the Gunner, the *English* Dog has given excellent Advice; but it is just the way to bring us all to the Gallows; the Rogue has given Devilish Advice, indeed, to go a Thieving, till from a little Vessel we come to a great Ship, and so we shall turn downright Pyrates, the End of which is to be hanged.

You may call us Pyrates, says another, if you will, and if we fall into bad Hands, we may be used like Pyrates; but I care not for that, I'll be a Pyrate, or any thing, nay, I'll be hang'd for a Pyrate, rather than starve here; and therefore I think the Advice is very good; and so they cry'd all, Let us have a Canoe. The Gunner over-ruled by the rest, submitted; but as we broke up the Council, he came to me, takes me by the Hand, and looking into the Palm of my Hand, and into my Face too, very gravely, My Lad, *says he*, thou art born to do a World of Mischief; thou hast commenced Pyrate very young, but have a Care of the Gallows, young Man; have a Care, I say, for thou wilt be an eminent Thief.

I laugh'd at him, and told him, I did not know what I might come to hereafter; but as our Case was now, I should make no Scruple to take the first Ship I came at, to get our Liberty: I only wish'd we could see one, and come at her. Just while we were talking, one of our Men that was at the Door of our Hutt, told us, that the Carpenter, who, it seems, was upon a Hill at a Distance, cried out, *a Sail, a Sail*.

We all turn'd out immediately; but tho' it was very clear Weather, we could see nothing; but the Carpenter continuing to holloo to us, *a Sail, a Sail*, away we run up the Hill, and there we saw a Ship plainly; but it was at a very great Distance, too far for us to make any Signal to her. However, we made a Fire upon the Hill, with all the Wood we could get together, and made as much Smoke as possible. The Wind was down, and it was almost calm; but as we thought by a Perspective Glass[38] which the Gunner had in his Pocket, her Sails were full, and she stood away large with the

Wind at E.N.E. taking no Notice of our Signal, but making for the Cape *de bona Speranza*; so we had no Comfort from her.

We went therefore immediately to Work about our intended Canoe, and having singled out a very large Tree to our Mind, we fell to Work with her; and having three good Axes among us, we got it down, but it was four Days time first, tho' we worked very hard too. I do not remember what Wood it was, or exactly what Dimensions: but I remember that it was a very large one, and we were as much encouraged when we launched it, and found it swam upright and steady, as we would have been at another time, if we had a good Man of War at our Command.

She was so very large, that she carried us all very easily, and would have carried two or three Ton of Baggage with us; so that we began to consult about going to Sea directly to *Goa*; but many other Considerations check'd that Thought, especially when we came to look nearer into it; such as Want of Provisions, and no Casks for fresh Water; no Compass to steer by; no Shelter from the Breach of the high Sea, which would certainly founder us; no Defence from the Heat of the Weather, and the like; so that they all came readily into my project, to cruise about where we were, and see what might offer.

Accordingly, to gratify our Fancy, we went one Day all out to Sea in her together, and we were in a very fair Way to have had enough of it; for when she had us all on Board; and that we were gotten about Half a League to Sea, there happening to be a pretty high Swell of the Sea, tho' little or no Wind, yet she wallow'd so in the Sea, that we all of us thought she would at last wallow her self Bottom up; so we set all to Work to get her in nearer the Shore, and giving her fresh Way[39] in the Sea, she swam more steady, and with some hard Work we got her under the Land again.

We were now at a great Loss; the Natives were civil enough to us, and came often to discourse with us; one time they brought one whom they shew'd Respect to as a King, with them, and they set up a long Pole between them and us, with a great Tossel[40] of Hair hanging, not on the Top, but something above the Middle of it, adorn'd with little Chains, Shells, Bits of Brass, and the like; and this we understood afterwards was a Token of Amity and Friendship, and they brought down to us Victuals in Abundance, Cattel, Fowls, Herbs, Roots, but we were in the utmost Confusion on our Side; for we had nothing to buy with, or exchange for; and as to giving us things for nothing, they had no Notion of that again. As to our Money, it was meer Trash to them, they had no Value for it; so that we were in a fair Way to be starved. Had we had but some Toys and Trinckets, Brass Chains, Baubles, Glass Beads, or in a Word, the veriest Trifles that a Ship Loading would not have been worth the Freight, we might have bought

Cattel and Provisions enough for an Army, or to Victual a Fleet of Men of War, but for Gold or Silver we could get nothing.

Upon this we were in a strange Consternation. I was but a young Fellow, but I was for falling upon them with our Fire Arms; and taking all the Cattel from them, and send them to the Devil to stop their Hunger, rather than be starved our selves; but I did not consider that this might have brought Ten Thousand of them down upon us the next Day; and tho' we might have killed a vast Number of them, and perhaps have frighted the rest, yet their own Desperation, and our small Number, would have animated them so, that one time or other they would have destroy'd us all.

In the Middle of our Consultation, one of our Men who had been a kind of a Cutler, or Worker in Iron, started up, and ask'd the Carpenter, if among all his Tools he could not help him to a File. Yes, says the Carpenter, I can, but it is a small one. The smaller the better, says the other. Upon this he goes to Work, and first by heating a Piece of an old broken Chissel in the Fire, and then with the Help of his File, he made himself several Kinds of Tools for his Work; and then he takes three or four Pieces of Eight, and beats them out with a Hammer upon a Stone, till they were very broad and thin, then he cut them out into the Shape of Birds and Beasts; he made little Chains of them for Bracelets and Necklaces, and turn'd them into so many Devices, of his own Head, that it is hardly to be exprest.

When he had for about a Fortnight exercised his Head and Hands at this Work, we try'd the Effect of his Ingenuity; and having another Meeting with the Natives, were surprized to see the Folly of the poor People. For a little Bit of Silver cut out in the Shape of a Bird, we had two Cows; and, which was our Loss, if it had been in Brass, it had been still of more Value. For one of the Bracelets made of Chain-work, we had as much Provision of several Sorts, as would fairly have been worth in *England*, Fifteen or Sixteen Pounds; and so of all the rest. Thus, that which when it was in Coin was not worth Six-pence to us, when thus converted into Toys and Trifles, was worth an Hundred Times its real Value, and purchased for us any thing we had Occasion for.

In this Condition, we lived upwards of a Year, but all of us began to be very much tir'd of it, and whatever came of it, resolv'd to attempt an Escape. We had furnished our selves with no less than three very good Canoes; and as the *Monsoones*, or Trade-Winds, generally affect that Country, blowing in most Parts of this Island one six Months of a Year one Way, and the other six Months another Way, we concluded we might be able to bear the Sea well enough. But always when we came to look nearer into it, the Want of fresh Water was the thing that put us off from such an Adventure, for it is a prodigious Length, and what no Man on Earth could be able to perform without Water to drink.

Being thus prevailed upon by our own Reason to set the Thoughts of that Voyage aside, we had then but two things before us; one was, to put to Sea the other Way, *viz.* West, and go away for the *Cape of Good Hope*, where first or last we should meet with some of our own Country Ships, or else to put for the main Land of *Africa*, and either travel by Land, or sail along the Coast towards the Red Sea; where we should first or last find a Ship of some Nation or other, that would take us up, or perhaps we might take them up; which, by the bye, was the thing that always run in my Head.

It was our ingenious Cutler, whom ever after we called *Silver-Smith*, that proposed this; but the Gunner told him, that he had been in the Red Sea, in a *Malabar* Sloop, and he knew this, that if we went into the Red Sea, we should either be killed by the wild *Arabs*, or taken and made Slaves of by the *Turks*; and therefore he was not for going that Way.

Upon this I took Occasion to put in my Vote again. *Why*, said I; *do we talk of being killed by the* Arabs; *or made Slaves of by the* Turks? *Are we not able to board almost any Vessel we shall meet with in those Seas; and instead of their taking us, we to take them?* Well done, Pyrate, said the Gunner, he that had look'd in my Hand, and told me I should come to the Gallows; *I'll say that for him, says he, he always looks the same Way. But I think o' my Conscience, 'tis our only Way now.* Don't tell me, *says I*, of being a Pyrate, *we must be Pyrates, or any thing, to get fairly out of this cursed Place.*

In a Word, they concluded all by my Advice, that our Business was to cruize[41] for any thing we could see. Why then, *said I* to them, our first Business is to see, if the People upon this Island have no Navigation, and what Boats they use; and if they have any better or bigger than ours, let us take one of them. First indeed all our Aim was to get, if possible, a Boat with a Deck and a Sail; for then we might have saved our provisions, which otherwise we could not.

We had, to our great good Fortune, one Sailor among us, who had been Assistant to the Cook, he told us, that he would find a Way how to preserve our Beef, without Cask or Pickle; and this he did effectually by curing it in the Sun, with the Help of Salt-Petre, of which there was great Plenty in the Island; so that before we found any Method for our Escape, we had dry'd the Flesh of six or seven Cows and Bullocks, and ten or twelve Goats, and it relished so well, that we never gave our selves the Trouble to boil it when we eat it, but either broiled[42] it, or eat it dry: But our main Difficulty about fresh Water still remained; for we had no Vessel to put any into, much less to keep any for our going to Sea.

But our first Voyage being only to coast the Island, we resolved to venture, whatever the Hazard or Consequence of it might be; and in order to preserve as much fresh Water as we could, our Carpenter made a Well thwart the Middle of one of our Canoes, which he separated from the other Parts of the Canoe, so as to make it tight to hold the Water, and cover'd so as we might step upon it; and this was so large, that it held near a Hogshead[43] of Water very well. I cannot better describe this Well, than by the same Kind which the small Fisher-Boats in *England* have to preserve their Fish alive in; only, that this, instead of having Holes to let the Salt Water in, was made sound every Way to keep it out; and it was the first Invention, I believe, of its Kind, for such an Use: But Necessity is a Spur to Ingenuity, and the Mother of Invention.

It wanted but a little Consultation to resolve now upon our Voyage. The first Design was only to coast it round the Island, as well to see if we could seize upon any Vessel fit to embark our selves in, as also to take hold of any Opportunity which might present for our passing over to the Main;[44] and therefore our Resolution was to go on the Inside, or West Shore of the Island, where at least at one Point, the Land stretching a great Way to the North-West, the Distance is not extraordinary great from the Island to the Coast of *Africk*.

Such a Voyage, and with such a desperate Crew, I believe was never made; for it is certain we took the worst Side of the Island to look for any Shipping, especially for Shipping of other Nations, this being quite out of the Way: However, we put to Sea, after taking all our Provisions and Ammunition, Bag and Baggage on Board; we had made both Mast and Sail for our two large Periagua's and the other we paddl'd along as well as we could; but when a Gale sprung up, we took her in Tow.

We sail'd merrily forward for several Days, meeting with nothing to interrupt us. We saw several of the Natives in small Canoes, catching Fish, and sometimes we endeavoured to come near enough to speak with them, but they were always shye, and afraid of us, making in for the Shore, as soon as we attempted it; till one of our Company remember'd the Signal of Friendship which the Natives made us from the South Part of the Island, *viz.* of setting up a long Pole, and put us in Mind, that perhaps it was the same thing to them as a Flag of Truce was to us: So we resolved to try it; and accordingly the next time we saw any of their Fishing Boats at Sea, we put up a Pole in our Canoe that had no Sail, and rowed towards them. As soon as they saw the Pole, they staid for us, and as we came nearer, paddl'd towards us. When they came to us, they shewed themselves very much pleased, and gave us some large Fish, of which we did not know the Names, but they were very good. It was our Misfortune still, that we had nothing to give them in Return; but our Artist, of whom I spoke before, gave them two little thin Plates of Silver, beaten, as I said before, out of a Piece of Eight; they were cut in a Diamond Square, longer one way than t'other, and a Hole punch'd at one of the longest Corners. This they were so fond of, that they made us stay till they had cast their Lines and Nets again, and gave us as many Fish as we cared to have.

All this while we had our Eyes upon their Boats, view'd them very narrowly, and examined whether any of them were fit for our Turn; but they were poor sorry things; their Sail was made of a large Matt, only one that was of a Piece of Cotton Stuff, fit for little, and their Ropes were twisted Flags,[45] of no Strength; so we concluded we were better as we were, and let them alone. We went forward to the North, keeping the Coast close on Board for twelve Days together; and having the Wind at East, and E.S.E. we made very fresh Way. We saw no Towns on the Shore, but often saw some Hutts by the Water Side, upon the Rocks, and always Abundance of People about them, who we could perceive run together to stare at us.

It was as odd a Voyage as ever Men went: We were a little Fleet of three Ships, and an Army of between Twenty and Thirty as dangerous Fellows as ever they had among them; and had they known what we were they would have compounded to give us every thing we desired, to be rid of us.

On the other Hand, we were as miserable as Nature could well make us to be; for we were upon *a* Voyage and *no* Voyage, we were bound *some* where and *no* where; for tho' we knew what we intended to do, we did really not know what we were doing: We went forward and forward by a Northerly Course; and as we advanced, the Heat increased, which began to be intolerable to us who were upon the Water, without any Covering from Heat or Wet; besides we were now in the Month of *October*, or there-abouts, in a Southern Latitude, and as we went every Day nearer the Sun, the Sun came also every Day nearer to us, till at last we found our selves in the Latitude of 20 Degrees, and having past the Tropick[46] about five or six Days before that, in a few Days more the Sun would be in the Zenith, just over our Heads.

Upon these Considerations we resolved to seek for a good Place to go on Shore again, and pitch our Tents till the Heat of the Weather abated. We had by this time measured Half the Length of the Island, and were come to that Part where the Shore tending away to the North-West, promised fair to make our Passage over to the main Land of *Africk*, much shorter than we expected. But notwithstanding that, we had good Reason to believe it was about 120 Leagues.

So, the Heats consider'd, we resolved to take Harbour; besides, our Provisions were exhausted, and we had not many Days Store left. Accordingly, putting in for the Shore early in the Morning, as we usually did once in three or four Days, for fresh Water, we sat down and considered, whether we should go on, or take up our Standing there; but upon several Considerations too long to repeat here, we did not like the Place, so we resolved to go on for a few Days longer.

After Sailing on N.W. by N. with a fresh Gale at S.E. about six Days, we found at a great Distance, a large Promontory, or Cape of Land, pushing out a long Way into the Sea; and as we were exceeding fond of seeing what was beyond the Cape, we resolved to double it before we took into Harbour; so we kept on our Way, the Gale continuing, and yet it was four Days more before we reach'd the Cape. But it is not possible to express the Discouragement and Melancholy that seized us all when we came thither; for when we made the Head Land of the Cape, we were surprized to see the Shore fall away on the other Side, as much as it had advanced on this Side, and a great deal more; and that, in short, if we would adventure over to the Shore of *Africk*, it must be from hence; for that if we went further, the Breadth of the Sea still increased, and to what Breadth it might increase, we knew not.

While we mused upon this Discovery, we were surprized with very bad Weather, and especially violent Rains, with Thunder and Lighting most unusually terrible to us. In this Pickle we run for the Shore, and getting under the Lee of the Cape, run our Frigates[47] into a little Creek, where we saw the Land overgrown with Trees, and made all the Haste possible to get on Shore, being exceeding wet, and fatigued with the Heat, the Thunder, Lightning and Rain.

Here we thought our Case was very deplorable indeed, and therefore our Artist, of whom I have spoken so often, set up a great Cross of Wood on the Hill, which was within a Mile of the Head Land, with these Words, but in the *Portuguese* Language,

Point Desperation. Jesus have Mercy!

We set to work immediately to build us some Hutts, and so get our Clothes dry'd, and tho' I was young, and had no Skill in such Things, yet I shall never forget the little City we built, for it was no less; and we fortify'd it accordingly; and the Idea is so fresh in my Thought, that I cannot but give a short Description of it.

Our Camp was on the South Side of a little Creek on the Sea, and under the Shelter of a steep Hill, which lay, tho' on the other Side of the Creek, yet within a Quarter of a Mile of us N.W. by N. and very happily intercepted the Heat of the Sun all the after Part of the Day. The Spot we pitched on had a little fresh Water, Brook, or a Stream running into the

Creek by us, and we saw Cattle feeding in the Plains and low Ground, East and to the South of us a great Way.

Here we set up twelve little Hutts, like Soldiers Tents, but made of the Boughs of Trees stuck into the Ground, and bound together on the Top with Withes,[48] and such other things as we could get; the Creek was our Defence on the North, a little Brook on the West, and the South and East Sides we fortify'd with a Bank, which entirely covered our Hutts; and being drawn oblique from the North West to the South East, made our City a Triangle. Behind the Bank, or Line, our Hutts stood, having three other Hutts behind them at a good Distance. In one of these, which was a little one, and stood further off, we put our Gun-powder, and nothing else, for fear of Danger; in the other, which was bigger, we drest our Victuals, and put all our Necessaries; and in the third, which was biggest of all, we eat our Dinners, called our Councils, and sat and diverted our selves with such Conversation as we had one with another, which was but indifferent truly at that time.

Our Correspondence with the Natives was absolutely necessary, and our Artist, the Cutler, having made Abundance of those little Diamond cut Squares of Silver, with these we made Shift to Traffick with the black People for what we wanted; for indeed they were pleased wonderfully with them: And thus we got Plenty of Provisions. At first, and in particular, we got about fifty Head of Black Cattel and Goats, and our Cook's Mate took care to cure them, and dry them, salt and preserve them for our grand Supply; nor was this hard to do, the Salt and Salt-Petre being very good, and the Sun excessively hot; and here we lived about four Months.

The Southern Solstice was over, and the Sun gone back towards the *Equinoctial*, when we considered of our next Adventure which was to go over the Sea of *Zanquebar*,[49] as the *Portuguese* call it, and to land, if possible, upon the Continent of *Africa*.

We talked with many of the Natives about it, such as we could make our selves intelligible to; but all that we could learn from them was, that there was a great Land of Lions beyond the Sea, but that it was a great Way off; we knew as well as they that it was a long Way, but our People differed mightily about it: Some said it was 150 Leagues, others not above 100. One of our Men that had a Map of the World shewed us by his Scale, that it was not above 80 Leagues. Some said there were Islands all the Way to touch at; some that there were no Islands at all: For my Part, I knew nothing of this Matter one way or another, but heard it all without Concern, whether it was near or far off; however, this we learned from an old Man who was blind, and led about by a Boy, that if we stay'd till the End of

August, we should be sure of the Wind to be fair, and the Sea smooth all the Voyage.

This was some Encouragement, but staying again was very unwelcome News to us, because that then the Sun would be returning again to the South, which was what our Men were very unwilling to. At last we called a Council of our whole Body; their Debates were too tedious to take Notice of, only to note, that when it came to *Captain Bob*, (for so they called me ever since I had taken State upon me before one of their great Princes) truly I was on no Side, it was not one Farthing Matter to me, I told them, whether we went or stayed, I had no home, and all the World was alike to me; so I left it entirely to them to determine.

In a Word, they saw plainly there was nothing to be done where we were, without Shipping; that if our Business indeed was only to eat and drink, we could not find a better Place in the World; but if our Business was to get away, and get home into our own Country, we could not find a Worse.

I confess, I liked the Country wonderfully, and even then had strange Notions of coming again to live there; and I used to say to them very often, that if I had but a Ship of 20 Guns, and a Sloop, and both well Manned, I would not desire a better Place in the World to make my self as rich as a King.

But to return to the Consultations they were in about going: Upon the whole, it was resolved to venture over for the Main; and venture we did, madly enough, indeed; for it was the wrong time of the Year to undertake such a Voyage in that Country; for, as the Winds hang Easterly all the Months from *September* to *March*, so they generally hang Westerly all the rest of the Year, and blew right in our Teeth, so that as soon as we had, with a kind of a Land Breeze, stretched over about 15 or 20 Leagues, and, as I may say, just enough to lose our selves, we found the Wind set in a steady fresh Gale or Breeze from the Sea, at West W.S.W. or S.W. by W. and never further from the West; so that, in a Word we could make nothing of it.

On the other Hand, the Vessel, such as we had would not lye close upon a Wind;[50] if so, we might have stretched away N.N.W. and have met with a great many Islands in our Way, as we found afterwards; but we could make nothing of it, tho' we tried, and by the trying had almost undone us all; for, stretching away to the North, as near the Wind as we could, we had forgotten the Shape and Position of the Island of *Madagascar* it self; how that we came off at the Head of a Promontory or Point of Land that lies about the Middle of the Island, and that stretches out West a great way into the Sea; and that now being run a Matter of 40 Leagues to the North, the Shore of the Island fell off again above 200 Miles to the East, so that we were by this Time in the wide Ocean, between the Island and the Main, and almost 100 Leagues from both.

Indeed as the Winds blew fresh at West, as before, we had a smooth Sea, and we found it pretty good going before it, and so taking our smallest Canoe in Tow, we stood in for the Shore with all the Sail we could make. This was a terrible Adventure; for if the least Gust of Wind had come, we had been all lost, our Canoes being deep, and in no Condition to make Way in a high Sea.

This Voyage, however, held us eleven Days in all, and at length having spent most of our Provisions, and every Drop of Water we had, we spied Land, to our great Joy, tho' at the Distance of ten or eleven Leagues, and as under the Land, the Wind came off like a Land Breeze, and blew hard against us, we were two Days more before we reached the Shore, having all that while excessive hot Weather, and not a Drop of Water, or any other Liquor, except some Cordial Waters, which one of our Company had a little of left in a Case of Bottles.

This gave us a Taste of what we should have done, if we had ventured forward with a scant Wind and uncertain Weather, and gave us a Surfeit of our Design for the Main, at least till we might have some better Vessels under us; so we went on Shore again, and pitched our Camp, as before, in as convenient Manner as we could, fortifying our selves against any Surprize; but the Natives here were exceeding courteous, and much civiller than on the South Part of the Island; and tho' we could not understand what they said, or they us, yet we found Means to make them understand that we were Sea-faring Men, and Strangers; and that we were in Distress for want of Provisions.

The first Proof we had of their Kindness was that, as soon as they saw us come on Shore, and begin to make our Habitation, one of their Captains or Kings, for we knew not what to call them, came down with five or six Men and some Women, and brought us five Goats and two young fat Steers, and gave them to us for nothing; and when we went to offer them any thing, the Captain, or the King, would not let any of them touch it, or take any thing of us. About two Hours after came another King or Captain, with forty or fifty Men after him; we began to be afraid of him, and laid Hands upon our Weapons; but he perceiving it, caused two Men to go before him carrying two long Poles in their Hands,[51] which they held upright, as high as they could, which we presently perceiv'd was a Signal of Peace, and these two Poles they set up afterwards sticking them up in the Ground; and when the King and his Men came to these two Poles, they stuck all their Lances up in the Ground, and came on unarmed, leaving their Lances, as also their Bows and Arrows behind them.

This was to satisfy us, that they were come as Friends, and we were very glad to see it; for we had no Mind to quarrel with them, if we could help it. The Captain of this Gang seeing some of our Men making up their Hutts, and that they did it but bunglingly, he becken'd to some of his Men to go and help us. Immediately 15 or 16 of them came and mingled among us, and went to Work for us; and, indeed, they were better Workmen than we were, for they run up three or four Hutts for us in a Moment, and much handsomer done than ours.

After this they sent us Milk, Plantanes,[52] Pumpkins, and Abundance of Roots and Greens that were very good, and then took their Leave, and would not take any thing from us that we had. One of our Men offer'd the King or Captain of these Men a Dram, which he drank, and was mightily pleased with it, and held out his Hand for another, which we gave him; and, in a Word, after this, he hardly failed coming to us two or three times a Week, always bringing us something or other, and one time sent us seven Head of Black Cattle, some of which we cured and dried as before.

And here I cannot but remember one thing, which afterwards stood us in great stead, *viz.* that the Flesh of their Goats and their Beef also, but especially the former, when we had dried and cured it, looked red, and eat hard and firm, as dry'd Beef in *Holland*; they were so pleased with it, and it was such a Dainty to them, that at any time after they would Trade with us for it, not knowing, or so much as imagining, what it was; so that for Ten or Twelve Pound Weight of smoked dry'd Beef, they would give us a whole Bullock, or Cow, or any thing else we could desire.

Here we observed two Things that were very material to us, even essentially so; first, we found they had a great deal of Earthen-Ware here, which they make use of many ways, as we did: Particularly they had long deep Earthen Pots, which they used to sink into the Ground to keep the Water which they drank cool and pleasant; and the other was, that they had larger Canoes than their Neighbours had.

By this we were prompted to enquire if they had no larger Vessels than those we saw there; or if any other of the Inhabitants had not such. They signified presently, that they had no larger Boats than that they shewed us; but that on the other Side of the Island they had larger Boats, and that with Decks upon them, and large Sails; and this made us resolve to Coast round the whole Island to see them; so we prepared and victualled our Canoe for the Voyage, and, in a Word, went to Sea for the third time.

It cost us a Month or six Weeks time to perform this Voyage, in which time we went on Shore several times for Water and Provisions, and found the Natives always very free and courteous; but we were surprized one Morning early, being at the Extremity of the Northermost Part of the Island, when one of our Men cried out *a Sail, a Sail*: We presently saw a Vessel a great Way out at Sea; but after we had looked at it with our Perspective Glasses, and endeavoured all we could to make out what it was, we could not tell what to think of it; for it was neither Ship, Ketch,[53] Gally, Galliot,[54] or like any thing that we had ever seen before: All that we could make of it was, that it went from us standing out to Sea. In a Word, we soon lost Sight of it, for we were in no Condition to chase any thing, and we never saw it again, but by all we could perceive of it, from what we saw of such things afterwards, it was some *Arabian* Vessel which had been trading to the Coast of *Mosambique*, or *Zanguebar*, the same Place where we afterwards went, as you shall hear.

I kept no Journal of this Voyage, nor indeed did I all this while understand any thing of Navigation, more than the common Business of a Foremast Man; so I can say nothing to the Latitudes or Distances of any Places we were at, how long we were going, or how far we sailed in a Day; but this I remember, that being now come round the Island, we sailed up the Eastern Shore due South, as we had done down the Western Shore due North before.

Nor do I remember that the Natives differed much from one another, either in Stature or Complexion, or in their Manners, their Habits their Weapons, or indeed in any thing; and yet we could not perceive that they had any Intelligence one with another; but they were extremely kind and civil to us on this Side, as well as on the other.

We continued our Voyage South for many Weeks, tho' with several Intervals of going on Shore to get Provisions and Water. At length, coming round a Point of Land which lay about a League farther than ordinary into the Sea, we were agreeably surprized with a Sight, which, no doubt, had been as disagreeable to those concern'd, as it was pleasant to us. This was the Wreck of an *European* Ship, which had been cast away upon the Rocks, which in that Place run a great Way into the Sea.

We could fee plainly at Low Water, a great deal of the Ship lay dry; even at High Water, she was not entirely covered; and that at most she did not lye above a League from the Shore. It will easily be believ'd, that our Curiosity led us, the Wind and Weather also permitting, to go directly to her, which we did without any Difficulty, and presently found that it was a *Dutch*-built Ship, and that she could not have been very long in that Condition, a great deal of the upper Work of her Stern remaining firm, with the Mizen Mast[55] standing. Her Stern seem'd to be jamm'd in between two

Ridges of the Rock, and so remained fast, all the Fore-part of the Ship having been beaten to Pieces.

We could see nothing to be gotten out of the Wreck that was worth our while; but we resolv'd to go on Shore, and stay sometime there-abouts, to see if perhaps we might get any Light into the Story of her, and we were not without Hopes that we might hear something more particular about her Men, and perhaps find some of them on Shore there, in the same Condition that we were in, and so might increase our Company.

It was a very pleasant Sight to us, when coming on Shore, we saw all the Marks and Tokens of a Ship-Carpenter's Yard; as a Launch Block and Craddles,[56] Scaffolds and Planks, and Pieces of Planks, the Remains of the Building a Ship or Vessel; and, in a Word, a great many things that fairly invited us to go about the same Work, and we soon came to understand, that the Men belonging to the Ship that was lost, had saved themselves on Shore, perhaps in their Boat, and had built themselves a Bark or Sloop, and so were gone to Sea again; and enquiring of the Natives which Way they went, they pointed to the South and South-West, by which we could easily understand that they were gone away to the *Cape of Good Hope*.

No body will imagine we could be so dull as not to gather from hence, that we might take the same Method for our Escapes; so we resolved first in general, that we would try, if possible, to build us a Boat of one Kind or other, and go to Sea as our Fate should direct.

In order to this, our first Work was to have the two Carpenters search about to see what Materials the *Dutchmen* had left behind them that might be of Use; and in particular, they found one that was very useful, and which I was much employ'd about, and that was a Pitch-Kettle, and a little Pitch in it.

When we came to set close to this Work, we found it very laborious and difficult, having but few Tools, no Iron Work, no Cordage, no Sails; so that, in short, whatever we built, we were oblig'd to be our own Smiths, Rope-Makers, Sail-Makers, and indeed to practise twenty Trades that we knew little or nothing of: However, Necessity was the Spur to Invention, and we did many things which before we thought impracticable, that is to say, in our Circumstances.

After our two Carpenters had resolved upon the Dimensions of what they would build, they set us all to Work, to go off in our Boats, and split up the Wreck of the old Ship, and to bring away every thing we could; and particularly, that, if possible, we should bring away the Mizen Mast, which was left standing, which with much Difficulty we effected, after above twenty Days Labour of fourteen of our Men.

At the same time we got out a great deal of Iron-Work; as Bolts, Spikes, Nails, &c. all which our Artist, of whom I have spoken already, who was now grown a very dexterous Smith, made us Nails and Hinges for our Rudder, and Spikes such as we wanted.

But we wanted an Anchor, and if we had had an Anchor, we could not have made a Cable; so we contented our selves with making some Ropes with the Help of the Natives, of such Stuff as they made their Matts of, and with these we made such a kind of cable or *Tow Line*, as was sufficient to fasten our Vessel to the Shore, which we contented our selves with for that time.

To be short, we spent four Months here, and work'd very hard too; at the End of which time we launch'd our Frigate, which, in a few Words, had many Defects, but yet, all things considered, it was as well as we could expect it to be.

In short, it was a kind of a Sloop, of the Burthen of near 18 or 20 Ton, and had we had Masts and Sails, standing, and running Rigging, as is usual in such Cases, and other Conveniences, the Vessel might have carry'd us wherever we could have had a Mind to go; but of all the Materials we wanted, this was the worst, *viz*, that we had no Tar or Pitch to pay the Seams, and secure the Bottom; and tho' we did what we could with Tallow and Oil, to make a Mixture to supply that Part, yet we could not bring it to answer our End fully; and when we launch'd her into the Water, she was so leaky, and took in the Water so fast, that we thought all our Labour had been lost, for we had much ado to make her swim; and as for Pumps, we had none, nor had we any Means to make one.

But at length one of the Natives, a black *Negro-man*, shewed us a Tree, the Wood of which being put into the Fire, sends forth a Liquid that is as glutinous, and almost as strong as Tar, and of which, by boiling, we made a Sort of Stuff which serv'd us for Pitch, and this answered our End effectually; for we perfectly made our Vessel sound and tight, so that we wanted no Pitch or Tar at all. This Secret has stood me in stead upon many Occasions since that time, in the same Place.

Our Vessel being thus finished, out of the Mizen Mast of the Ship, we made a very good Mast to her, and fitted our Sails to it as well as we could; then we made a Rudder and Tiller; and, in a Word, every thing that our present Necessity called upon us for; and having victualled her, and put as much fresh Water on Board as we thought we wanted, or as we knew how to stow (for we were yet without Casks) we put to Sea with a fair Wind.

We had spent near another Year in these Rambles, and in this Piece of Work; for it was now, as our Men said, about the Beginning of our *February*, and the Sun went from us apace, which was much to our Satisfaction, for the Heats were exceeding violent. The Wind, as I said, was fair, for as I have since learnt, the Winds generally spring up to the Eastward, as the Sun goes from them to the North.

Our Debate now was, which Way we should go, and never were Men so irresolute; some were for going to the East, and stretching away directly for the Coast of *Malabar*; but others who considered more seriously the Length of that Voyage, shook their Heads at the Proposal, knowing very well, that neither our Provisions, especially of Water; or our Vessel, were equal to such a Run as that is, of near 2000 Miles, without any Land to touch at in the Way.

These Men too had all along had a great Mind to a Voyage for the main Land of *Africk*, where they said we should have a fair Cast[57] for our Lives, and might be sure to make our selves rich which Way soever we went, if we were but able to make our Way through, whether by Sea or by Land.

Besides, as the Case stood with us, we had not much Choice for our Way; for if we had resolv'd for the East, we were at the wrong Season of the Year, and must have staid till *April* or *May* before we had gone to Sea. At length, as we had the Wind at S.E. and E.S.E. and fine promising Weather, we came all into the first Proposal, and resolved for the Coast of *Africa*; nor were we long in disputing as to our Coasting the Island, which we were upon; for we were now on the wrong Side of the Island for the Voyage we intended; So we stood away to the North, and having rounded the Cape, we hall'd away Southward under the Lee of the Island, thinking to reach the West Point of Land, which, as I observed before, runs out so far towards the Coast of *Africa*, as would have shorten'd our Run almost 100 Leagues. But when we had sailed about thirty Leagues, we found the Winds variable under the Shore, and right against us; so we concluded to stand over directly, for then we had the Wind fair, and our Vessel was but very ill fitted to lye near the Wind, or any Way indeed but just afore it.

Having resolv'd upon it therefore, we put in to the Shore, to furnish our selves again with fresh Water and other Provisions, and about the latter End of *March*, with more Courage than Discretion, more Resolution than Judgment, we launch'd for the main Coast of *Africa*.

As for me, I had no Anxieties about it; so that we had but a View of reaching some Land or other, I cared not what or where it was to be, having at this time no Views of what was before me, nor much Thought of what might, or might not befal me; but with as little Consideration as any one can be supposed to have at my Age, I consented to every thing that was proposed, however hazardous the thing it self, however improbable the Success.

The Voyage, as it was undertaken with a great deal of Ignorance and Desperation, so really it was not carry'd on with much Resolution or Judgment; for we knew no more of the Course we were to steer, than this, that it was any where about the West, within two or three Points N. or S. and as we had no Compass with us, but a little Brass Pocket Compass, which one of our Men had more by Accident than otherwise, so we could not be very exact in our Course.

However, as it pleased God that the Wind continued fair at S.E. and by E. we found that N.W. by W. which was right afore it, was as good a Course for us as any we could go, and thus we went on.

The Voyage was much longer than we expected; our Vessel also, which had no Sail that was proportion'd to her, made but very little Way in the Sea, and sail'd heavily. We had indeed no great Adventures happen'd in this Voyage, being out of the Way of every thing that could offer to divert us; and as for seeing any Vessel, we had not the least Occasion to hail any thing in all the Voyage; for we saw not one Vessel small or great, the Sea we were upon being entirely out of the way of all Commerce; for the People of *Madagascar* knew no more of the Shores of *Africa* than we did, only that there was a Country of Lions, as they call *it, that Way.*

We had been eight or nine Days under Sail, with a fair Wind, when, to our great Joy one of our Men cry'd out, *Land.* We had great Reason to be glad of the Discovery; for we had not Water enough left for above two or three Days more, tho' at a short Allowance. However, tho' it was early in the Morning when we discover'd it, we made it near Night before we reach'd it, the Wind slackening almost to a Calm, and our ship being, as I said, a very dull Sailer.

We were sadly baulk'd upon our coming to the Land, when we found, that instead of the main Land of *Africk*, it was only a little Island, with no Inhabitants upon it, at least, none that we could find; nor any Cattel, except a few Goats, of which we killed three only. However, they served us for fresh Meat, and we found very good Water; and it was fifteen Days more before we reach'd the Main, which, however, at last we arriv'd at; and which was most essential to us, we came to it just as all our Provisions were spent. Indeed we may say they were spent first; for we had but a Pint of Water a Day to each Man for the last two Days. But to our great Joy, we saw the Land, tho' at a great Distance, the Evening before, and by a pleasant Gale in the Night, were, by Morning, within two Leagues of the Shore.

We never scrupled going ashore at the first Place we came at, tho' had we had Patience, we might have found a very fine River a little farther North. However, we kept our Frigate on Float by the Help of two great Poles which we fasten'd into the Ground to *More*[58] her, like Piles; and the little weak Ropes, which, as I said, we had made of Matting, served us well enough to make the Vessel fast.

As soon as we had viewed the Country a little, got fresh Water, and furnished our selves with some Victuals, which we found very scarce here, we went on board again with our Stores. All we got for Provision, was some Fowls that we killed, and a kind of wild Buffloe, or Bull, very small, but good Meat: I say, having got these things on Board, we resolved to sail on along the Coast, which lay away N.N.E. till we found some Creek or River that we might run up into the Country, or some Town or People; for we had Reason enough to know the Place was inhabited, because we several times saw Fires in the Night, and Smoke in the Day, every way at a Distance from us.

At length we came to a very large Bay, and in it several little Creeks or Rivers emptying themselves into the Sea, and we run boldly into the first Creek we came at; where seeing some Hutts and wild People about them, on the Shore, we run our Vessel into a little Cove on the North Side of the Creek, and held up a long Pole with a white Bit of Cloath on it, for a Signal of Peace to them. We found they understood us presently, for they came flocking to us both Men, Women, and Children, most of them of both Sexes stark naked. At first they stood wondering and staring at us, as if we had been Monsters, and as if they had been frighted; but we found they inclined to be familiar with us afterwards. The first thing we did to try them, was, we held up our Hands to our Mouths, as if we were to drink, signifying that we wanted Water. This they understood presently, and three of their Women and two Boys ran away up the Land, and came back in about Half a Quarter of an Hour, with several Pots made of Earth pretty enough, and bak'd, I suppose, in the Sun; these they brought us full of Water, and set them down near the Sea-shore, and there left them, going back a little, that we might fetch them, which we did.

Sometime after this, they brought us Roots and Herbs, and some Fruits which I cannot remember, and gave us; but as we had nothing to give them, we found them not so free as the people in *Madagascar* were. However, our Cutler went to Work, and as he had saved some Iron out of the Wreck of the Ship, he made Abundance of Toys, Birds, Dogs, Pins, Hooks, and Rings, and we helped to file them, and make them bright for him; and when we gave them some of these, they brought us all the Sorts of Provisions they had, such as Goats, Hogs, and Cows, and we got Victuals enough.

We were now landed upon the Continent of *Africa*, the most desolate, desart, and unhospitable Country in the World, even *Greenland* and *Nova Zembla*[59] it self not excepted; with this difference only, that even the worst

Part of it we found inhabited; tho' taking the Nature and Quality of some of the Inhabitants, it might have been much better to us if there had been none.

And, to add to the Exclamation I am making on the Nature of the Place, it was here, that we took one of the rashest and wildest, and most desperate Resolutions that ever was taken by man, or any Number of Men, in the World; this was, to travel over Land through the Heart of the Country, from the Coast of *Mozambique*, on the East-Ocean to the Coast of *Angola* or *Guinea* on the Western or *Atlantick* Ocean, a Continent of Land of at least 1800 Miles; in which we had excessive Heats to support, unpassable Desarts to go over, no Carriages, Camels or Beasts of any kind to carry our Baggage, innumerable Numbers of wild and ravenous Beasts to encounter with, such as Lions, Leopards, Tigers, Lizards, and Elephants; we had the Equinoctial Line to pass under, and consequently were in the very Center of the Torrid Zone; we had Nations of Savages to encounter with, barbarous and brutish to the last Degree, Hunger and Thirst to struggle with; and, in one Word, Terrors enough to have daunted the stoutest hearts that ever were placed in Cases of Flesh and Blood.

Yet, fearless of all these, we resolved to adventure, and accordingly made such Preparation for our Journey, as the Place we were in would allow us, and such as our little Experience of the Country seem'd to dictate to us.

It had been some time already that we had been used to tread barefooted upon the Rocks, the Gravel, the Grass and the Sand on the Shore; but as we found the worst thing for our Feet was, the walking or travelling on the dry burning Sands, within the Country; so we provided our selves with a sort of Shoes made of the Skins of Wild Beasts, with the Hair inward, and being dryed in the Sun, the Out-side were thick and hard, and would last a great while. In short, as I called them, so I think the Term very proper still, we made us Gloves for our Feet, and we found them very convenient and very comfortable.

We conversed with some of the Natives of the Country who were friendly enough. What Tongue they spoke, I do not yet pretend to know. We talked as far as we could make them understand us, not only about our Provisions, but also about our Undertaking; and ask'd them what Country lay that Way, pointing West with our Hands. They told us but little to our Purpose, only we thought by all their Discourse, that there were People to be found of one Sort or other every where; that there were many great Rivers, many Lions and Tygers, Elephants, and furious wild Cats (which in the End we found to be Civet Cats)[60] and the like.

When we ask'd them, if any one had ever travelled that Way, they told us Yes, some had gone to where the Sun sleeps, meaning to the West; but they could not tell us who they were. When we ask'd for some to guide us, they shrunk up their Shoulders as *Frenchmen* do when they are afraid to undertake a thing. When we ask'd them about the Lions and wild Creatures they laught, and let us know they would do us no Hurt, and directed us to a good way indeed to deal with them, and that was to make some Fire, which would always fright them away, and so indeed we found it.

Upon these Encouragements we resolved upon our Journey, and many Considerations put us upon it, which, had the thing it self been practicable, we were not so much to blame for, as it might otherwise be supposed; I'll name some of them, not to make the Account too tedious.

First, We were perfectly destitute of Means to work about our own Deliverance any other way; we were on shore in a Place perfectly remote from all *European* Navigation; so that we could never think of being relieved, and fetch'd off by any of our own Country-men in that Part of the World. Secondly, If we had adventured to have sailed on along the Coast of *Mozambique*, and the desolate Shores of *Africa* to the North, till we came to the Red Sea, all we could hope for there, was to be taken by the *Arabs*, and be sold for Slaves to the *Turks*, which to all of us was little better than Death. We could not build any thing of a Vessel that would carry us over the great *Arabian* Sea to *India*, nor could we reach the Cape *de Bona Speranza*, the Winds being too variable, and the Sea in that Latitude too tempestuous; but we all knew, if we could cross this Continent of Land, we might reach some of the great Rivers that run into the *Atlantick* Ocean, and that on the Banks of any of those Rivers we might there build us Canoes which would carry us down, if it were Thousands of Miles; so that we could want nothing but Food, of which we were assured we might kill sufficient with our Guns: And, to add to the Satisfaction of our Deliverance, we concluded we might every one of us get a Quantity of Gold, which, if we came safe, would infinitely recompence us for our Toil.

I cannot say, that in all our Consultations I ever began to enter into the Weight and Merit of any Enterprize we went upon till now. My View before was, as I thought, very good, *viz.* that we should get into the *Arabian* Gulph, or the Mouth of the Red Sea, and waiting for some Vessel passing, or repassing there, of which there is Plenty, have seized upon the first we came at, by Force, and not only have enriched our selves with her Cargo, but have carried our selves to what part of the World we had pleased: But when they came to talk to me of a March of 2 or 3000 Miles on Foot, of Wandering in Desarts, among Lions and Tygers, I confess my Blood run chill, and I used all the Arguments I could to perswade them against it.

But they were all positive, and I might as well have held my Tongue; so I submitted, and told them, I would keep to our first Law, to be governed by the Majority, and we resolved upon our Journey. The first thing we did, was to take an Observation, and see whereabouts in the World we were, which we did, and found we were in the Latitude of 12 Degrees, 35 Minutes South of the Line. The next thing was to look on the Charts, and see the Coast of the Country we aimed at, which we found to be from 8 to 11 Degrees South Latitude, if we went for the Coast of *Angola*, or in 12 to 19 Degrees North Latitude, if we made for the River *Niger*, and the Coast of *Guiney*.

Our Aim was for the Coast of *Angola*, which by the Charts we had, lying very near the same Latitude we were then in, our Course thither was due West, and as we were assured we should meet with Rivers, we doubted not, but that by their Help we might ease our Journey, especially if we could find Means to cross the great Lake,[61] or Inland Sea, which the Natives call *Coalmucoa*, out of which it is said the River *Nile* has its Source or Beginning; but we reckoned without our Host, as you will see in the Sequel of our Story.

The next thing we had to consider was, how to carry our Baggage, which we were first of all determined not to travel without; neither indeed was it possible for us to do so, for even our Ammunition which was absolutely necessary to us, and on which our Subsistence, I mean for Food, as well as our Safety; and particularly our Defence against wild Beasts, and wild Men depended: I say, even our Ammunition was a Load too heavy for us to carry in a Country where the Heat were such, that we should be Load enough for our selves.

We enquired in the Country, and found there was no Beast of Burthen known among them; that is to say, neither Horses or Mules or Asses, Camels or Dromedaries; the only Creature they had, was a kind of Buffloe, or tame Bull, such a one as we had killed, and that some of these they had brought so to their Hand, that they taught them to go and come with their Voices, as they called them to them, or sent them from them; that they made them carry Burthens, and particularly, that they would swim over Rivers and Lakes upon them, the Creatures swimming very high and strong in the Water.

But we understood nothing of the Management or Guiding such a Creature, or how to bind a Burthen upon them; and this last Part of our Consultation puzzled us extremely: At last I proposed a Method for them, which after some Consideration, they found very convenient; and this was to quarrel with some of the Negro Natives, take ten or twelve of them Prisoners, and binding them as Slaves, cause them to travel with us, and make them carry our Baggage; which I alledged would be convenient and useful many ways, as well to shew us the Way, as to converse with other Natives for us.

This Counsel was not accepted at first, but the Natives soon gave them Reason to approve it; and also gave them an Opportunity to put it in Practice; for as our little Traffick with the Natives was hitherto upon the Faith of their first Kindness, we found some Knavery among them at last; for having bought some Cattel of them for our Toys, which, as I said, our Cutler had contrived, one of our Men differing with his Chapman,[62] truly they huff'd him[63] in their Manner, and keeping the things he had offered them for the Cattel, made their Fellows drive away the Cattel before his Face, and laugh at him; our Man crying out loud of this Violence, and calling to some of us, who were not far off, the Negro he was dealing with threw a Lance at him, which came so true, that if he had not with great Agility jumped aside, and held up his Hand also to turn the Lance as it came, it had struck through his Body, and, as it was, it wounded him in the Arm; at which the Man enraged took up his Fuzee,[64] and shot the Negro through the Heart.

The others that were near him, and all those that were with us at a Distance, were so terribly frighted; first, at the Flash of Fire; secondly, at the Noise: And thirdly, at seeing their Countryman killed, that they stood like Men stupid and amazed, at first, for some time: But after they were a little recovered from their Fright, one of them, at a good Distance from us, set up a sudden screaming Noise, which, it seems, is the Noise they make when they go to Fight; and all the rest understanding what he meant, answered him, and run together to the Place where he was, and we not knowing what it meant, stood still looking upon one another like a Parcel of Fools.

But we were presently undeceived, for in two or three Minutes more we heard the screaming roaring Noise go on from one Place to another, through all their little Towns; nay, even over the Creek to the other Side; and, on a sudden we saw a naked Multitude running from all Parts to the Place where the first Man began it, as to a Rendezvous; and, in less than an Hour, I believe there was near 500 of them gotten together, armed some with Bows and Arrows, but most with Lances, with which they throw, at a good Distance, so nicely, that they will strike a Bird flying.

We had but a very little time for Consultation, for the Multitude was encreasing every Moment; and I verily believe, if we had stay'd long, they would have been 10000 together in a little time. We had nothing to do therefore, but to fly to our Ship or Bark, where indeed we could have defended our selves very well, or to advance and try what a Volley or two of small Shot would do for us.

We resolved immediately upon the latter, depending upon it, that the Fire and Terror of our Shot would soon put them to Flight; so we drew up all in a Line, and marched boldly up to them; they stood ready to meet us, depending, I suppose, to destroy us all with their Lances; but before we came near enough for them to throw their Lances, we halted, and standing at a good Distance from one another, to stretch our Line as far as we could, we gave them a Salute with our Shot, which besides what we wounded that we knew not of, knocked sixteen of them down upon the Spot, and three more were so lamed, that they fell about 20 or 30 Yards from them.

As soon as we had fired, they set up the horridest Yell, or Howling, partly raised by those that were wounded, and partly by those that pitied and condoled the Bodies they saw lye dead, that I never heard any thing like it before or since.

We stood stock still after we had fired, to load our Guns again, and finding they did not stir from the Place, we fired among them again; we killed about nine of them at the second Fire; but as they did not stand so thick as before, all our Men did not fire, seven of us being ordered to reserve our Charge, and to advance as soon as the other had fired, while the rest loaded again; of which I shall speak again presently.

As soon as we had fired the second Volley we shouted as loud as we could, and the seven Men advanced upon them, and, coming about 20 Yards nearer, fired again, and those that were behind having loaded again, with all Expedition, follow'd but when they saw us advance, they run screaming away as if they were bewitched.

When we came up to the Field of Battle, we saw a great Number of Bodies lying upon the Ground, many more than we could suppose were killed or wounded, nay more than we had Bullets in our Pieces when we fired; and we could not tell what to make of it; but at length, we found how it was *viz*. that they were frighted out of all manner of Sense; nay, I do believe several of those that were really dead, were frighted to Death, and had no Wound about them.

Of those that were thus frighted, as I have said, several of them, as they recovered themselves, came and worshipped us (taking us for Gods or Devils, I know not which, nor did it much matter to us) some kneeling, some throwing themselves flat on the Ground, made a Thousand antick Gestures, but all with Tokens of the most profound Submission. It presently came into my Head, that we might now by the Law of Arms[65] take as many Prisoners as we would, and make them travel with us, and carry our Baggage: As soon as I proposed it, our Men were all of my Mind; and accordingly we secured about 60 lusty young Fellows, and let them know they must go with us; which they seemed very willing to do: But the next Question we had among our selves, was, how we should do to trust them, for we found the People not like those of *Madagasar*, but fierce, revengeful and treacherous, for which Reason we were sure, that we should have no Service from them but that of meer Slaves, no Subjection that would continue any longer than the Fear of us was upon them, nor any Labour but by Violence.

Before I go any farther, I must hint to the Reader, that from this time forward I began to enter a little more seriously into the Circumstance I was in, and concern'd my self more in the Conduct of our Affairs; for, tho' my Comerades were all older Men, yet I began to find them void of Counsel, or, as I now call it, Presence of Mind, when they came to the Execution of a thing. The first Occasion I took to observe this, was in their late Engagement with the Natives, when, tho' they had taken a good Resolution to attack them, and fire upon them, yet when they had fired the first time, and found that the Negroes did not run as they expected, their Hearts began to fail, and I am perswaded if their Bark had been near Hand, they would every Man have run away.

Upon this Occasion, I began to take upon me a little to hearten them up, and to call upon them to load again, and give them another Volley, telling them that I would engage, if they would be ruled by me, I'd make the Negroes run fast enough. I found this heartned them, and therefore, when they fired a second time, I desired them to reserve some of their Shot to an Attempt by it self, as I mentioned above.

Having fired a second time, I was indeed forced to command, as I may call it. Now, *Seigniors*, said I, let us give them a Chear; so I open'd my Throat, and shouted three times, as our *English* Sailors do on like Occasions; and now follow me, said I to the seven that had not fired, and *I'll warrant you we will make Work with them*; and so it proved indeed: For as soon as they saw us coming, away they run as above.

From this Day forward they would call me nothing but *Seignior Capitanio*; but I told them, I would not be called *Seignior*. Well then, said the Gunner, who spoke good *English*, you shall be called Captain *Bob*, and so they gave me my Title ever after.

Nothing is more certain of the *Portuguese* than this, take them nationally or personally; if they are animated and hearten'd up by any body to go before, and encourage them by Example, they will behave well enough; but if they have nothing but their own Measures to follow, they sink immediately: These Men had certainly fled from a Parcel of naked Savages, tho' even by flying they could not have saved their Lives, if I had not shouted and halloo'd, and made rather Sport with the thing, than a Fight, to keep up their Courage.

Nor was there less need of it upon several Occasions hereafter; and I do confess, I have often wonder'd how a Number of Men, who, when they came to the Extremity, were so ill supported by their own Spirits, had at first Courage to propose, and to undertake the most desperate and impracticable attempt that ever Men went about in the World.

There were indeed two or three indefatigable Men among them, by whose Courage and Industry all the rest were upheld; and indeed those two or three were the Managers of them from the Beginning; that was the Gunner, and that Cutler whom I call the Artist; and the third, who was pretty well, tho' not like either of them, was one of the Carpenters. These indeed were the Life and Soul of all the rest, and it was to their Courage that all the rest ow'd the Resolution they shewd upon any Occasion. But when those saw me take a little upon me, as above, they embraced me, and treated me with particular Affection ever after.

This Gunner was an excellent Mathematician, a good Scholar, and a compleat Sailor; and it was in conversing intimately with him, that I learnt afterwards the Grounds of what Knowledge I have since had in all the Sciences useful for Navigation, and particularly in the Geographical Part of Knowledge.

Even in our Conversation, finding me eager to understand and learn, he laid the Foundation of a general Knowledge of things in my Mind, gave me just Ideas of the Form of the Earth and of the Sea, the Situation of Countries, the Course of Rivers, the Doctrine of the Spheres, the Motion of the Stars; and, in a Word, taught me a kind of System of Astronomy, which I afterwards improv'd.

In especial Manner, he filled my Head with aspiring Thoughts, and with an earnest Desire after learning every thing that could be taught me; convincing me, that nothing could qualify me for great Undertakings, but a Degree of Learning superior to what was usual in the Race of Seamen; he told me, that to be ignorant, was to be certain of a mean Station in the World, but that Knowledge was the first Step to Preferment. He was always flattering me with my Capacity to Learn; and tho' that fed my Pride, yet on the other Hand, as I had a secret Ambition which just at that time fed it self in my Mind, it prompted in me an insatiable Thirst after Learning in general, and I resolved, if ever I came back to *Europe*, and had any thing left to purchase it, I would make my self Master of all the Parts of Learning needful to the making of me a compleat Sailor; but I was not so just to my self afterwards, as to do it when I had an Opportunity.

But to return to our Business; the Gunner when he saw the Service I had done in the Fight, and heard my Proposal for keeping a Number of Prisoners for our March, and for carrying our Baggage, turns to me before them all, Captain *Bob, says he*, I think you must be our Leader, for all the Success of this Enterprize is owing to you. *No, no, said I*, do not compliment me, you shall be our *Seignior Capitanio*, you shall be *General*, I am too young for it; so in short, we all agreed he should be our Leader; but he would not accept of it alone, but would have me join'd with him, and all the rest agreeing, I was oblig'd to comply.

The first Piece of Service they put me upon in this new Command, was as difficult as any they could think of, and that was to manage the Prisoners; which however I chearfully undertook, as you shall hear presently: But the immediate Consultation was yet of more Consequence; and that was, *First*, Which Way we should go, and *Secondly*, How to furnish our selves for the Voyage with Provisions.

There was among the Prisoners one tall, well-shap'd, handsom Fellow, to whom the rest seem'd to pay great Respect, and who, as we understood afterwards, was the Son of one their Kings, his Father was, it seems, killed at our first Volley, and he wounded with a Shot in his Arm, and with another just on one of his Hips or Haunches., The Shot in his Haunch being in a fleshy Part, bled much, and he was half dead with the Loss of Blood. As to the Shot in his Arm, it had broke his Wrist, and he was by both these Wounds quite disabled, so that we were once going to turn him away, and let him die; and if we had, he would have died indeed in a few Days more: But as I found the Man had some Respect shew'd him, it presently occurred to my Thoughts, that we might bring him to be useful to us, and perhaps make him a kind of Commander over them. So I caused our Surgeon to take him in Hand, and gave the poor Wretch good Words, that is to say, I spoke to him as well as I could by Signs, to make him understand that we would make him well again.

This created a new Awe in their Minds of us, believing that as we could kill at a Distance by something invisible to them (for so our Shot was to be sure) so we could make them well again too. Upon this the young Prince (for so we called him afterwards) called six or seven of the Savages to him, and said something to them; what it was we knew not, but immediately all the seven came to me, and kneel'd down to me, holding up their Hands, and making Signs of Entreaty, pointing to the Place where one of those lay whom we had killed.

It was a long time before I or any of us could understand them; but one of them run and lifted up a dead Man, pointing to his Wound, which was in his Eye, for he was shot into the Head at one of his Eyes. Then another pointed to the Surgeon, and at last we found it out, that the Meaning was, that he should heal the Prince's Father too, who was dead, being shot thro' the Head, as above.

We presently took the Hint, and would not say we could not do it, but let them know, the Men that were kill'd were those that had first fallen upon us, and provoked us, and we would by no Means make them alive again; and that if any other did so, we would kill them too, and never let them live any more: But that if he (the Prince) would be willing to go with us, and do as we should direct him, we would not let him dye, and would make his Arm well. Upon this he bid his Men go and fetch a long Stick or Staff, and lay on the Ground. When they brought it, we saw it was an Arrow; he took it with his left Hand, (for his other was lame with the Wound) and pointing up at the Sun, broke the Arrow in two, and set the Point against his Breast, and then gave it to me. This was as I understood afterwards, wishing the Sun, whom they worship, might shoot him into the Breast with an Arrow, if ever he failed to be my Friend; and giving the Point of the Arrow to me, was to be a Testimony, that I was the Man he had sworn to; and never was Christian more punctual to an Oath, than he was to this, for he was a sworn Servant to us for many a weary Month after that.

When I brought him to the Surgeon, he immediately dress'd the Wound in his Haunch or Bottock, and found the Bullet had only graz'd upon the Flesh, and pass'd, as it were, by it, but it was not lodg'd in the Part; so that it was soon healed and well again: But as to his Arm, he found one of the Bones broken, which are in the Fore-part from the Wrist to the Elbow; and this he set, and splinter'd it up, and bound his Arm in a Sling, hanging it about his Neck, and making Signs to him that he should not stir it; which he was so strict an Observer of, that he set him down, and never mov'd one Way or other, but as the Surgeon gave him Leave.

I took a great deal of Pains to acquaint this Negroe what we intended to do, and what Use we intended to make of his Men; and particularly, to teach him the Meaning of what we said: Especially to teach him some Words, such as *Yes* and *No*, and what they meant, and to innure him to our Way of Talking, and he was very willing and apt to learn any thing I taught him.

It was easy to let him see, that we intended to carry our Provision with us from the first Day; but he made Signs to us to tell us we need not, for that we should find Provisions enough every where for fourty Days. It was very difficult for us to understand how he express'd Forty; for he knew no Figures, but some Words they used to one another that they understood it by. At last, one of the Negroes, by his Order, laid fourty little Stones one by another, to shew us how many Days we should travel, and find Provisions sufficient.

Then I shew'd him our baggage, which was very heavy, particularly our Powder and Shot, Lead, Iron, Carpenters Tools, Seamens Instruments, Cases of Bottles, and other Lumber. He took some of the things up in his Hand to see the Weight, and shook his Head at them; so I told our People, they must resolve to divide their Things into small Parcels, and make them portable; and accordingly they did so, by which means we were fain to leave all our Chests behind us, which were Eleven in Number.

Then he made Signs to us, that he would procure some Buffloes, or young Bulls, *as I called them*, to carry things for us, and made Signs too, that if we were weary, we might be carry'd too; but that we slighted, only were willing to have the Creatures, because at last, when they could serve us no farther for Carriage, we might eat them all up if we had any Occasion for them.

I then carry'd him to our Bark, and shewed him what things we had there; he seem'd amaz'd at the Sight of our Bark, having never seen any thing of that Kind before, for their Boats are most wretched things, such as I never saw before, having no Head or Stern, and being made only of the Skins of Goats sewed together with dried Guts of Goats and Sheep, and done over with a kind of slimy Stuff like Rosin and Oil, but of a most nauseous, odious Smell, and they are poor miserable things for Boats, the worst that any Part of the World ever saw; a Canoe is an excellent Contrivance compared to them.

But to return to our Boat: We carried our new Prince into it, and help'd him over the Side, because of his Lameness. We made Signs to him, that his Men must carry our Goods for us, and shewed him what we had; he answer'd, *Ce Seignior*,[66] or, *Yes Sir*, (for we had taught him that Word, and the Meaning of it) and taking up a Bundle, he made Signs to us, that when his Arm was well, he would carry some for us.

I made Signs again, to tell him, that if he would make his Men carry them, we would not let him carry any thing. We had secured all the Prisoners in a narrow Place, where we had bound them with Matt Cords, and set up Stakes like a Palisado round them; so when we carry'd the Prince on Shore, we went with him to them, and made Signs to him, to ask them if they were willing to go with us to the Country of Lions. Accordingly he made a long Speech to them, and we could understand by it, that he told them, if they were willing, they must say, *Ce Seignior*, telling them what it signify'd. They immediately answered, *Ce Seignior*, and clapt their Hands, looking up to the Sun, which the Prince signify'd to us, was Swearing to be faithful. But as soon as they had said so, one of them made a long Speech to the Prince, and in it, we perceived by his Gestures, which were very antick,[67] that they desired something from us, and that they were in great Concern about it. So I ask'd him as well as I could, what it was they desired of us; he told us by Signs, that they desired we should clap our Hands to the Sun (that was to swear) that we would not kill them, that we would give them *Chiaruck*, that is to say, Bread, would not starve them, and would not let the Lions eat them. I told him we would promise all that; then he pointed to the Sun, and clapt his Hands, signing to me, that I should do so too, which I did; at which all the Prisoners fell flat on the Ground, and rising up again, made the oddest, wildest Cries that ever I heard.

I think it was the first time in my Life that ever any religious Thought affected me; but I could not refrain some Reflections, and almost Tears, in considering how happy it was, that I was not born among such Creatures as these, and was not so stupidly ignorant and barbarous: But this soon went off again, and I was not troubled again with any Qualms of that Sort for a long time after.

When this Ceremony was over, our Concern was to get some Provisions, as well for the present Subsistence of our Prisoners, as our selves; and making Signs to our Prince, that we were thinking upon that Subject, he made Signs to me, that if I would let one of the Prisoners go to his Town, he should bring Provisions, and should bring some Beasts to carry our Baggage. I seemed loath to trust him, and supposing that he would run away, he made great Signs of Fidelity, and with his own Hands tied a Rope about his Neck, offering me one End of it, intimating, that I should hang him, if the Man did not come again. So I consented, and he gave him Abundance of Instructions, and sent him away, pointing to the Light of the Sun, which it seems was to tell him, at what time he must be back.

The Fellow run as if he was mad, and held it till he was quite out of Sight, by which I supposed he had a great Way to go. The next Morning, about two Hours before the Time appointed, the Black Prince, for so I always called him, beckoning with his Hand to me, and hollooing after his Manner, desired me to come to him, which I did, when pointing to a little Hill about two Miles off, I saw plainly a little Drove of Cattel, and several People with them; those he told me by Signs were the Man he had sent, and several more with him, and Cattel for us.

Accordingly by the time appointed, he came quite to our Hutts, and brought with him a great many Cows, young Runts, about 16 Goats, and, four young Bulls, taught to carry Burthens.

This was a Supply of Provisions sufficient; as for Bread we were obliged to shift with some Roots which we had made use of before. We then began to consider of making some large Bags like the Soldiers Knapsacks, for their Men to carry our Baggage in, and to make it easy to them; and the Goats being killed, I ordered the Skins to be spread in the Sun, and they were as dry in two Days as could be desired; so we found means to make such little Bags as we wanted, and began to divide our Baggage into them: When the Black Prince found what they were for, and how easy they were of Carriage when we put them on, he smiled a little, and sent away the Man again to fetch Skins, and he brought two Natives more with him, all loaded with Skins better cured than ours, and of other kinds, such as we could not tell what Names to give them.

These two Men brought the Black Prince two Lances of the sort they use in their Fights, but finer than ordinary, being made of black smooth Wood, as fine as Ebony, and headed at the Point with the End of a long Tooth of some Creature, we could not tell of what Creature; the Head was so firm put on, and the Tooth so strong, tho' no bigger than my Thumb, and sharp at the End, that I never saw any thing like it in any Place in the World.

The Prince would not take them till I gave him Leave, but made Signs that they should give them to me; however I gave him Leave to take them himself, for I saw evident Signs of an honourable just Principle in him.

We now prepared for our March, when the Prince coming to me, and pointing towards the several Quarters of the World, made Signs to know, which way we intended to go; and when I shewed him pointing to the West, he presently let me know, there was a great River a little further to the North, which was able to carry our Bark many Leagues into the Country due West. I presently took the Hint, and enquired for the Mouth of the River, which I understood by him was above a Day's March, and by our Estimation we found it about seven Leagues further; I take this to be the great River marked by our Chart-Makers at the Northmost Part of the Coast of *Mozambique*, and called there *Quilloa*.[68]

Consulting thus with our selves, we resolved to take the Prince, and as many of the Prisoners as we could stow in our Frigate, and go about by the Bay into the River; and that eight of us with our Arms should march by Land, to meet them on the River-side; for the Prince carrying us to a rising Ground, had shew'd us the River very plain a great Way up the Country, and in one Place it was not above six Miles to it.

It was my Lot to march by Land, and be Captain of the whole Carravan: I had eight of our own Men with me, and Seven and Thirty of our Prisoners, without any Baggage, for all our Luggage was yet on board. We drove the young Bulls with us; nothing was ever so tame, so willing to work, or carry any thing. The Negroes would ride upon them four at a Time, and they would go very willingly; they would eat out of our Hand, lick our Feet, and were as tractable as a Dog.

We drove with us six or seven Cows for Food; but our Negroes knew nothing of curing the Flesh by salting and drying it, till we shew'd them the Way, and then they were mighty willing to do so as long as we had any Salt to do it with, and to carry Salt a great Way too, after we found we should have no more.

It was an easy March to the River Side for us that went by Land, and we came thither in a Piece of a Day, being as above not above six *English* Miles; whereas it was no less than five Days before they came to us by Water, the Wind in the Bay having failed them, and the Way, by Reason of a great Turn or Reach in the River being above fifty Miles about.

We spent this time in a thing which the two Strangers, which brought the Prince the two Lances, put into the Head of the Prisoners; (*viz.*) to make Bottles of the Goats-Skins to carry fresh Water in, which it seems they knew we should come to want; and the Men, did it so dexterously, having dried Skins fetched them by those two Men, that before our Vessel came up, they had every Man a Pouch like a Bladder, to carry fresh Water in, hanging over their Shoulder by a Thong made of other Skins, about three Inches broad, like the Sling of a Fuzee.

Our Prince, to assure us of the Fidelity of the Men in this March, had ordered them to be tied two and two by the Wrist, as we handcuff Prisoners in *England*; and made them so sensible of the Reasonableness of it, that he made them do it themselves, appointing four of them, to bind the rest; but we found them so honest, and particularly so obedient to him, that after we were gotten a little further off of their own Country, we set them all at Liberty, tho' when he came to us, he would have them tied again, and they continued so for a good while.

All the Country on the Bank of the River was a high Land, no marshy swampy Ground in it, the Verdure good, and Abundance of Cattel feeding upon it, wherever we went, or which Way soever we look'd; there was not much Wood indeed, at least not near us, but further up we saw Oak, Cedar, and Pine Trees, some of which were very large.

The River was a fair open Channel about as broad as the *Thames* below *Gravesend*, and a strong Tide of Flood, which we found held us about 60 Miles, the Channel deep; nor did we find any Want of Water for a great Way. In short, we went merrily up the River with the Flood, and the Wind blowing still fresh at E. and E.N.E., we stemm'd the Ebb easily also, especially while the River continued broad and deep; but when we came past the Swelling of the Tide, and had the natural Current of the River to go against, we found it too strong for us, and began to think of quitting our

Bark; but the Prince would by no means agree to that, for finding we had on board pretty good Store of Roping made of Matts and Flags,[69] which I described before, he ordered all the Prisoners which were on shore, to come and take hold of those Ropes, and tow us along by the Shore Side; and as we hoisted our Sail too, to ease them, the Men run along with us at a very great Rate.

In this Manner the River carry'd us up by our Computation near 200 Miles, and then it narrowed apace, and was not above as broad as the *Thames* is at *Windsor*, or thereabouts; and after another Day, we came to a great Water-fall or Cataract, enough to fright us, for I believe the whole Body of Water fell at once perpendicularly down a Precipice, above sixty Foot high, which made a Noise enough to deprive men of their Hearing, and we heard it above Ten Miles before we came to it.

Here we were at a full Stop, and now our Prisoners went first on Shore; they had worked very hard, and very cheerfully, relieving one another, those that were weary being taken into the Bark. Had we had Canoes, or any Boats which might have been carried by Mens Strength, we might have gone 200 Miles more up this River in small Boats, but our great Boat could go no farther.

All this Way the Country looked green and pleasant, and was full of Cattel, and some People we saw, tho' not many; but this we observ'd now, that the People did no more understand our Prisoners here, than we could understand them; being it seems of different Nations, and of different Speech. We had yet seen no wild Beasts, or at least none that came very near us; except two Days before we came at the Water-fall, when we saw three of the most beautiful Leopards that ever were seen, standing upon the Bank of the River on the North-side, our Prisoners being all on the other Side of the Water. Our Gunner espy'd them first, and ran to fetch his Gun, putting a Ball extraordinary in it; and coming to me, now Captain *Bob*, says he, where's your Prince, so I called him out, now, says he, tell your Men not to be afraid, tell them they shall see that Thing in his Hand, speak in Fire to one of those Beasts, and make it kill it self.

The poor Negroes looked as if they had been all going to be killed, notwithstanding what their Prince said to them, and stood staring to expect the Issue, when on a sudden the Gunner fired; and as he was a very good Marks-Man, he shot the Creature with two Sluggs just in the Head. As soon as the Leopard felt her self struck, she rear'd up on her two hind Legs bolt upright, and throwing her Fore-Paws about in the Air, fell backward, growling and struggling, and immediately died; the other two frighted with the Fire and the Noise, fled, and were out of Sight in an Instant.

But the two frighted Leopards were not in half the Consternation that our Prisoners were; four or five of them fell down as if they had been shot, several others fell on their Knees, and lifted up their Hands to us; whether to worship us, or pray us not to kill them, we did not know; but we made Signs to their Prince to encourage them, which he did, but it was with much ado that he brought them to their Sense; nay, the Prince, notwithstanding all that was said to prepare him for it, yet when the Piece went off, he gave a Start as if he would have leap'd into the River.

When we saw the Creature killed, I had a great Mind to have the Skin of her, and made Signs to the Prince, that he should send some of his Men over to take the Skin off. As soon as he spoke but a Word, four of them that offered themselves were untied, and immediately they jump'd into the River, and swam over, and went to work with him: The Prince having a Knife that we gave him, made four wooden Knives so clever, as I never saw any thing like them in my Life, and in less than an Hour's time, they brought me the Skin of the Leopard, which was a monstrous great one, for it was from the Ears to the Tail about seven Foot, and near five Foot Broad on the Back, and most admirably spotted all over; the Skin of this Leopard I brought to *London* many Years after.

We were now all upon a Level, as to our travelling; being unshipp'd, for our Bark would swim no farther, and she was too heavy to carry on our Backs; but as we found the Course of the River went a great Way farther, we consulted our Carpenters, whether we could not pull the Bark in Pieces, and make us three or four small Boats to go on with. They told us, we might do so, but it would be very long a-doing; and, that when we had done, we had neither Pitch or Tar to make them sound, to keep the Water out, or Nails to fasten the Plank; but one of them told us, that as soon as he could come at any large Tree, near the River he would make us a Canoe or two in a Quarter of the Time, and which would serve us as well for all the Uses we could have any Occasion for as a Boat; and such, that if we came to any Water-falls, we might take them up, and carry them for a Mile or two by Land, upon our Shoulders.

Upon this we gave over the Thoughts of our Frigate, and hauling her into a little Cove, or Inlet, where a small Brook came into the main River, we laid her up for those that came next, and marched forward. We spent indeed two Days dividing our Baggage, and loading our tame Buffloes and our Negroes: Our Powder and Shot, which was the thing we were most careful of, we ordered thus: First the Powder we divided into little Leather Bags, that is to say, Bags of dried Skins with the Hair inward, that the Powder might not grow damp; and then we put those Bags into other Bags made of Bullocks Skins, very thick and hard, with the Hair outward, that no Wet might come in; and this succeeded so well, that in the greatest Rains we had, whereof some were very violent and very long, we always kept our Powder dry. Besides these Bags which held our chief Magazine, we divided to every one a Quarter of a Pound of Powder, and Half a Pound of Shot to carry always about us; which as it was enough for our present Use, so we were willing to have no Weight to carry more than was absolutely necessary, because of the Heat.

We kept still on the Bank of the River, and for that Reason had very little Communication with the People of the Country; for, having also our Bark stored with Plenty of Provisions, we had had no Occasion to look abroad for a Supply; but now we came to march on Foot, we were obliged often to seek out for Food. The first Place we came to on the River that gave us any Stop, was a little Negro Town, containing about 50 Hutts, and there appeared about 400 People, for they all came out to see us, and wonder at us. When our Negroes appeared, the Inhabitants began to fly to Arms, thinking there had been Enemies coming upon them; but our Negroes, tho' they could not speak their Language, made Signs to them, that they had no Weapons, and were tied two and two together, as Captives; that there were People behind who came from the Sun,[70] and that could kill them all, and make them alive again, if they pleased; but that they would do them no Hurt, and came with Peace. As soon as they understood this, they laid down their Lances, and Bows and Arrows, and came and stuck twelve large Stakes in the Ground, as a Token of Peace, bowing themselves to us in Token of Submission. But as soon as they saw white Men with Beards, that is to say, Mustachoes, they run screaming away as in a Fright.

We kept at a Distance from them, not to be too familiar; and when we did appear, it was but two or three of us at a time. But our Prisoners made them understand, that we required some Provisions of them; so they brought us some black Cattel, for they have Abundance of Cows and Buffloes all over that Side of the Country, as also great Numbers of Deer. Our Cutler, who had now a great Stock of things of his Handy-work, gave them some little Knick Knacks, as Plates of Silver and of Iron, cut Diamond Fashion, and cut into Hearts and into Rings, and they were mightily pleased. They also brought several Sorts of Fruits and Roots, which we did not understand, but our Negroes fed heartily on them, and after we had seen them eat them, we did so too.

Having stock'd our selves here with Flesh and Roots as much as we could well carry, we divided the Burthens among our Negroes, appointing about 30 to 40 Pound Weight to a Man; which we thought indeed was Load enough in a hot Country; and the Negroes did not at all repine at it, but would sometimes help one another when they began to be weary, which did happen now and then, tho' not often: besides, as most of their Luggage was our Provision, it lighten'd every Day like Æsop's Basket of Bread,[71] till we came to get a Recruit. Note, when we loaded them, we untied their Hands, and tied them two and two together by one Foot. The third Day of our March from this Place, our chief Carpenter desired us to halt, and set up some Hutts, for he had found out some Trees that he liked, and resolved to make us some Canoes; for as he told me, he knew we should have Marching enough on Foot after we left the River, and he was resolved to go no farther by Land than needs must.

We had no sooner given Order for our little Camp, and given Leave to our Negroes to lay down their Loads, but they fell to Work to build our Hutts; and tho' they were tied, as above, yet they did it so nimbly, as surprized us. Here we set some of the Negroes quite at Liberty, that is to say, without tying them, having the Prince's Word pass'd for their Fidelity; and some of these were ordered to help the Carpenters, which they did very handily, with a little Direction, and others were sent to see whether they could get any Provision near Hand; but instead of Provisions, three of them came in with two Bows and Arrows, and five Lances. They could not easily make us understand how they came by them, only that they had surprized some Negroe Women, who were in some Hutts, the Men being from Home, and they had found the Lances and Bows in the Hutts or Houses, the Women and Children flying away at the Sight of them, as from Robbers. We seem'd very angry at them, and made the Prince ask them, if they had not kill'd any of the Women or Children, making them believe, that if they had kill'd any Body, we would make them kill themselves too; but they protested their Innocence, so we excused them. Then they brought us the Bows and Arrows and Lances; but at a Motion of their black Prince, we gave them back the Bows and Arrows, and gave them Leave to go out to see what they could kill for Food; and here we gave them the Law of Arms, viz. That if any Men appeared to assault them, or shoot at them, or offer any Violence to them, they might kill them; but that they should not offer to kill or hurt any that offer'd them Peace, or laid down their Weapons, nor any Women or Children, upon any Occasion whatsoever. These were our Articles of War.

These two Fellows had not been gone out above three or four Hours, but one of them came running to us without his Bow and Arrows, hallooing and hooping a great while before he came at us, *Okoamo, Okoamo*, which it seems was, *Help, Help*. The rest of the Negroes rose up in a Hurry, and by Two's, as they could, run forward toward their Fellows to know what the Matter was. As for me, I did not understand it, nor any of our People; the

Prince look'd as if something unlucky had fallen out, and some of our Men took up their Arms, to be ready on Occasion. But the Negroes soon discover'd the Thing; for we saw four of them presently after coming along with a great Load of Meat upon their Backs. The Case was, that the first two who went out with their Bows and Arrows, meeting with a great Herd of Deer in the Plain, had been so nimble as to shoot three of them; and then one of them came running to us for Help, to fetch them away. This was the first Venison we had met with upon all our March, and we feasted upon it very plentifully; and this was the first time we began to prevail with our Prince to eat his Meat drest our Way; after which, his Men were prevailed with by his Example, but before that, they eat most of the Flesh they had quite raw.

We wish'd now we had brought some Bows and Arrows out with us, which we might have done; and we began to have so much Confidence in our Negroes, and to be so familiar with them, that we oftentimes let them go, or the greatest Part of them, unty'd, being well assured they would not leave us, and that they did not know what Course to take without us; but one thing we resolved not to trust them with, and that was the Charging our Guns; but they always believed our Guns had some heavenly Power in them, that they would send forth Fire and Smoke, and speak with a dreadful Noise, and kill at a Distance whenever we bid them.

In about eight Days we finished three Canoes, and in them we embarked our white Men and our Baggage, with our Prince, and some of the Prisoners. We also found it needful to keep some of our selves always on Shore, not only to manage the Negroes, but to defend them from Enemies and wild Beasts. Abundance of little Incidents happened upon this March, which it is not possible to crowd into this Account; particularly, we saw more wild Beasts now than we did before, some Elephants, and two or three Lions; none of which Kinds we had seen any of before; and we found our Negroes were more afraid of them a great deal than we were; principally because they had no Bows and Arrows, or Lances, which were the particular Weapons they were bred up to the Exercise of.

But we cured them of their Fears, by being always ready with our Fire-Arms. However, as we were willing to be sparing of our Powder, and the Killing any of the Creatures now was no Advantage to us, seeing their Skins were too heavy for us to carry, and their Flesh not good to eat, we resolved therefore to keep some of our Pieces uncharg'd, and only prim'd; and causing them to flash in the Pan,[72] the Beasts, even the Lions themselves, would always start, and fly back when they saw it, and immediately march off.

We past Abundance of Inhabitants upon this upper Part of the River, and with this Observation, that almost every ten Miles we came to a several Nation, and every several Nation had a different Speech, or else their Speech had differing Dialects, so that they did not understand one another. They all abounded in Cattel, especially on the River Side; and the eighth Day of this second Navigation, we met with a little Negroe Town, where they had growing a Sort of Corn like Rice, which eat very sweet; and as we got some of it of the People, we made very good Cakes of Bread of it, and making a Fire, bak'd them on the Ground, after the Fire was swept away very well; so that hitherto we had no Want of Provisions of any kind we could desire.

Our Negroes towing our Canoes, we travelled at a considerable Rate, and by our own Account, could not go less than 20 or 25 *English* Miles a Day, and the River continuing to be much at the same Breadth, and very deep all the Way, till on the tenth Day we came to another Cataract; for a Ridge of high Hills crossing the whole Channel of the River, the Water came tumbling down the Rocks from one Stage to another in a strange Manner: So that it was a continued Link of Cataracts from one to another, in the Manner of a Caskade; only, that the Falls were sometimes a Quarter of a Mile from one another, and the Noise confused and frightful.

We thought our Voyaging was at a full Stop now; but three of us, with a Couple of our Negroes, mounting the Hills another Way, to view the Course of the River, we found a fair Channel again after about half a Mile's March, and that it was like to hold us a good Way farther. So we set all Hands to Work, unloaded our Cargo, and hauled our Canoes on Shore, to see if we could carry them.

Upon Examination, we found that they were very heavy; but our Carpenters spending but one Day's Work on them, hew'd away so much of the Timber from their Outsides, as reduced them very much, and yet they were as fit to swim as before. When this was done, ten Men with Poles took up one of the Canoes, and made nothing to carry it. So we ordered twenty Men to each Canoe, that one Ten might relieve another; and thus we carried all our Canoes, and launch's them into the Water again, and then fetch'd our Luggage, and loaded it all again into the Canoes, and all in an Afternoon; and the next Morning early we mov'd forward again. When we had towed about four Days more, our Gunner, who was our Pilot, begun to observe that we did not keep our right Course so exactly as we ought, the River winding away a little towards the North, and gave us Notice of it accordingly. However, we were not willing to lose the Advantage of Water-Carriage, at least not till we were forced to it; so we jogg'd on, and the River served us about Threescore Miles further; but then we found it grew very small and shallow, having pass'd the Mouths of several little Brooks or Rivulets which come into it, and at Length it became but a Brook it self.

We tow'd up as far as ever our Boats would swim, and we went two Days the further, having been about twelve Days in this last Part of the River, by Lightning the Boats, and taking our Luggage out, which we made the Negroes carry, being willing to ease our selves as long as we could; but at the End of these two Days, in short, there was not Water enough to swim a *London* Wherry.

We now set forward wholly by Land, and without any Expectation of more Water Carriage. All our Concern for more Water, was to be sure to have a Supply for our Drinking; and therefore upon every Hill that we came near, we clamber'd up to the highest Part, to see the Country before us, and to make the best Judgment we could which way to go to keep the lowest Grounds, and as near some Stream of Water as we could.

The Country held verdant, well grown with Trees, and spread with Rivers and Brooks, and tolerably well with Inhabitants, for about thirty Days March. After our leaving the Canoes, during which time things went pretty well with us; we did not tye our selves down when to march, and when to halt, but order'd those things as our convenience, and the Health and Ease of our People, as well our Servants, as our selves, required.

About the Middle of this March, we came into a low and plain Country, in which we perceived a greater Number of Inhabitants than in any other Country we had gone thro'; but that which was worse for us, we found them a fierce, barbarous, treacherous People, and who at first look'd upon us as Robbers, and gathered themselves in Numbers to attack us.

Our Men were terrified at them at first, and began to discover an unusual Fear; and even our black Prince seemed in a great deal of Confusion: But I smiled at him, and shewing him some of our Guns, I asked him, if he thought that which killed the spotted Cat, (for so they called the Leopard in their Language) could not make a Thousand of those naked Creatures die at one Blow? Then he laugh'd, and said Yes, he believ'd it would. Well then, said I, tell your Men not to be afraid of these People, for we shall soon give them a Taste of what we can do, if they pretend to meddle with us. However, we considered we were in the Middle of a vast Country, and we knew not what Numbers of People and Nations we might be surrounded with; and above all, we knew not how much we might stand in Need of the Friendship of these that we were now among; so that we ordered the Negroes to try all the Methods they could, to make them Friends.

Accordingly, the two Men who had gotten Bows and Arrows, and two more to whom we gave the Prince's two fine Lances, went foremost with five more having long Poles in their Hands; and after them ten of our Men advanced toward the Negro Town that was next to us, and we all stood ready to succour them if there should be Occasion.

When they came pretty near their Houses, our Negroes halloo'd in their screaming Way, and called to them as loud as they could; upon their calling, some of the Men came out, and answer'd, and immediately after the whole Town, Men Women and Children appeared: Our Negroes with their long Poles went forward a little, and stuck them all in the Ground, and left them, which in their country was a Signal of Peace, but the other did not understand the Meaning of that. Then the two Men with Bows, laid down their Bows and Arrows, went forward unarmed, and made Signs of Peace to them, which at last the other began to understand; so two of their Men laid down their Bows and Arrows, and came towards them: Our Men made all the Signs of Friendship to them that they could think of, putting their Hands up to their Mouths, as a Sign that they wanted Provisions to eat, and the other pretended to be pleased and friendly, and went back to their Fellows, and talk'd with them a while, and they came forward again, and made Signs that they would bring some Provisions to them before the Sun set; and so our Men came back again very well satisfied for that time.

But an Hour before Sun-set our Men went to them again, just in the same Posture as before, and they came according to their Appointment, and brought Deers Flesh, Roots, and the same kind of Corn like Rice, *which I mentioned above*, and our Negroes being furnish'd with such Toys as our Cutler had contrived, gave them some of them, which they seem'd infinitely pleas'd with, and promis'd to bring more Provisions the next Day.

Accordingly, the next Day they came again, but our Men perceived they were more in Number by a great many than before; however, having sent out ten Men with Fire-Arms to stand ready, and our whole Army being in View also, we were not much surprised; nor was the Treachery of the Enemy so cunningly ordered as in other cases; for they might have surrounded our Negroes, which were but nine, under a Shew of Peace; but when they saw our Men advance almost as far as the Place where they were the Day before, the Rogues snatch'd up their Bows and Arrows, and come running upon our Men like so many Furies, at which our ten Men called to the Negroes to come back to them, which they did with Speed enough at the first Word, and stood all behind our Men. As they fled, the other advanced, and let fly near a 100 of their Arrows at them, by which two of our Negroes were wounded, and one we thought had been killed. When they came to the five Poles that our Men had stuck in the Ground, they stood still a while, and gathering about the Poles, looked at them, and handled them as wondering at what they meant. We then who were drawn up behind all, sent one of our Number to our ten Men, to bid them fire among them, while they stood so thick, and to put some small shot into their Guns, besides the ordinary Charge, and to tell them, that we would be up with them immediately.

Accordingly they made ready, but by that time they were ready to fire, the Black Army had left their wondering about the Poles, and began to stir as if they would come on, tho' seeing more Men stand at some Distance behind our Negroes, they could not tell what to make of us; but if they did not understand us before, they understood us less afterwards, for as soon as ever our Men found them begin to move forward, they fired among the thickest of them, being about the Distance of 120 Yards, as near as we could guess.

It is impossible to express the Fright, the Screaming and Yelling of those Wretches upon this first Volley; we killed six of them, and wounded 11 or 12, I mean as we knew of; for, as they stood thick, and the small Shot, as we called it, scattered among them, we had Reason to believe we wounded more that stood farther off; for our small Shot was made of Bits of Lead, and Bits of Iron, Heads of Nails, and such things as our diligent Artificer the Cutler help'd us to.

As to those that were killed and wounded, the other frighted Creatures were under the greatest Amazement in the World, to think what should hurt them; for they could see nothing but Holes made in their Bodies they knew not how. Then the Fire and the Noise amazed all their Women and Children, and frighted them out of their Wits, that they ran staring and howling about like mad Creatures.

However, all this did not make them fly, which was what we wanted; nor did we find any of them die as it were with Fear, as at first, so we resolved upon a second Volley, and then to advance as we did before. Whereupon our reserved Men advancing, we resolved to fire only three Men at a time, and move forward like an Army firing in Platoons; so being all in Line we fired first three on the Right, then three on the Left, and so on; and every time we killed or wounded some of them; but still they did not fly, and yet they were so frighted, that they used none of their Bows and Arrows, or of their Lances; and we thought their Numbers encreased upon our Hands; particularly we thought so by the Noise; so I called to our Men to halt, and bid them pour in one whole Volley, and then shout, as we did in our first Fight, and so run in upon them, and knock them down with our Musquets.

But they were too wise for that too, for as soon as we had fired a whole Volley, and shouted, they all run away, Men, Women, and Children, so fast, that in a few Moments we could not see one Creature of them, except some that were wounded and lame, who lay wallowing and screaming here and there upon the Ground, as they happen'd to fall.

Upon this we came up to the Field of Battle, where we found we had killed 37 of them, among which were three Women, and had wounded about 64 among which were two Women; by wounded I mean, such as were so maimed, as not to be able to go away, and those our Negroes killed afterwards in a cowardly manner in cold Blood, for which we were very angry, and threatened to make them go to them if they did so again.

There was no great Spoil to be got, for they were all stark naked as they came into the World, Men and Women together; some of them having Feathers stuck in their Hair, and others a kind of Bracelets about their Necks, but nothing else; but our Negroes got a Booty here which we were very glad of, and this was the Bows and Arrows of the vanquished, of which they found more than they knew what to do with, belonging to the killed and wounded Men; these we ordered them to pick up, and they were very useful to us afterwards. After the Fight, and our Negroes had gotten Bows and Arrows, we sent them out in Parties to see what they could get, and they got some Provisions; but, which was better than all the rest, they brought us four more young Bulls, or Buffloes, that had been brought up to Labour, and to carry Burthens: They knew them, it seems, by the Burthens they had carry'd having galled their Backs; for, they have no Saddles to cover them with in that Country.

Those Creatures not only eased our Negroes, but gave us an Opportunity to carry more Provisions, and our Negroes loaded them very hard at this Place, with Flesh and Roots, such as we wanted very much afterwards.

In this Town we found a very little young Leopard, about two Spans high; it was exceeding tame, and purr'd like a Cat when we stroked it with our hands, being, as I suppose, bred up among the Negroes like a House-Dog. It was our Black Prince, it seems, who making his Tour among the abandoned Houses or Hutts, found this Creature there, and making much of him, and giving a Bit or two of Flesh to him, the Creature followed him like a Dog; of which more hereafter.

Among the Negroes that were killed in this Battle, there was one who had a little thin Bit or Plate of Gold, about as big as a Six-Pence, which hung by a little Bit of a twisted Gutt, upon his Forehead, by which we supposed he was a Man of some Eminence among them; but that was not all, for this Bit of Gold put us upon searching very narrowly, if there was not more of it to be had thereabouts, but we found none at all.

From this Part of the Country we went on for about 15 Days, and then found our selves obliged to march up a high Ridge of Mountains frightful to behold, and the first of the Kind that we met with; and having no Guide but our little Pocket Compass, we had no Advantage of Information as to which was the best, or the worst Way, but were obliged to chuse by what we saw, and shift as well as we could. We met with several Nations of wild and naked people in the plain Country, before we came to those Hills, and we found them much more tractable and friendly than those Devils we had been forc'd to fight with; and tho' we could learn little from these People, yet we understood by the Signs they made, that there was a vast Desart beyond those Hills, and, *as our Negroes called them*, much Lion, much spotted Cat (so they called the Leopard) and they sign'd to us also, that we must carry Water with us. At the last of these Nations we furnished our selves with as much Provision as we could possibly carry, not knowing what we had to suffer, or what length we had to go; and to make our Way as Familiar to us as possible, I proposed, that of the last Inhabitants we could find, we should make some Prisoners, and carry them with us for Guides over the Desart, and to assist us in carrying Provisions, and perhaps in getting it too. The Advice was too necessary to be slighted; so finding by our dumb Signs to the Inhabitants, that there were some People that dwelt at the Foot of the Mountains, on the other Side, before we came to the Desart it self, we resolved to furnish our selves with Guides, by fair Means or soul.

Here, by a moderate Computation, we concluded our selves 700 Miles from the Sea Coast where we began. Our Black Prince was this Day set free from the Sling his Arm hung in, our Surgeon having perfectly restored it, and he shewed it to his own Countrymen quite well, which made them greatly wonder. Also our two Negroes began to recover, and their Wounds to heal apace, for our Surgeon was very skilful in managing their Cure.

Having with infinite Labour mounted these Hills, and coming to a View of the Country beyond them, it was indeed enough to astonish as stout a Heart as ever was created. It was a vast-howling Wilderness,[73] not a Tree, a River, or a Green thing to be seen, for as far as the Eye could look; nothing but a scalding Sand, which, as the Wind blew, drove about in Clouds, enough to overwhelm Man and Beast; nor could we see any End of it, either before us, which was our Way, or to the right Hand or left: So that truly our Men began to be discouraged, and talk of going back again; nor could we indeed think of venturing over such a horrid Place as that before us, in which we saw nothing but present Death.

I was as much affected with the Sight as any of them, but for all that I could not bear the Thoughts of going back again. I told them we had march'd 700 Miles of our Way, and it would be worse than Death to think of going back again; and that if they thought the Desart was not passable, I thought we should rather change our Course, and travel South till we came to the *Cape of Good Hope*, or North to the Country that lay along the

Nile, where perhaps we might find some Way or other over to the West Sea; for sure all *Africa* was not a Desart.

Our Gunner, who, as I said before, was our Guide as to the Situation of Places, told us, that he could not tell what to say to going for the Cape; for it was a monstrous Length, being from the Place where we now were, not less than 1500 Miles, and by his Account, we were come now a third Part of the Way to the Coast of *Angola*, where we should meet with the Western Ocean, and find Ways enough for our Escape Home. On the other Hand, he assured us, and shewed us a Map of it, that if we went Northward, the Western Shore of *Africk* went out into the Sea above a Thousand Miles West; so that we should have so much, and more Land, to travel afterwards; which Land might, for ought we knew, be as wild, barren, and desart, as this: And therefore, upon the whole, he proposed that we should attempt this Desart, and perhaps we should not find it so long as we feared; and however, he proposed that we should see how far our Provisions would carry us, and in particular, our Water; and that we should venture no farther than Half so far as our Water would last; and if we found no End of the Desart, we might come safely back again.

This Advice was so reasonable, that we all approved of it; and accordingly we calculated, that we were able to carry Provisions for 42 Days, but that we could not carry Water for above 20 Days, tho' we were to suppose it to stink too before that time expired. So that we concluded, that if we did not come at some Water in ten Days time, we would return, but if we found a Supply of Water, we could then travel 21 Days; and if we saw no End of the Wilderness in that time, we would return also.

With this Regulation of our Measures, we descended the Mountains, and it was the second Day before we quite reached the Plain, where however, to make us amends, we found a fine little Rivulet of very good Water, Abundance of Deer, a sort of Creature like a Hare, but not so nimble, and whose Flesh we found very agreeable; but we were deceived in our Intelligence, for we found no People; so we got no more Prisoners to assist us in carrying our Baggage.

The infinite Number of Deer and other Creatures which we saw here, we found was occasioned by the Neighbourhood of the Wast or Desart, from whence they retired hither for Food and Refreshment. We stored our selves here with Flesh and Roots of divers Kinds, which our Negroes understood better than we, and which served us for Bread; and with as much Water as, (by the Allowance of a Quart a Day to a Man for our Negroes, and three Pints a Day a Man for our selves, and three Quarts a Day each, for our Buffloes) would serve us 20 Days: And thus loaden for a long miserable March, we set forward, being all sound in Health, and very chearful, but not alike strong for so great a Fatigue; and which was our Grievance, were without a Guide.

In the very first Entrance of the Wast, we were exceedingly discouraged; for we found the Sand so deep, and it scalded our Feet so much with the Heat, that after we had, as I may call it, waded rather than walk'd thro' it, about seven or eight Miles, we were all heartily tired and faint; even the very Negroes lay down and panted, like Creatures that had been push'd beyond their Strength.

Here we found the Difference of Lodging greatly injurious to us; for (as before) we always made us Hutts to sleep under, which cover'd us from the Night Air, which is particularly unwholesom in those hot Countries: But we had here no Shelter, no Lodging after so hard a March; for here were no Trees, no not a Shrub near us: And which was still more frightful, towards Night we began to hear the Wolves howl, the Lions bellow, and a great many wild Asses braying, and other ugly Noises which we did not understand.

Upon this we reflected upon our own Indiscretion, that had not at least brought Poles or Stakes in our Hands, with which we might have, as it were pallisadoed our selves in for the Night; and so we might have slept secure, whatever other Inconveniences we suffer'd. However, we found a Way at last to relieve our selves a little. For first we set up the Lances and Bows we had, and endeavoured to bring the Tops of them as near to one another as we could, and so hung our Coats on the Top of them, which made us a kind of a sorry Tent; the Leopard's Skin, and a few other Skins we had put together, made us a tolerable Covering, and thus we lay down to Sleep, and slept very heartily too for the first Night, setting however a good Watch, being two of our own Men with their Fuzees, whom we reliev'd in an Hour at first, and two Hours afterwards; and it was very well we did this; for they found the Wilderness swarm'd with raging Creatures of all Kinds, some of which came directly up to the very Enclosure of our Tent. But our Centinels were ordered not to alarm us with Firing in the Night, but to flash in the Pan at them, which they did, and found it effectual; for the Creatures went off always as soon as they saw it, perhaps with some Noise or Howling, and pursued such other Game as they were upon.

If we were tired with the Day's Travel; we were all as much tired with the Night's Lodging: But our Black Prince told us in the Morning, he would give us some Counsel, and indeed it was very good Counsel. He told us we should all be kill'd if we went on this Journey, and thro' this Desart, without some Covering for us at Night; so he advised us to march back again to a little River Side where we lay the Night before, and stay there till we could make us Houses, as he called them, to carry with us to lodge in every Night. As he began a little to understand our Speech, and we very well to understand his Signs, we easily knew what he meant, and that we should there make Matts; (for we remembered that we saw a great deal of Matting, or Bass[74] there that the Natives make Matts of) I say, that we should make large Matts there for Covering our Hutts or Tents to lodge in at Night.

We all approv'd this Advice, and immediately resolved to go back that one Day's Journey, resolving, tho' we carried less Provisions, we would carry Matts with us to cover us in the Night. Some of the nimblest of us got back to the River with more Ease than we had travell'd it out the Day before; but as we were not in Haste, the rest made a Halt, encamp'd another Night, and came to us the next Day.

In our Return of this Day's Journey, our Men that made two Days of it, met with a very surprizing thing, that gave them some Reason to be careful how they parted Company again. The Case was this. The second Day in the Morning, before they had gone Half a Mile, looking behind them, they saw a vast Cloud of Sand or Dust rise in the Air, as we see sometimes in the Roads in Summer, when it is very dusty, and a large Drove of Cattel are coming, only very much greater; and they could easily perceive that it came after them, and that it came on faster than they went from it. The Cloud of Sand was so great, that they could not see what it was that raised it, and concluded, that it was some Army of Enemies that pursued them; but then considering that they came from the vast uninhabited Wilderness, they knew, it was impossible any Nation or People that Way should have Intelligence of them, or of the Way of their March: And therefore, if it was an Army, it must be of such as they were, travelling that Way by Accident. On the other Hand, as they knew that there were no Horses in the Country, and that they came on so fast, they concluded, that it must be some vast Collection of wild Beasts, perhaps making to the Hill Country for Food or Water, and that they should be all devoured or trampled under Foot by their Multitude.

Upon this Thought, they very prudently observed which Way the Cloud seem'd to point, and they turned a little out of their Way to the North, supposing it might pass by them. When they were about a Quarter of a Mile, they halted to see what it might be. One of the Negroes, a nimbler Fellow than the rest, went back a little, and come again in a few Minutes, running as fast as the heavy Sand would allow, and by Signs gave them to know, that it was a great Herd or Drove, or whatever it might be called, of vast monstrous Elephants.

As it was a Sight our Men had never seen, they were desirous to see it, and yet a little uneasy at the Danger too; for tho' an Elephant is a heavy, unwieldy Creature, yet in the deep Sand, which was nothing at all to them, they marched at a great Rate, and would soon have tired our People, if they had had far to go, and had been pursued by them.

Our Gunner was with them, and had a great Mind to have gone close up to one of the outermost of them, and to have clapt his Piece to his Ear, and to have fired into him, because he had been told no Shot would penetrate them; but they all disswaded him, lest, upon the Noise, they should all turn upon, and pursue us; so he was reasoned out of it, and let them pass, which in our People's Circumstance was certainly the right Way.

They were between 20 and 30 in Number, but prodigious great ones; and tho' they often shew'd our Men that they saw them, yet they did not turn out of their Way, or take any other Notice of them, than, *as we might say*, just to look at them. We that were before, saw the Cloud of Dust they raised, but we thought it had been our own Carravan, and so took no Notice; but as they bent their Course one Point of the Compass, or thereabouts, to the Southward of the East, and we went due East, they pass'd by us at some little Distance; so that we did not see them, or know any thing of them till Evening, when our Men came to us, and gave us this Account of them. However, this was a useful Experiment for our future Conduct in passing the Desart, as you shall hear in its Place.

We were now upon our Work, and our Black Prince was Head Surveyor, for he was an excellent Matt-Maker himself, and all his Men understood it; so that they soon made us near a Hundred Matts: And as every Man, I mean of the Negroes, carried one, it was no Manner of Load, and we did not carry an Ounce of Provisions the less. The greatest Burthen was to carry six long Poles, besides some shorter Stakes; but the Negroes made an Advantage of that, for carrying them between two, they made the Luggage of Provisions which they had to carry, so much the lighter, binding it upon two Poles, and so made three Couple of them. As soon as we saw this, we made a little Advantage of it too; for having three or four of our Baggs called Bottles, (I mean Skins or Bladders to carry Water) more than the Men could carry, we got them fill'd, and carried them this Way, which was a Day's Water and more for our Journey.

Having now ended our Work, made our Matts, and fully recruited our Stores of all things necessary, and having made us Abundance of small Ropes of Matting for ordinary Use, as we might have Occasion, we set forward again, having interrupted our Journey eight Days in all, upon this Affair. To our great Comfort, the Night before we set out, there fell a very violent Shower of Rain, the Effects of which we found in the Sand; tho the Heat of one Day dry'd the Surface as much as before, yet it was harder at Bottom, not so heavy, and was cooler to our Feet, by which Means we march'd, as we reckoned, about fourteen Miles instead of seven, and with much more Ease.

When we came to encamp, we had all things ready, for we had fitted our Tent, and set it up for Trial where we made it; so that in less than an Hour, we had a large Tent raised, with an Inner and Outer Apartment, and two Entrances. In one we lay our selves, in the other our Negroes, having light pleasant Matts over us, and others at the same time under us. Also we had a little Place without all for our Buffloes, for they deserved our Care, being very useful to us, besides carrying Forage and Water for themselves. Their Forage was a Root which our Black Prince directed us to find, not much unlike a Pasnip, very moist and nourishing, of which there was Plenty wherever we came, this horrid Desart excepted.

When we came the next Morning to decamp, our Negroes took down the Tent, and pull'd up the Stakes, and all was in Motion in as little time as it was set up. In this Posture we march'd eight Days, and yet could see no End, no Change of our Prospect, but all looking as wild and dismal as at the Beginning. If there was any Alteration, it was, that the Sand was no where so deep and heavy as it was the first three Days. This we thought might be, because for six Months of the Year the Winds blowing West, (as for the other six, they blew constantly East) the Sand was driven violently to the Side of the Desart where we set out, where the Mountains lying very high, the Easterly *Monsoons*, when they blew, had not the same Power to drive it back again; and this was confirm'd by our finding the like Depth of Sand on the farthest Extent of the Desart to the West.

It was the ninth Day of our Travel in this Wilderness, when we came to the View of a great Lake[75] of Water, and you may be sure this was a particular Satisfaction to us, because we had not Water left for above two or three Days more, at our shortest Allowance; I mean, allowing Water for our Return, if we had been driven to the Necessity of it. Our Water had served us two Days longer than we expected, our Buffloes having found for two or three Days, a kind of Herb like a Broad flat Thistle, tho without any Prickle, spreading on the Ground and growing in the Sand, which they eat freely of, and which supplied them for Drink as well as Forage.

The next Day, which was the tenth from our setting out, we came to the Edge of this Lake, and very happily for us, we came to it at the South Point of it, for to the North we could see no End of it; so we passed by it, and travelled three Days by the Side of it, which was a great Comfort to us, because it lightened our Burthen, there being no need to carry Water, when we had it in View; and yet, tho' here was so much Water, we found but very little Alteration in the Desart, no Trees, no Grass or Herbage, except that Thistle, as I call'd it, and two or three more Plants, which we did not understand, of which the Desart began to be pretty full.

But as we were refreshed with the Neighbourhood of this Lake of Water, so we were now gotten among a prodigious Number of ravenous Inhabitants, the like whereof, 'tis most certain the Eye of Man never saw: For as I firmly believe, that never Man, nor a Body of Men, passed this Desart since the Flood, so I believe there is not the like Collection of fierce, ravenous, and devouring Creatures in the World; I mean not in any particular Place.

For a Day's Journey before we came to this Lake, and all the three Days we were pasting by it, and for six or seven Days March after it, the Ground was scattered with Elephants Teeth, in such a Number, as is incredible; and as some of them may have lain there for some Hundreds of Years, so seeing the Substance of them scarce ever decayes, they may lye there for ought I know to the End of Time. The Size of some of them is, it seems, to those to whom I have reported it, as incredible as the Number, and I can assure you, there were several so heavy, as the strongest Man among us could not lift. As to Number, I question not but there are enough to load a thousand Sail of the biggest Ships in the World, by which I may be understood to mean, that the Quantity is not to be conceived of; seeing that as they lasted in View for above eighty Miles Travelling, so they might continue as far to the right Hand, and to the left as far, and many times as far, for ought we knew; for it seems the Number of Elephants hereabouts is prodigious great. In one Place in particular, we saw the Head of an Elephant, with several Teeth in it, but one the biggest that ever I saw: The Flesh was consumed to be sure many Hundred Years before, and all the other Bones; but three of our strongest Men could not lift this Scull and Teeth: The great Tooth, I believe, weighed at least 300 Weight, and this was particularly remarkable to me, that I observed the whole Scull was as good Ivory as the Teeth, and I believe all together weighed at least 600 Weight, and tho' I do not know but, by the same Rule, all the Bones of the Elephant may be Ivory; yet I think there is this just Objection against it from the Example before me, that then all the other Bones of this Elephant would have been there as well as the Head.

I proposed to our Gunner, that seeing we had travelled now 14 Days without Intermission, and that we had Water here for our Refreshment, and no Want of Food yet, or any Fear of it; we should rest our People a little, and see at the same time, if perhaps we might kill some Creatures that were proper for Food. The Gunner, who had more Forecast of that kind, than I had, agreed to the Proposal, and added, why might we not try to catch some Fish out of the Lake? The first thing we had before us, was to try if we could make any Hooks, and this indeed put our Artificer to his

Trumps;[76] however, with some Labour and Difficulty he did it, and we catched fresh Fish of several kinds. How they came there, none but he that made the Lake, and all the World, knows; for to be sure no human Hands ever put any in there, or pulled any out before.

We not only catched enough for our present Refreshment, but we dried several large Fishes of Kinds which I cannot describe, in the Sun, by which we lengthen'd out our Provision considerably; for the Heat of the Sun dried them so effectually without Salt, that they were perfectly cured dry and hard in one Day's time.

We rested our selves here five Days, during which time we had Abundance of pleasant Adventures with the wild Creatures, too many to relate: One of them was very particular, which was a Chase between a She Lion, or Lioness, and a large Deer; and tho' the Deer is naturally a very nimble Creature, and she flew by us like the Wind, having perhaps about 300 Yards the Start of the Lion, yet we found the Lion by her Strength, and the Goodness of her Lungs, got Ground of her. They past by us within about a Quarter of a Mile, and we had a View of them a great Way, when having given them over, we were surprized about an Hour after, to see them come thundering back again on the other Side of us, and then the Lion was within 30 or 40 Yards of her, and both straining to the Extremity of their Speed, when the Deer coming to the Lake, plunged into the Water, and swam for her Life, as she had before run for it.

The Lioness plunged in after her, and swam a little way, but came back again; and when she was got upon the Land, she set up the most hideous Roar that ever I heard in my Life, as if done in the Rage of having lost her Prey.

We walked out Morning and Evening constantly; the Middle of the Day we refreshed our selves under our Tent; but one Morning early we saw another Chase, which more nearly concern'd us than the other; for our Black Prince, walking by the Side of the Lake, was set upon by a vast great Crocodile, which came out of the Lake upon him; and tho' he was very light of Foot, yet it was as much as he could do to get away: He fled amain to us, and the Truth is, we did not know what to do, for we were told no Bullet would enter her; and we found it so at first, for tho' three of our Men fired at her, yet she did not mind them; but my Friend the Gunner, a ventrous Fellow, of a bold Heart, and great Presence of Mind, went up so near as to thrust the Muzzle of his Piece into her Mouth, and fired but let his Piece fall, and run for it the very Moment he had fired it: The Creature raged a great while, and spent its Fury upon the Gun, making Marks upon the very Iron with her Teeth, but after some time fainted and died.

Our Negroes spread the Banks of the Lake all this while, for Game, and at length killed us three Deer, one of them very large, the other two very small. There was Water-Fowl also in the Lake, but we never came near enough to them to shoot any; and, as for the Desart, we saw no Fowls any where in it, but at the Lake.

We likewise killed two or three Civet Cats, but their Flesh is the worst of Carrion; we saw Abundance of Elephants at a Distance, and observed, that they always go in very good Company, that is to say, Abundance of them together, and always extended in a fair Line of Battle; and this, they say, is the way they defend themselves from their Enemies; for if Lions or Tygers, Wolves or any Creatures, attack them, they being drawn up in a Line, sometimes reaching five or six Miles in Length, whatever comes in their Way is sure to be trod under Foot, or beaten in Pieces with their Trunks, or lifted up in the Air with their Trunks; so that if a hundred Lions or Tygers were coming along, if they meet a Line of Elephants, they will always fly back till they see Room to pass by to the Right Hand or to the Left; and if they did not, it would be impossible for one of them to escape; for the Elephant, tho' a heavy Creature, is yet so dexterous and nimble with his Trunk, that he will not fail to lift up the heaviest Lion, or any other wild Creature, and throw him up in the Air quite over his Back, and then trample him to Death with his Feet. We saw several Lines of Battle thus, we saw one so long, that indeed there was no End of it to be seen, and, I believe, their might be 2000 Elephants in a Row, or Line. They are not Beasts of Prey, but live upon the Herbage of the Field, as an Ox does, and, it is said, that tho' they are so great a Creature, yet that a smaller Quantity of Forage supplies one of them, than will suffice a Horse.

The Numbers of this kind of Creature that are in those Parts are inconceivable, as may be gather'd from the prodigious Quantity of Teeth, which as I said we saw in this vast Desart, and indeed we saw a 100 of them to one of any other Kinds.

One Evening we were very much surprized; we were most of us laid down upon our Matts to Sleep, when our Watch came running in among us, being frighted with the sudden Roaring of some Lions just by them, which it seems they had not seen, the Night being dark, till they were just upon them. There was, as it proved, an old Lion and his whole Family, for there was the Lioness and three young Lions, besides the old King, who was a monstrous great one: One of the young ones, who were good large well grown ones too, leapt up upon one of our Negroes, who stood Centinel, before he saw him, at which he was heartily frighted, cried out, and run into the Tent: Our other Man, who had a Gun, had not Presence of Mind at first to shoot him, but struck him with the But-End of his Piece, which made him whine a little, and then growl at him fearfully; but the Fellow retired, and we being all alarmed, three of our Men snatched up their Guns, run to the Tent-Door, where they saw the great old Lion by the Fire of his Eyes, and first fired at him, but, we supposed, missed him, or at least did not kill him; for they went all off, but raised a most hideous Roar, which, as if they had called for Help, brought down a prodigious Number of Lions, and other furious Creatures, we know not what about them, for we could not see them; but their was a Noise and Yelling, and Howling, and all sort of such Wilderness Musick on every Side of us, as if all the Beasts of the Desart were assembled to devour us.

We asked our Black Prince what we should do with them? *Me go*, says he, *fright them all*; so he snatches up two or three of the worst of our Matts, and, getting one of our Men to strike some Fire, he hangs the Matt up at the End of a Pole, and set it on Fire, and it blazed abroad a good while; at which the Creatures all moved off, for we heard them roar, and make their bellowing Noise at a great Distance. Well, says our Gunner, if that will do, we need not burn our Matts, which are our Beds to lay under us, and our Tilting to cover us. Let me alone, says he, so he comes back into our Tent, and falls to making some artificial Fire-Works, and the like; and he gave our Centinels some to be ready at Hand, upon Occasion, and particularly he placed a great Piece of Wild-fire[77] upon the same Pole that the Matt had been tied to, and set it on Fire, and that burnt there so long, that all the Wild Creatures left us for that time.

However, we began to be weary of such Company, and, to be rid of them, we set forward again two Days sooner than we intended. We found now, that tho' the Desart did not end, nor could we see any Appearance of it, yet that the Earth was pretty full of green Stuff, of one sort or another, so that our Cattle had no Want. And secondly, that there were several little Rivers which run into the Lake, and so long as the Country continued low, we found Water sufficient, which eased us very much in our Carriage, and we went on yet sixteen Days more without yet coming to any Appearance of better Soil: After this we found the Country rise a little, and by that we perceived, that the Water would fail us, so, for fear of the worst, we filled our Bladder Bottles with Water; we found the Country rising gradually thus for three Days continually, when, on the sudden, we perceived, that tho' we had mounted up insensibly, yet that we were on the Top of a very high ridge of Hills, tho' not such as at first.

When we came to look down on the other Side of the Hills we saw, to the great Joy of all our Hearts, that the Desart was at an End; that the Country was clothed with Green, Abundance of Trees, and a large River, and we made no doubt but that we should find People and Cattel also; and here, by our Gunner's Account, who kept our Computations, we had marched above 400 Miles over this dismal Place of Horrour, having been four and thirty Days a-doing of it, and consequently were come about 1100 Miles of our Journey.

We would willingly have descended the Hills that Night, but it was too late; the next Morning we saw every thing more plain, and rested our selves under the Shade of some Trees; which were now the most refreshing things imaginable to us, who had been scorched above a Month without a Tree to cover us. We found the Country here very pleasant, especially considering that we came from, and we killed some Deer here also, which we found very frequent under the Cover of the Woods; also we killed a creature like a Goat, whose Flesh was very good to eat, but it was no Goat: We found also a great Number of Fowls like Partridge, but something smaller, and were very tame, so that we lived here very well, but found no People, at least none that would be seen, no not for several Days Journey; and, to allay our Joy, we were almost every Night disturbed with Lions and Tygers; Elephants indeed we saw none here.

In three Days March we came to a River, which we saw from the Hills, and which we called the Golden River, and we found it run Northward, which was the first Stream we had met with that did so; it run with a very rapid current, and our Gunner pulling out his Map, assured me that this was either the River *Nile*, or run into the great Lake; out of which the River *Nile* was said to take its Beginning; and he brought out his Carts[78] and Maps, which by his Instruction, I began to understand very well; and told me, he would convince me of it, and indeed he seemed to make it so plain to me, that I was of the same Opinion.

But I did not enter into the Gunner's Reason for this Enquiry, not in the least, till he went on with it farther, and stated it thus; if this is the River *Nile*, why should not we build some more Canoes, and go down this Stream rather than to expose our selves to any more Desarts and scorching Sands, in Quest of the Sea, which when we are come to, we shall be as much at a Loss how to get home as we were at *Madagascar*.

The Argument was good, had there been no Objections in the Way, of a Kind which none of us were capable of answering; but upon the whole it was an Undertaking of such a Nature, that every one of us thought it impracticable, and that upon several Accounts; and our Surgeon, who was himself a good Scholar, and a Man of Reading, tho' not acquainted with the Business of Sailing, opposed it; and some of his Reasons, I remember, were such as these; first, the Length of the Way, which both he and the Gunner allowed by the Course of the Water and Turnings of the River, would be at least 4000 Miles. Secondly, The innumerable Crocodiles in the

River, which we should never be able to escape. Thirdly, The dreadful Desarts in the Way; and lastly, the approaching rainy Season, in which the Streams of the *Nile* would be so furious, and rise so high, spreading far and wide over all the plain Country, that we should never be able to know when we were in the Channel of the River, and when not, and should certainly be cast away, over-set, or run a-ground so often, that it would be impossible to proceed by a River so excessively dangerous.

This last Reason he made so plain to us, that we began to be so sensible of it our selves; so that we agreed to lay that Thought aside, and proceed in our first Course Westward towards the Sea: But as if we had been loath to depart, we continued, by way of refreshing our selves, to loyter two Days upon this River, in which time our Black Prince, who delighted much in wandering up and down, came one Evening and brought us several little Bits of something, he knew not what; but he found it felt heavy, and looked well, and shewed it to me, as what he thought was some Rarity. I took not much Notice of it to him, but stepping out, and calling the Gunner to me, I shewed it him, and told him what I thought, *viz.* that it was certainly Gold: He agreed with me in that, and also in what follow'd, that we would take the Black Prince out with us the next Day, and make him shew us where he found it, that if there was any Quantity to be found, we would tell our Company of it, but if there was but little, we would keep Counsel, and have it to our selves.

But we forgot to engage the Prince in the Secret, who innocently told so much to all the rest, as that they guessed what it was, and came to us to see; when we found it was publick, we were more concerned to prevent their suspecting that we had any Design to conceal it, and openly telling our Thoughts of it, we called our Artificer, who agreed presently that it was Gold; so I proposed, that we should all go with the Prince to the Place where he found it, and if any Quantity was to be had, we would lye here some time, and see what we could make of it.

Accordingly, we went every Man of us, for no Man was willing to be left behind in a Discovery of such a Nature. When we came to the Place, we found it was on the West Side of the River, not in the main River, but in another small River or Stream which came from the West, and run into the other River at that Place. We fell to raking in the Sand, and washing it in our Hands, and we seldom took up a Handful of Sand, but we washed some little round Lumps as big as a Pin's Head, or sometimes as big as a Grapestone, into our Hands, and we found in two or three Hours time, that every one had got some, so we agreed to leave off, and go to Dinner.

While we were eating, it came into my Thoughts, that while we work'd at this Rate in a thing of such Nicety and Consequence, it was ten to one if the Gold, which was the *Makebait*[79] of the World, did not first or last set us together by the Ears to break our good Articles and our Understanding one among another, and perhaps cause us to part Companies, or worse; I therefore told them, that I was indeed the youngest Man of the Company, but as they had always allowed me to give my Opinion in things, and had sometimes been pleased to follow my Advice, so I had something to propose now, which I thought, would be for all our Advantages, and I believed they would all like it very well. I told them we were in a Country where we all knew there was a great deal of Gold, and that all the World sent Ships thither to get it; that we did not indeed know where it was, and so we might get a great deal, or a little, we did not know whether; but I offered it to them to consider whether it would not be the best Way for us, and to preserve the good Harmony and Friendship that had been always kept among us, and which was so absolutely necessary to our Safety, that what we found should be brought together to one common Stock, and be equally divided at last, rather than to run the Hazard of any Difference which might happen among us, from any one's having found more or less than another. I told them, that if we were all upon one Bottom,[80] we should all apply our selves heartily to the Work, and besides that, we might then set our Negroes all to Work for us, and receive equally the Fruit of their Labour, and of our own, and being all exactly alike Sharers, there could be no just Cause of Quarrel or Disgust among us.

They all approv'd the Proposal, and every one jointly swore, and gave their Hands to one another, that they would not conceal the least Grain of Gold from the rest; and consented, that if any one or more should be found to conceal any, all that he had should be taken from him, and divided among the rest: And one thing more was added to it by our Gunner, from Considerations equally good and just; that if any one of us, by any Play, Bett, Game, or Wager, won any Money or Gold, or the Value of any from another, during our whole Voyage till our Return quite to *Portugal*, he should be obliged by us all to restore it again on the Penalty of being disarm'd, and turn'd out of the Company, and of having no Relief from us on any Account whatsoever. This was to prevent Wagering and Playing for Money, which our Men were apt to do by several Means, and at several Games, tho' they had neither Cards or Dice.

Having made this wholesom Agreement, we went chearfully to Work, and shew'd our Negroes how to work for us; and working up the Stream on both Sides, and in the Bottom of the River, we spent about three Weeks Time dabbling in the Water; by which time, as it lay all in our Way, we had gone about six Miles, and not more; and still the higher we went, the more Gold we found; till at last, having pass'd by the Side of a Hill, we perceived on a sudden, that the Gold stopp'd, and that there was not a Bit taken up beyond that Place; it presently occurr'd to my Mind, that it must then be from the Side of that little Hill that all the Gold we found was work'd down.

Upon this, we went back to the Hill, and fell to Work with that. We found the Earth loose, and of a yellowish loamy Colour, and in some Places, a white hard Kind of Stone, which in describing since to some of our Artists, they tell me was the Spar[81] which is found by the Oar, and surrounds it in the Mine. However, if it had been all Gold, we had no Instrument to force it out; so we passed that: But scratching into the loose Earth with our Fingers, we came to a surprizing Place, where the Earth for the Quantity of two Bushels, I believe, or thereabouts, crumbled down with little more than touching it, and apparently shewed us that there was a great deal of Gold in it. We took it all carefully up, and washing it in the Water, the loamy Earth wash'd away, and left the Gold Dust free in our Hands; and that which was more remarkable, was, that when this loose Earth was all taken away, and we came to the Rock or hard Stone, there was not one Grain of Gold more to be found.

At Night we came all together to see what we had got, and it appeared we had found in that Day's Heap of Earth, about Seven and Fifty Pound Weight of Gold Dust, and about Thirty Four Pound more in all the rest of our Works in the River.

It was a happy Kind of Disappointment to us, that we found a full Stop put to our Work; for had the Quantity of Gold been ever so small, yet had any at all come, I do not know when we should have given over; for having rummaged this Place, and not finding the least Grain of Gold in any other Place, or in any of the Earth there, except in that loose Parcel, we went quite back down the small River again, working it over and over again, as long as we could find any thing how small soever; and we did get six or seven Pound more the second time. Then we went into the first River, and tried it up the Stream and down the Stream, on the one Side and on the other. Up the Stream we found nothing, no not a Grain; down the Stream we found very little, not above the Quantity of Half an Ounce in two Miles working; so back we came again to the Golden River, as we justly called it, and work'd it up the Stream and down the Stream twice more a-piece, and every time we found some Gold, and perhaps might have done so, if we had stay'd there till this time; but the Quantity was at last so small, and the Work so much the harder, that we agreed by Consent to give it over, lest we should fatigue our selves and our Negroes so, as to be quite unfit for our Journey. When we had brought all our Purchase together, we had in the whole three Pound and a Half of Gold to a Man, Share and Share alike, according to such a Weight and Scale as our ingenious Cutler made for us to weigh it by, which he did indeed by guess, but which, as he said he was sure was rather more than less, and so it prov'd at last; for it was near two Ounces more than Weight in a Pound. Besides this, there was seven or eight Pound Weight left, which we agreed to leave in his Hands, to work it into such Shapes as we thought fit to give away to such People as we might yet meet with, from whom we might have Occasion to buy Provisions, or even to buy Friendship, or the like; and particularly we gave about a Pound to our Black Prince, which he hammer'd and work'd by his own indefatigable Hand, and some Tools our Artificer lent him, into little round Bits, as round almost as Beads, tho' not exact in Shape, and drilling Holes thro' them, put them all upon a String, and wore them about his black Neck, and they look'd very well there I assure you; but he was many Months a-doing it. And thus ended our first Golden Adventure.

We now began to discover what we had not troubled our Heads much about before; and that was, that let the Country be good or bad that we were in, we could not travel much farther, for a considerable time. We had been now five Months and upwards in our Journey, and the Season began to change; and Nature told us, that being in a Climate that had a Winter as well as Summer, tho' of a differing Kind from what our own Country produced, we were to expect a wet Season, and such as we should not be able to travel in, as well by reason of the Rain it self, as of the Floods which it would occasion wherever we should come; and tho' we had been no Strangers to those wet Seasons in the Island of *Madagascar*, yet we had not thought much of them since we begun our Travels; for setting out when the Sun was about the Solstice, that is, when it was at the greatest Northern Distance from us, we had found the Benefit of it in our Travels. But now it drew near us apace, and we found it began to rain; upon which we called another General Council, in which we debated our present Circumstances, and in particular, whether we should go forward, or seek for a proper Place upon the Bank of our Golden River, which had been so lucky to us to fix our Camp for the Winter.

Upon the whole, it was resolved to abide where we were; and it was not the least Part of our Happiness that we did so, as shall appear in its Place.

Having resolved upon this, our first Measures were to set our Negroes to Work, to make Hutts or Houses for our Habitation; and this they did very dexterously; only that we changed the Ground where we had at first intended it, thinking, as indeed it happen'd, that the river might reach it upon any sudden Rain. Our Camp was like a little Town, in which our Hutts were in the Center, having one large one in the Center of them also, into which all our particular Lodgings opened; so that none of us went into our Apartments, but thro' a publick Tent where we all eat and drank together, and kept our Councils and Society, and our Carpenters made us Tables, Benches, and Stools in Abundance, as many as we could make use of.

We had no Need of Chimneys, it was hot enough without Fire; but yet we found our selves at last oblig'd to keep a Fire every Night upon a particular Occasion: For tho' we had in all other Respects a very pleasant and agreeable Scituation, yet we were rather worse troubled with the unwelcome Visits of wild Beasts here, than in the Wilderness it self; for as the Deer, and other gentle Creatures came hither for Shelter and Food, so the Lions, and Tigers, and Leopards, haunted these Places continually for Prey.

When first we discovered this, we were so uneasy at it, that we thought of removing our Scituation; but after many Debates about it, we resolved to fortify our selves in such a Manner, as not to be in any Danger from it; and this our Carpenters undertook, who first palisadoed our Camp quite round with long Stakes (for we had Wood enough) which Stakes were not stuck in one by another like Pales, but in an irregular Manner; a great Multitude of them so placed, that they took up near two Yards in Thickness, some higher, some lower, all sharpened at the Top, and about a Foot asunder; so that had any Creature jump'd at them, unless he had gone clean over, which it was very hard to do, he would be hung upon twenty or thirty Spikes.

The Entrance into this, had larger Stakes than the rest, placed so before one another, as to make three or four short Turnings, which no four-footed Beast bigger than a Dog could possibly come in at; and that we might not be attack'd by any Multitude together, and consequently be alarm'd in our Sleep, as we had been, or be oblig'd to waste our Ammunition, which we were very chary of, we kept a great Fire every Night without the Entrance of our Palisade; having a Hutt for our two Centinels to stand in free from the Rain, just within the Entrance, and right against the Fire.

To maintain this Fire, we cut a prodigious deal of Wood, and piled it upon a Heap to dry, and with the green Boughs made a second Covering over our Hutts, so high and thick, that it might cast the Rain off from the first, and keep us effectually dry.

We had scarce finished all these Works, but that the Rain came on so fierce, and so continued, that we had little time to stir abroad for Food, except indeed that our Negroes, who wore no Clothes, seem'd to make nothing of the Rain, tho' to us *Europeans* in those hot Climates, nothing is more dangerous.

We continued in this Posture for four Months, that is, from the Middle of *June* to the Middle of *October*; for tho' the Rains went off, at least the greatest Violence of them, about the *Equinox*, yet as the Sun was then just over our Heads, we resolved to stay a while till it was pass'd us a little to the Southward.

During our Encampment here, we had several Adventures with the ravenous Creatures of that Country, and had not our Fire been always kept burning, I question much whether all our Fence, tho' we strengthen'd it afterwards with twelve or fourteen Rows of Stakes more, would have kept us secure. It was always in the Night that we had the Disturbance of them, and sometimes they came in such Multitudes, that we thought all the Lions, and Tigers, and Leopards, and Wolves of *Africa* were come together to attack us. One Night being clear Moonshine, one of our Men being upon the Watch, told us, he verily believed he saw Ten Thousand wild Creatures of one Sort or another, pass by our little Camp; and ever as they saw the Fire, they sheer'd off, but were sure to howl or roar, or whatever it was, when they were past.

The Musick of their Voices was very far from being pleasant to us, and sometimes would be so very disturbing, that we could not sleep for it; and often our Centinels would call us, that were awake to come and look at them. It was one windy tempestuous Night after a very rainy Day, that we were indeed all called up; for such innumerable Numbers of Devilish Creatures came about us, that our Watch really thought they would attack us. They would not come on the Side where the Fire was; and tho' we thought our selves secure every where else, yet we all got up, and took to our Arms. The Moon was near the Full, but the Air full of flying Clouds, and a strange Hurricane of Wind to add to the Terror of the Night; when looking on the Back Part of our Camp, I thought I saw a Creature within our Fortification, and so indeed he was, except his Haunches; for he had taken a running Leap, I suppose, and with all his Might had thrown himself clear over our Palisadoes, except one strong Pile which stood higher than the rest, and which had caught hold of him, and by his Weight he had hang'd himself upon it, the Spike of the Pile running into his Hinder-Haunch or Thigh, on the Inside, and by that he hung growling and biting the Wood for Rage. I snatch up a Lance from one of the Negroes that stood just by me, and running to him, struck it three or four Times into him, and dispatch'd him; being unwilling to shoot, because I had a Mind to have a Volley fired among the rest, whom I could see standing without as thick as a Drove of Bullocks going to a Fair. I immediately called our People out, and shewed them the Object of Terror which I had seen, and without any farther Consultation, fired a full Volley among them, most of our Pieces being loaden with two or three Sluggs or Bullets a-piece. It made a horrible Clutter[82] among them, and in general they all took to their Heels, only that we could observe, that some walk'd off with more Gravity and Majesty than others, being not so much frighted at the Noise and Fire; and we could perceive that some were left upon the Ground struggling as for Life, but we durst not stir out to see what they were.

Indeed they stood so thick, and were so near us, that we could not well miss killing or wounding some of them, and we believe they had certainly the Smell of us, and of our Victuals we had been killing; for we had killed a Deer, and three or four of those Creatures like Goats, the Day before; and some of the Offal had been thrown out behind our Camp, and this we suppose drew them so much about us; but we avoided it for the future.

Tho' the Creatures fled, yet we heard a frightful Roaring all Night at the Place where they stood, which we supposed was from some that were wounded; and as soon as Day came, we went out to see what Execution we had done, and, indeed, it was a strange Sight; there were three Tygers and two Wolves quite killed, besides the Creature I had killed within our Palisado, which seem'd to be of an ill-gendered kind, between a Tyger and a Leopard. Besides this, there was a noble old Lion alive, but with both his Fore Legs broke, so that he could not stir away, and he had almost beat himself to Death with struggling all Night; and we found, that this was the wounded Soldier that had roared so loud, and given us so much Disturbance: Our Surgeon, looking at him, smiled; Now, says he, if I could be sure this Lion would be as grateful to me, as one of his Majesty's Ancestors was to *Andronicus* the *Roman* Slave, I would certainly set both his Legs again, and cure him. I had not heard the Story of *Andronicus*,[83] so he told it me at large; but as to the Surgeon, we told him, he had no Way to know whether the Lion would do so or not, but to cure him first, and trust to his Honour; but he had no Faith; so to dispatch him, and put him out of his Torment, he shot him into the Head, and killed him, for which we called him the King-Killer ever after.

Our Negroes found no less than five of these ravenous Creatures wounded and dropt at a Distance from our Quarters; whereof, one was a Wolf, one a fine spotted young Leopard, and the other were Creatures that we knew not what to call them.

We had several more of these Gentle-folks about us after that, but no such general Rendezvous of them as that was, any more; but this ill Effect it had to us, that it frighted the Deer and other Creatures from our Neighbourhood, of whose Company we were much more desirous, and who were necessary for our Subsistence: However, our Negroes went out every Day a-Hunting, as they called it, with Bow and Arrow, and they scarce ever failed of bringing us home something or other; and particularly we found in this Part of the Country, after the Rains had fallen some time, Abundance of Wild-fowl, such as we have in *England*; Duck, Teal, Widgeon, &c. some Geese, and some Kinds that we had never seen before, and we frequently killed them. Also we catched a great Deal of fresh Fish out of the River, so that we wanted no Provision; if we wanted any thing, it was Salt to eat with our fresh Meat, but we had a little left, and we used it sparingly; for, as to our Negroes, they would not taste it, nor did they care to eat any Meat that was seasoned with it.

The Weather began now to clear up, the Rains were down, and the Floods abated, and the Sun, which had passed our Zenith, was gone to the Southward a good Way, so we prepared to go on of our Way.

It was the 12th of *October* or thereabouts, that we began to set forward, and having an easy Country to travel in, as well as to supply us with Provisions, tho' still without Inhabitants, we made more Dispatch, travelling some times, as we calculated it 20 or 25 Miles a Day; nor did we halt any where in eleven Days March, one Day excepted, which was to make a Raft to carry us over a small River, which having swelled with the Rains was not yet quite down.

When we were past this River, which by the Way run to the Northward too, we found a great Row of Hills in our Way; we saw indeed the Country open to the Right at a great Distance, but as we kept true to our Course due West, we were not willing to go a great Way out of our Way, only to shun a few Hills; so we advanced; but we were surprized, when being not quite come to the Top, one of our Company who with two Negroes was got up before us, cry'd out the *Sea!* the *Sea!* and fell a-dancing and jumping as Signs of Joy.

The Gunner and I were most surprized at it, because we had but that Morning been calculating, that we must have yet above a 1000 Miles to the Sea-side, and that we could not expect to reach it till an other rainy Season would be upon us, so that when our Man cry'd out the Sea, the Gunner was angry, and said he was mad.

But we were both in the greatest Surprize imaginable, when coming to the Top of the Hill, and tho' it was very high, we saw nothing but Water, either before us, or to the right Hand or the left, being a vast Sea without any Bound but the Horizon.

We went down the Hill full of Confusion of Thought, not being able to conceive where-abouts we were, or what it must be, seeing by all our Charts the Sea was yet a vast Way off.

It was not above three Miles from the Hills before we came to the Shore, or Water-edge of this Sea, and there, to our further Surprize, we found the Water fresh and pleasant to drink; so that in short: we knew not what Course to take: The Sea, as we thought it to be, put a full stop to our Journey, (I mean Westward) for it lay just in the Way. Our next Question was which Hand to turn to, to the Right or the Left, but this was soon resolved; for as we knew not the Extent of it, we considered that our Way, if it had been the Sea really, must be to the North; and therefore, if we went to the South now, it must be just so much out of our Way at last: So having spent a good Part of the Day in our Surprize at the Thing, and consulting what to do, we set forward to the North.

We travelled upon the Shore of this Sea full 23 Days, before we could come to any Resolution about what it was; at the End of which, early one Morning, one of our Seamen cried out Land, and it was no false Alarm, for we saw plainly the Tops of some Hills at a very great Distance, on the further Side of the Water, due West; but tho' this satisfied us that it was not the Sea, but an Inland Sea or Lake, yet we saw no Land to the Northward, that is so say, no End of it; but were obliged to travel eight Days more, and near a 100 Miles further, before we came to the End of it, and then we found this Lake or Sea ended in a very great River, which run N. or N. by E. as the other River had done, which I mention'd before.

My Friend the Gunner, upon examining, said, that he believed that he was mistaken before, and that this was the River *Nile*, but was still of the Mind, that we were of before, that we should not think of a Voyage into *Egypt* that Way; so we resolved upon crossing this River, which however was not so easy as before, the River being very rapid, and the Channel very broad.

It cost us therefore a Week here to get Materials to waft our selves and Cattel over this River; for tho' here were Store of Trees, yet there were none of any considerable Growth, sufficient to make a Canoe.

During our March on the Edge of this Bank, we met with great Fatigue, and therefore travell'd fewer Miles in a Day than before, there being such a prodigious Number of little Rivers that came down from the Hills on the East Side, emptying themselves into this Gulph, all which Waters were pretty high, the Rains having been but newly over.

In the last three Days of our Travel we met with some Inhabitants, but we found they lived upon the little Hills, and not by the Water Side; nor were we a little put to it for Food in this March, having killed nothing for four or five Days, but some Fish we caught out of the Lake, and that not in such Plenty as we found before.

But to make us some amends, we had no Disturbance upon all the Shore of this Lake, from any wild Beasts; the only Inconveniency of that Kind was, that we met an ugly, venemous, deformed kind of a Snake or Serpent in the wet Grounds near the Lake, that several times pursued us, as if it would attack us; and if we struck at, or threw any thing at it, would raise it self up, and hiss as loud it might be heard a great Way; it had a hellish, ugly, deformed Look and Voice, and our Men would not be perswaded but it was the Devil, only that we did not know what Business Satan could have there, where there were no People.

It was very remarkable that we had now travelled a 1000 Miles without meeting with any People, in the Heart of the whole Continent of *Africa*, where to be sure never Man set his Foot since the Sons of *Noah*[84] spread themselves over the Face of the whole Earth; here also our Gunner took an Observation with his Forestaff[85] to determine our Latitude, and he found now, that having marched about 33 Days Northward, we were in 6 Degrees 22 Minutes South Latitude.

After having with great Difficulty got over this River, we came into a strange wild Country, that began a little to affright us; for tho' the Country was not a Desart of dry scalding Sand, as that was we had passed before, yet it was mountainous, barren and infinitely full of most furious wild Beasts, more than any Place we had past yet. There was indeed a kind of coarse Herbage on the Surface, and now and then a few Trees or rather Shrubs; but People we could see none, and we began to be in great Suspense about Victuals; for we had not killed a Deer a great while, but had lived chiefly upon Fish and Fowl alway by the Water Side, both which seemed to fail us now; and we were in the more Consternation, because we could not lay in a Stock here to proceed upon, as we did before, but were obliged to set out with Scarcity, and without any Certainty of a Supply.

We had however no Remedy but Patience; and having killed some Fowls, and dried some Fish, as much as with short Allowance we reckoned would last us five Days, we resolved to venture, and venture we did; nor was it without Cause that we were apprehensive of the Danger, for we travelled the five Days, and met neither with Fish, or Fowl, or four-footed Beast whose Flesh was fit to eat; and we were in a most dreadful Apprehension of being famished to Death; on the sixth Day we almost fasted, or, as we may say, we eat up all the Scraps of what we had left, and at Night lay down supperless upon our Matts with heavy Hearts, being obliged the eighth Day to kill one of our poor faithful Servants the Buffloes, that carry'd our Baggage; the flesh of this Creature was very good, and so sparingly did we eat of it, that it lasted us all three Days and a half, and was just spent; and we were upon the point of killing another, when we saw before us a Country that promised better, having high Trees and a large River in the middle of it.

This encouraged us, and we quicken'd our March for the River Side, tho' with empty Stomachs, and very faint and weak; but before we came to this River we had the good Hap to meet with some young Deer, a Thing we had long wished for. In a Word, having shot three of them, we came to a full Stop to fill our Bellies, and never gave the Flesh time to cool before we eat it; nay 'twas much we could stay to kill it, and had not eaten it alive, for we were in short almost famished.

Through all that unhospitable Country we saw continually Lions, Tygers, Leopards, Civet Cats, and Abundance of Kinds of Creatures that we did not understand; we saw no Elephants, but every now and then we met with an Elephant's Tooth lying on the Ground, and some of them lying as it were half buried by the Length of Time that they had lain there.

When we came to the Shore of this River, we found it run Northerly still, as all the rest had done, but with this Difference, that as the Course of the other Rivers were N. by E. or N.N.E. the Course of this lay N.N.W.

On the farther Bank of this River we saw some Sign of Inhabitants, but met with none for the first Day; but the next Day we came into an Inhabited Country, the People all Negroes, and stark naked, without Shame, both Men and Women.

We made Signs of Friendship to them, and found them a very frank, civil, and friendly sort of People. They came to our Negroes without any Suspition, nor did they give us any Reason to suspect them of any Villainy, as the others had done; we made Signs to them that we were hungry, and immediately some naked Women ran and fetched us great Quantities of Roots, and of Things like Pumpkins, which we made no Scruple to eat; and our Artificer shewed them some of his Trinkets that he had made, some of Iron, some of Silver, but none of Gold: They had so much Judgment to chuse that of Silver before the Iron, but when we shewed them some Gold, we found they did not value it so much as either of the other.

For some of these Things they brought us more Provisions, and three living Creatures as big as Calves, but not of that Kind; neither did we ever see any of them before; their Flesh was very good; and after that they brought us twelve more, and some smaller Creatures, like Hares, all which were very welcome to us who were indeed at a very great Loss for Provisions.

We grew very intimate with these People, and indeed they were the civillest and most friendly People that we met with at all, and mightily pleased with us; and which was very particular, they were much easier to be made to understand our Meaning, than any we had met with before.

At last, we began to enquire our Way, pointing to the West, they made us understand easily that we could not go that Way, but they pointed to us, that we might go North-West, so that we presently understood that there was another Lake in our Way, which proved to be true; for in two Days more we saw it plain, and it held us till we past the Equinoctial Line, lying all the Way on our left Hand, tho' at a great Distance.

Travelling thus Northward, our Gunner seemed very anxious about our Proceedings; for he assured us, and made me sensible of it by the Maps, which he had been teaching me out of, that when we came into the Latitude of six Degrees, or thereabouts, North of the Line, the land trended away to the West, to such a Length, that we should not come at the Sea under a March of above 1500 Miles farther Westward than the Country we desired to go to. I asked him if there were no Navigable Rivers that we might meet with, which running into the West Ocean, might perhaps carry us down their Stream, and then if it were 1500 Miles, or twice 1500 Miles, we might do well enough, if we could but get Provisions.

Here he shewed me the Maps again, and that there appeared no River whose Stream was of any such Length as to do us any Kindness, till we came perhaps within 2 or 300 Miles of the Shore, except the *Rio Grande*,[86] as they call it, which lay farther Northward from us, at least 700 Miles; and that then he knew not what kind of Country it might carry us through; for he said it was his Opinion, that the Heats on the North of the Line, even in the same Latitude, were violent, and the Country more desolate, barren, and barbarous than those of the South; and that when we came among the Negroes in the North Part of *Africa*, next the Sea, especially those who had seen and trafficked with the *Europeans*, such as *Dutch*, *English*, *Portuguese*, *Spaniards*, &c. that they had most of them been so ill used at some time or other, that they would certainly put all the Spight they could upon us in meer Revenge.

Upon these Considerations, he advised us, that as soon as we had passed this Lake, we should proceed W. S. W. that is to say, a little enclining to the South, and that in Time we should meet with the great River *Congo*, from whence the Coast is called *Congo*, being a little North of *Angola*, where we intended at first to go.

I asked him, if ever he had been on the Coast of *Congo*; he said yes he had, but was never on Shore there: Then I asked him, how we should get from thence to the Coast where the *European* Ships came, seeing if the Land trended away West for 1500 Miles, we must have all that Shore to traverse, before we could double the West Point of it.

He told me, it was ten to one but we should hear of some *European* Ships to take us in, for that they often visited the Coast of *Congo* and *Angola*, in Trade with the Negroes; and that if we could not, yet, if we could but find Provisions, we should make our Way as well along the Sea-Shore, as along the River, till we came to the Gold Coast, which he said was not above 4 or 500 Miles North of *Congo*, besides the turning of the Coast West about 300 more; that Shore being in the Latitude of six or seven Degrees, and that there the *English*, or *Dutch*, or *French*, had Settlements or Factories, perhaps all of them.

I confess, I had more Mind all the while he argued, to have gone Northward, and Shipt our selves in the *Rio Grand*, or as the Traders call it, the River *Negro* or *Niger*, for I knew that at last it would bring us down to the *Cape de Verd*, where we were sure of Relief; whereas at the Coast we were going to now, we had a prodigious Way still to go, either by Sea or Land, and no Certainty which way to get Provisions but by Force; but for the present I held my Tongue, because it was my Tutor's Opinion.

But when, according to his Desire, we came to turn Southward, having passed beyond the second great Lake, our Men began all to be uneasy, and said, we were now out of our Way for certain, for that we were going farther from home, and that we were indeed far enough off already.

But we had not marched above twelve Days more, eight whereof was taken up in rounding the Lake, and four more Southwest, in order to make for the River *Congo*, but we were put to another full Stop, by entring a Country so desolate, so frightful, and so wild, that we knew not what to think or do; for besides that it appeared as a terrible and boundless Desart, having neither Woods, Trees, Rivers, or Inhabitants; so even the Place where we were, was desolate of Inhabitants, nor had we any Way to gather in a Stock of Provisions for the passing this Desart, as we did before at our entering the first, unless we had marched back four Days to the Place where we turned the Head of the Lake.

Well, notwithstanding this we ventured, for to Men that had passed such wild Places as we had done, nothing could seem too desperate to undertake: We ventured I say, and the rather because we saw very high Mountains in our way at a great Distance, and we imagined, wherever there was Mountains, there would be Springs and Rivers, where Rivers, there would be Trees and Grass, where Trees and Grass, there would be Cattel, and where Cattel, some Kind of Inhabitants.

At last, in Consequence of this speculative Philosophy, we entered this Wast, having a great Heap of Roots and Plants for our Bread, such as the *Indians*[87] gave us, a very little Flesh, or Salt, and but a little Water.

We travelled two Days towards those Hills, and still they seemed as far off as they did at first, and it was the fifth Day before we got to them; indeed we travelled but softly, for it was excessive hot, and we were much about the very *Equinoctial* Line, we hardly knew whether to the South or the North of it.

As we had concluded that, where there were Hills there would be Springs, so it happened; but we were not only surprized, but really frighted, to find the first Spring we came to, and which looked admirably clear and beautiful, be salt as Brine: It was a terrible Disappointment to us, and put us under melancholy Apprehensions at first; but the Gunner who was of a Spirit never discouraged, told us we should not be disturbed at that, but be very thankful, for Salt was a Bait[88] we stood in as much Need of as any thing, and there was no Question but we should find fresh Water as well as Salt; and here our Surgeon steps in to encourage us, and told us, that if we did not know, he would shew us a Way how to make that salt Water fresh,[89] which indeed made us all more chearful, tho' we wondered what he meant.

Mean time our Men, without bidding, had been seeking about for other Springs, and found several, but still they were all salt; from whence we concluded, that there was a salt Rock or Mineral Stone in those Mountains, and perhaps they might be all of such a Substance: But still I wondered by what Witchcraft it was that our Artist the Surgeon would make this salt Water turn fresh, and I long'd to see the Experiment, which was indeed a very odd one; but he went to Work with as much Assurance, as if he had try'd it on the very Spot before.

He took two of our large Matts, and sow'd them together, and they made a kind of a Bag four Foot broad, three Foot and a Half high, and about a Foot and a Half thick when it was full.

He caused us to fill this Bag with dry Sand, and tread it down as close as we could, not to burst the Matts. When thus the Bag was full within a Foot, he sought some other Earth, and filled up the rest with it, and still trod it all in as hard as he could. When he had done, he made a Hole in the upper Earth, about as broad as the Crown of a large Hat, or something bigger about, but not so deep, and bad a Negroe fill it with Water, and still as it shrunk away, to fill it again, and keep it full. The Bag he had placed at first cross two Pieces of Wood, about a Foot from the Ground, and under it he ordered some of our Skins to be spread, that would hold Water. In about an Hour, and not sooner, the Water began to come dropping thro' the Bottom of the Bag, and to our great Surprize, was perfect fresh and sweet; and this continued for several Hours: But in the End, the Water began to be a little brackish. When we told him that, Well then, *said he*, turn the Sand out, and fill it again; whether he did this by way of Experiment from his own Fancy, or whether he had seen it done before, I do not remember.

The next Day we mounted the Tops of the Hills, where the Prospect was indeed astonishing; for as far as the Eye could look, South, or West, or North-West, there was nothing to be seen but a vast howling Wilderness, with neither Tree or River, or any green thing. The Surface we found, as the Part we passed the Day before, had a kind of thick Moss upon it, of a blackish dead Colour, but nothing in it that look'd like Food, either for Man or Beast.

Had we been stored with Provisions to have entred for ten or twenty Days upon this Wilderness as we were formerly, and with fresh Water, we had Hearts good enough to have ventured; tho' we had been obliged to come back again; for if we went North, we did not know but we might meet with the same; but we neither had Provisions, neither were we in any Place where it was possible to get them. We killed some wild ferine[90] Creatures at the Foot of these Hills; but except two things like to nothing that we ever saw before, we met with nothing that was fit to eat. These were Creatures that seemed to be between the Kind of a Buffloe and a Deer, but indeed resembled neither; for they had no Horns, and had great Legs like a Cow, with a fine Head; and the Neck like a Deer. We killed also at several times a Tiger, two young Lions, and a Wolf, but, God be thanked, we were not so reduced as to eat Carrion.

Upon this terrible Prospect I renew'd my Motion of turning Northward, and making towards the River *Niger*, or *Rio Grand*, then to turn West towards the *English* Settlements on the Gold Coast, to which every one most readily consented, only our Gunner, who was indeed our best Guide, tho' he happen'd to be mistaken at this time. He moved, that as our Coast was *now* Northward, so we might slant away North West, that so by crossing the Country, we might perhaps meet with some other River that run into the *Rio Grand* Northward, or down to the Gold Coast Southward, and so both direct our Way, and shorten the Labour; as also, because, if any of the Country was inhabited and fruitful, we should probably find it upon the Shore of the Rivers, where alone we could be furnished with Provisions.

This was good Advice, and too rational not to be taken; but our present Business was, what to do to get out of this dreadful Place we were in; behind us was a Wast, which had already cost us five Days March, and we had not Provisions for five Days left to go back again the same Way. Before us was nothing but Horrour as above, so we resolv'd, seeing the Ridge of Hills we were upon had some Appearance of Fruitfulness, and that they seemed to lead away to the Northward a great Way, to keep under the Foot of them on the East Side, to go on as far as we could, and in the mean time to look diligently out for Food.

Accordingly we moved on the next Morning; for we had no time to lose, and to our great Comfort we came in our first Morning's March to very good Springs of fresh Water; and least we should have a Scarcity again, we filled all our Bladder Bottles, and carried it with us. I should also have observed, that our Surgeon who made the salt Water fresh, took the

Opportunity of those salt Springs, and made us the Quantity of three or four Pecks of very good Salt.

In our third March we found an unexpected Supply of Food, the Hills being full of Hares; they were of a kind something different from ours in *England*, larger, and not so swift of Foot, but very good Meat. We shot several of them, and the little tame Leopard, which I told you we took at the Negroe Town that we plundered, hunted them like a Dog, and killed us several every Day; but she would eat nothing of them unless we gave it her, which indeed in our Circumstance was very obliging. We salted them a little, and dried them in the Sun whole, and carry'd a strange Parcel along with us, I think it was almost three Hundred; for we did not know when we might find any more, either of these, or any other Food. We continued our Course under these Hills very comfortably eight or nine Days, when we found to our great Satisfaction, the Country beyond us began to look with something a better Countenance. As for the West Side of the Hills, we never examin'd it till this Day, when three of our Company, the rest halting for Refreshment, mounted the Hills again to satisfy their Curiosity, but found it all the same; nor could they see any End of it, no not to the North, the Way we were going; so the tenth Day finding the Hills made a Turn, and led as it were into the vast Desart, we left them, and continued our Course North; the Country being very tolerably full of Woods, some Wast, but not tediously long; till we came, by our Gunner's Observation, into the Latitude of 8 Degrees, 5 Minutes, which we were nineteen Days more a performing.

All this Way we found no Inhabitants, Abundance of wild ravenous Creatures, with whom we became so well acquainted now, that really we did not much mind them. We saw Lions and Tigers, and Leopards every Night and Morning in Abundance; but as they seldom came near us, we let them go about their Business; if they offer'd to come near us, we made false Fire with any Gun that was uncharged, and they would walk off as soon as they saw the Flash.

We made pretty good Shift for Food all this Way; for sometimes we killed Hares, sometimes some Fowls, but for my Life I cannot give Names to any of them, except a kind of Partridge, and another that was like our Turtles. Now and then we began to meet with Elephants again in great Numbers, those Creatures delighting chiefly in the woody Part of the Country.

This long continued March fatigued us very much, and two of our Men fell sick, indeed so very sick, we thought they would have died; and one of our Negroes died suddenly. Our Surgeon said it was an Apoplexy, but *he wondered at it, he said*, for he could never complain of his high Feeding.

Another of them was very ill, but our Surgeon with much ado perswading him, indeed it was almost forcing him, to be let Blood, he recover'd.

We halted here twelve Days for the sake of our sick Men, and our Surgeon perswaded me, and three or four more of us, to be let Blood during the time of Rest, which with other things he gave us, contributed very much to our continued Health, in so tedious a March, and in so hot a Climate.

In this March we pitched our matted Tents every Night, and they were very comfortable to us, tho' we had Trees and Woods to shelter us also in most Places. We thought it very strange, that in all this Part of the Country we yet met with no Inhabitants; but the principal Reason as we found afterwards was, that we having kept a Western Course first, and then a Northern Course, were gotten too much into the Middle of the Country, and among the Desarts: Whereas the Inhabitants are principally found among the Rivers, Lakes, and Low-Lands as well to the South-West, as to the North.

What little Rivulets we found here, were so empty of Water, that except some Pits, and little more than ordinary Pools, there was scarce any Water to be seen in them; and they rather shewed, that during the Rainy Months they had a Channel, than that they had really any running Water in them at that time: By which it was easy for us to judge, that we had a great Way to go; but this was no Discouragement so long as we had but Provisions, and some reasonable Shelter from the violent Heat, which indeed I thought was much greater now, than when the Sun was just over our Heads.

Our Men being recovered, we set forward again, very well stored with Provisions and Water sufficient, and bending our Course a little to the Westward of the North, travelled in Hopes of some favourable Stream which might bear a Canoe; but we found none till after twenty Days Travel, including eight Days Rest, for our Men being weak we rested very often; especially when we came to Places which were proper for our Purpose; where we found Cattel, Fowl, or any thing to kill for our Food. In those twenty Days March, we advanced four Degrees to the Northward, besides some Meridian[91] Distance Westward, and we met with Abundance of Elephants, and with a good Number of Elephants Teeth scatter'd up and down, here and there, in the Woody Grounds especially; some of which were very large. But they were no Booty to us; our Business was Provisions, and a good Passage out of the Country; and it had been much more to our Purpose, to have found a good fat Deer; and to have killed it for our Food, than a hundred Ton of Elephants Teeth; and yet as you shall presently hear, when we came to begin our Passage by Water, we once thought to have built a large Canoe on purpose to have loaded her with Ivory, but this was when we knew nothing of the Rivers, nor knew anything how dangerous, and how difficult a Passage it was that we were like to have in them, nor had considered the Weight of Carriage to lug them to the Rivers where we might Embark.

At the End of twenty Days Travel, as above, in the Latitude of three Degrees, sixteen Minutes, we discovered in a Valley, at some Distance from us, a pretty tolerable Stream, which we thought deserved the Name of a River, and which run its Course N.N.W. which was just what we wanted. As we had fixt our Thoughts upon our Passage by Water, we took this for the Place to make the Experiment, and bent our March directly to the Valley.

There was a small Thicket of Trees just in our Way, which we went by, thinking no harm, when on a sudden one of our Negroes was very dangerously wounded with an Arrow, shot into his Back slanting between his Shoulders. This put us to a full stop, and three of our Men with two Negroes spreading[92] the Wood, for it was but a small one, found a Negro with a Bow, but no Arrow, who would have escaped; but our Men that discovered him, shot him in Revenge of the Mischief he had done; so we lost the Opportunity of taking him Prisoner, which if we had done, and sent him home with good usage, it might have brought others to us in a friendly Manner.

Going a little farther, we came to five Negro Hutts or Houses, built after a differing Manner from any we had seen yet; and at the Door of one of them, lay seven Elephants Teeth piled up against the Wall or Side of the Hutt, as if they had been provided against a Market: Here were no Men, but seven or eight Women, and near twenty Children: We offered them no Uncivility of any kind, but gave them every one a Bit of Silver beaten out thin, as I observed before, and cut Diamond fashion, or in the Shape of a Bird; at which the Women were over-joy'd and brought out to us several Sorts of Food, which we did not understand, being Cakes of a Meal made of Roots, which they bake in the Sun, and which eat very well. We went a little Way farther, and pitched our Camp for that Night, not doubting but our Civility to the Women would produce some good Effect, when their Husbands might come Home.

Accordingly, the next Morning, the Women, with eleven Men, five young Boys, and two good big Girls, came to our Camp; before they came quite to us, the Women called aloud, and made an odd screeking Noise, to bring us out, and accordingly we came out, when two of the Women, shewing us what we had given them, and pointing to the Company behind, made such Signs as we could easily understand signified Friendship. When the Men advanced, having Bows and Arrows, they laid them down on the Ground, scraped, and threw Sand over their Heads, and turned round three times with their Hands laid up upon the Tops of their Heads. This it seems, was a solemn Vow of Friendship. Upon this we beckon'd them with our Hands to come nearer; then they sent the Boys and Girls to us first, which, it seems was to bring us more Cakes of Bread, and some green Herbs, to eat, which we receiv'd, and took the Boys up and kissed, them, and the little Girls too; then the Men came up close to us, and sat them down on the Ground, making Signs, that we should sit down by them, which we did. They said much to one another, but we could not understand them, nor could we find any way to make them understand us; much less whither we were going; or what we wanted, only that we easily made them understand we wanted Victuals; whereupon one of the Men casting his Eyes about him towards a rising Ground that was about half a Mile off, starts up as if he was frighted, flies to the Place where they had laid down their Bows and Arrows, snatches up a Bow and two Arrows, and run like a race Horse to the Place: When he came here, he let fly both his Arrows, and comes back again to us with the same Speed; we seeing he came with the Bow, but without the Arrows, were the more inquisitive, but the Fellow saying nothing to us, beckons to one of our Negroes to come to him, and we bid him go; so he led him back to the Place, where lay a kind of a Deer, shot with two Arrows, but not quite dead; and, between them, they brought it down to us. This was for a Gift to us, and was very welcome, I assure you, for our Stock was low. These People were all stark naked.

The next Day there came about a Hundred Men to us, and Women, making the same aukward Signals of Friendship; and dancing and shewing themselves very well pleased, and any thing they had they gave us. How the Man in the Wood came to be so butcherly and rude, as to shoot at our Men, without making any Breach first, we could not imagine; for the People were simple, plain, and inoffensive, in all our other Conversation with them.

From hence we went down the Bank of the little River I mentioned, and where I found we should see whole Nations of Negroes, but whether friendly to us, or not, that we could make no judgment of yet.

The River was of no Use to us, as to the Design of making Canoes, a great while, and we traversed the Country, on the Edge of it about five Days more, when our Carpenters finding the Stream encrease, proposed to pitch our Tents, and fall to work to make Canoes; but after we had begun the Work, and cut down two or three Trees, and spent five Days in the Labour, some of our Men wandring further down the River, brought us Word, that the Stream rather decreased than encreased, sinking away into the Sands, or drying up by the Heat of the Sun; so that the River appeared not able to carry the least Canoe, that could be any way useful to us, so we were obliged to give over our Enterprize, and move on.

In our further Prospect this Way, we march'd three Days full West the Country on the North Side, being extraordinary mountainous, and more parched and dry than any we had seen yet; whereas, in the Part which looks due West, we found a pleasant Valley, running a great way between two great Ridges of Mountains: The Hills look'd frightful, being entirely bare of Trees or Grass, and even white with the Driness of the Sand; but in the Valley we had Trees, Grass, and some Creatures that were fit for Food, and some Inhabitants.

We past by some of their Hutts or Houses, and saw People about them, but they run up into the Hills as soon as they saw us; at the End of this Valley we met with a peopled Country, and at first it put us to some doubt, whether we should go among them, or keep up towards the Hills Northerly; and as our Aim was principally, as before, to make our Way to the River *Niger*, we enclined to the latter, pursuing our Course by the Compass to the N.W. We march'd thus without Interruption seven Days more, when we met with a surprizing Circumstance, much more desolate and disconsolate than our own, and, which, in time to come, will scarce seem credible.

We did not much seek the conversing, or acquainting our selves with the Natives of the Country, except where we found the Want of them for our Provision, or their Direction for our Way; so that whereas we found the Country here begin to be very populous, especially towards our left Hand, that is, to the South, we kept at the more Distance Northerly, still stretching towards the West.

In this Tract we found something or other to kill and eat, which always supplied our Necessity, tho' not so well as we were provided in our first setting out; being thus, as it were, pushing to avoid the peopled Country, we at last came to a very pleasant, agreeable Stream of Water, not big enough to be called a River, but running to the N.N.W. which was the very Course we desired to go.

On the farthest Bank of this Brook we perceiv'd some Hutts of Negroes not many, and in a little low Spot of Ground some *Maise* or *Indian* Corn growing, which intimated presently to us, that there were some Inhabitants on that Side, less barbarous than what we had met with in other Places where we had been.

As we went forward our whole Carravan being in a Body, our Negroes, who were in the Front, cry'd out, that they saw a *White Man*; we were not much surprized at first, it being, as we thought, a Mistake of the Fellows, and asked them what they meant; when one of them stept to me, and pointing to a Hutt on the other Side of the Hill, I was astonished to see a White Man[93] indeed, but stark naked, very busy near the Door of his Hutt, and stooping down to the Ground with something in his Hand, as if he had been at some Work, and his back being towards us, he did not see us.

I gave Notice to our Negroes to make no Noise, and waited till some more of our Men were come up, to shew the Sight to them, that they might be sure I was not mistaken, and we were soon satisfied of the Truth; for the Man having heard some Noise, started up, and looked full at us, as much surprized, to be sure, as we were, but whether with Fear or Hope, we then knew not.

As he discovered us, so did the rest of the Inhabitants belonging to the Hutts about him, and all crouded together, looking at us at a Distance: A little Bottom, in which the Brook ran, lying between us, the white Man, and all the rest, as he told us afterwards, not knowing well whether they should stay, or run away: However, it presently came into my Thoughts, that if there were white Men among them, it would be much easier for us to make them understand what we meant, as to Peace or War, than we found it with others; so tying a Piece of white Rag to the End of a Stick, we sent two Negroes with it to the Bank of the Water, carrying the Pole up as high as they could; it was presently understood, and two of their Men, and the white Man, came to the Shore on the other Side.

However, as the white Man spoke no *Portuguese*, they could understand nothing of one another, but by Signs; but our Men made the white Man understand, that they had white Men with them too, at which they said the white Man laught. However, to be short, our Men came back, and told us they were all good Friends, and in about an Hour four of our Men, two Negroes, and the Black Prince went to the River Side, were the white Man came to them.

They had not been half a Quarter of an Hour, but a Negro came running to me, and told me the white Man was *Inglese*, as he called him; upon which I run back, eagerly enough you may be sure with him, and found as he said, that he was an *Englishman*; upon which he embraced me very passionately, the Tears running down his Face. The first Surprize of his seeing us was over before we came, but any one may conceive of it, by the brief Account he gave us afterwards of his very unhappy Circumstance; and of so unexpected a Deliverance, such as perhaps never happened to any Man in the World; for it was a Million to one odds, that ever he could have been relieved; nothing but an Adventure that never was heard or read of before, could have suited his Case, unless Heaven, by some Miracle that never was to be expected, had acted for him.

He appeared to be a Gentleman, not an ordinary bred Fellow, Seaman, or labouring Man; this shewed it self in his Behaviour, in the first Moment of our conversing with him, and in spight of all the Disadvantages of his miserable Circumstance.

He was a middle-aged Man, not above 37 or 38, tho' his Beard was grown exceeding long, and the Hair of his Head and face strangely covered him to the Middle of his Back and Breast, he was white, and his Skin very fine, tho' discoloured, and in some Places blistered and covered with a brown blackish Substance, scurfy, scaly, and hard which was the Effect of the scorching Heat of the Sun; he was stark naked, and had been so, as he told us, upwards of two Years.

He was so exceedingly transported at our meeting with him, that he could scarce enter into any Discourse at all with us for that Day, and when he could get away from us for a little, we saw him walking alone, and shewing all the most extravagant Tokens of an ungovernable Joy; and even afterwards he was never without Tears in his Eyes for several Days, upon the least Word spoken by us of his Circumstances, or by him of his Deliverance.

We found his Behaviour the most courteous and endearing I ever saw in any Man whatever, and most evident Tokens of a mannerly wellbred Person, appeared in all things he did or said; and our People were exceedingly taken with him. He was a Scholar, and a Mathematician; he could not speek *Portuguese* indeed, but he spoke *Latin* to our Surgeon, *French* to another of our Men, and *Italian* to a Third.

He had no Leisure in his Thoughts to ask us whence we came, whither we were going, or who we were; but would have it always as an Answer to himself, that to be sure wherever we were a-going, we came from Heaven, and were sent on purpose to save him from the most wretched Condition that ever Man was reduced to.

Our Men pitching their Camp on the Bank of a little River opposite to him, he began to enquire what Store of Provision we had, and how we proposed to be supplied; when he found that our Store was but small, he said he would talk with the Natives, and we should have Provisions enough; for he said they were the most courteous, good natured Part of the Inhabitants in all that Part of the Country, as, we might suppose by his living so safe among them.

The first things this Gentleman did for us were indeed of the greatest Consequence to us; for first he perfectly informed us where we were, and which was the properest Course for us to steer: secondly, he put us in a Way how to furnish our selves effectually with Provisions; and Thirdly, he was our compleat Interpreter and Peace-maker with all the Natives, who now began to be very numerous about us; and who were a more fierce and politick[94] People than those we had met with before; not so easily terrified with our Arms as those, and not so ignorant, as to give their Provisions and Corn for our little Toys, such as I said before our Artificer made; but as they had frequently traded and conversed with the *Europeans* on the Coast, or with other Negro Nations that had traded and been concerned with them, they were the less ignorant, and the less fearful, and consequently nothing was to be had from them but by Exchange for such things as they liked.

This I say of the Negro Natives, which we soon came among; but as to these poor People that he lived among, they were not much acquainted with Things, being at the Distance of above 300 Miles from the Coast, only that they found Elephants Teeth upon the Hills to the North, which they took and carried about sixty or seventy Miles South, where other trading Negroes usually met them, and gave them Beads, Glass, Shels, and Cowries[95] for them, such as the *English* and *Dutch* and other Traders, furnish them with from *Europe*.

We now began to be more familiar with our new Acquaintance; and first, tho' we made but a sorry Figure as to Clothes our selves, having neither Shoe, or Stocking, or Glove or Hat among us, and but very few Shirts, yet as well as we could we clothed him; and first our Surgeon having Scissers and Razors, shaved him, and cut his Hair; a Hat, as I say, we had not in all our Stores, but he supply'd himself by making himself a Cap of a Piece of a Leopard Skin, most artificially.[96] As for Shoes or Stockings, he had gone so long without them, that he cared not even for the Buskins and Foot-Gloves we wore, which I described above.

As he had been curious to hear the whole Story of our Travels, and was exceedingly delighted with the Relation; so we were no less to know, and pleased with the Account of his Circumstance, and the History of his coming to that strange Place alone, and in that Condition, which we found him in, as above.

This Account of his would indeed be in it self the Subject of an agreeable History, and would be as long and as diverting as our own, having in it many strange and extraordinary Incidents, but we cannot have Room here to launch out into so long a Digression; the Sum of his History was this.

He had been a Factor for the *English Guiney* Company[97] at *Siera Leon*, or some other of their Settlements which had been taken by the *French*, where he had been plundered of all his own Effects, as well as of what was intrusted to him by the Company. Whether it was, that the Company did not do him justice in restoring his Circumstances, or in further employing him, he quitted their Service, and was employed by those they called Separate Traders;[98] and being afterwards out of Employ there also, traded on his own Account; when passing unwarily into one of the Company's Settlements, he was either betray'd into the Hands of some of the Natives, or some how or other was surprized by them. However, as they did not kill him, he found Means to escape from them at that time, and fled to another Nation of the Natives, who being Enemies to the other, entertained him friendly, and with them he lived some time; but not liking his Quarters, or his Company, he fled again, and several times changed his Landlords; sometimes was carry'd by Force, sometimes hurried by Fear, as Circumstances altered with him (the Variety of which deserves a History by it self) till at last he had wandred beyond all Possibility of Return, and had taken up his Abode where we found him, where he was well received by the petty King of the Tribe he lived with; and he, in Return, instructed them how to value the Product of their Labour, and on what Terms to trade with those Negroes who came up to them for Teeth.

As he was naked, and had no Clothes, so he was naked of Arms for his Defence, having neither Gun, Sword, Staff, or any Instrument of War about him, no not to guard himself against the Attacks of a wild Beast, of which the Country was very full. We asked him how he came to be so entirely abandoned of all Concern for his Safety? He answered, That to him that had so often wish'd for Death, Life was not worth defending; and that as he was entirely at the Mercy of the Negroes, they had much the more Confidence in him, seeing he had no Weapons to hurt them. As for wild Beasts, he was not much concerned about that; for he scarce ever went from his Hutt; but if he did, the Negroe King and his Men went all with him, and they were all armed with Bows and Arrows, and Lances, with which they would kill any of the ravenous Creatures, Lions as well as others; but that they seldom came abroad in the Day; and if the Negroes wander any where in the Night, they always build a Hutt for themselves, and make a Fire at the Door of it, which is Guard enough.

We enquired of him, what we should next do towards getting to the Sea-side; he told us we were about 120 *English* Leagues from the Coast, where almost all the *European* Settlements and Factories were, and which is called the Gold Coast; but that there were so many different Nations of Negroes in the Way, that it was ten to one if we were not either fought with continually, or starv'd for Want of Provisions: But that there were two other Ways to go, which, if he had had any Company to go with him, he had often contrived to make his Escape by. The one was to travel full West, which, tho' it was farther to go, yet was not so full of People; and the People we should find, would be so much the civiller to us, or be so much the easier to fight with: Or, that the other Way was, if possible, to get to the *Rio Grand*, and go down the Stream in Canoes. We told him, that was the

Way we had resolved on before we met with him; but then he told us, there was a prodigious Desart to go over, and as prodigious Woods to go thro', before we came to it, and that both together were at least twenty Days March for us, travel as hard as we could.

We ask'd him, if there were no Horses in the Country, or Asses, or even Bullocks or Buffloes to make use of in such a Journey, and we shewed him ours, of which we had but three left; he said No, all the Country did not afford any thing of that kind.

He told us, that in this great Wood there were innumerable Numbers of Elephants, and upon the Desart, great Multitudes of Lions, Linxes, Tygers, and Leopards, &c. and that it was to that Wood, and to that Desart that the Negroes went to get Elephants Teeth, where they never failed to find a great Number.

We enquired still more, and particularly the Way to the Gold Coast, and if there were no Rivers to ease us in our Carriage; and told him, as to the Negroes fighting with us, we were not much concern'd at that; nor were we afraid of starving; for if they had any Victuals among them, we would have our Share of it: And therefore, if he would venture to shew us the Way, we would venture to go; and as for himself, we told him we would live and dye together, there should not a Man of us stir from him.

He told us, with all his Heart, if we resolv'd it, and would venture, we might be assured he would take his Fate with us, and he would endeavour to guide us such a Way, as we should meet with some friendly Savages who would use us well, and perhaps stand by us against some others who were less tractable: So, in a Word, we all resolved to go full South for the Gold Coast.

The next Morning he came to us again, and being all met in Council, as we may call it, he began to talk very seriously with us, that since we were now come after a long Journey to a View of the End of our Troubles, and had been so obliging to him, as to offer Carrying him with us, he had been all Night revolving in his Mind what he and we all might do to make our selves some Amends for all our Sorrows; and first he said, he was to let me know, that we were just then in one of the richest Parts of the World, tho' it was really otherwise, but a desolate, disconsolate Wilderness; for says he, there's not a River here but runs Gold, not a Desart but without Plowing bears a Crop of Ivory. What Mines of Gold, what immense Stores of Gold those Mountains may contain, from whence these Rivers come, or the Shores which these Waters run by, we know not, but may imagine that they must be inconceivably rich, seeing so much is washed down the Stream by the Water washing the Sides of the Land, that the Quantity suffices all the Traders which the *European* World send thither. We ask'd him how far they went for it, seeing the Ships only trade upon the Coast. He told us, that the Negroes on the Coast search the Rivers up for the Length of 150 or 200 Miles, and would be out a Month or two or three at a Time, and always come Home sufficiently rewarded; but, says he, they never come thus far, and yet hereabouts is as much Gold as there. Upon this he told us, that he believed he might have gotten a Hundred Pound Weight of Gold, since he came thither, if he had employed himself to look and work for it, but as he knew not what to do with it, and had long since despaired of being ever delivered from the Misery he was in, he had entirely omitted it. For what Advantage had it been to me, said he, or what richer had I been, if I had a Ton of Gold Dust, and lay and wallowed in it; the Richness of it, *said he*, would not give me one Moment's Felicity, or relieve me in the present Exigency. Nay, says he, as you all see, it would not buy me Clothes to cover me, or a Drop of Drink to save me from perishing. 'Tis of no Value here, says he; there are several People among these Hutts that would weigh Gold against a few Glass Beads, or a Cockle-Shell, and give you a Handful of Gold Dust for a Handful of Cowries. *N.B.* These are little Shells which our Children call Blackamores Teeth.

When he had said thus, he pulled out a Piece of an earthen Pot baked hard in the Sun: Here *says he*, is some of the Dirt of this Country, and if I would, I could have got a great deal more; and shewing it to us, I believe there was between two and three Pound Weight of Gold Dust, of the same Kind and Colour with that we had gotten already, as before. After we had look'd at it a while, he told us smiling, we were his Deliverers, and all he had, as well as his Life, was ours; and therefore, as this would be of Value to us when we came to our own Country, so he desired we would accept of it among us, and that this was the only time that he had repented that he had pickt up no more of it.

I spoke for: him as his Interpreter to my Comrades, and in their Names thank'd him; but speaking to them in *Portuguese*, I desired them to refer the Accepting his Kindness to the next Morning, and so I did, telling him we would further talk of this Part in the Morning; so we parted for that time.

When he was gone, I found they were all wonderfully affected with his Discourse, and with the Generosity of his Temper, as well as the Magnificence of his Present, which in another Place had been extraordinary. Upon the whole, not to detain you with Circumstances, we agreed, that seeing he was now one of our Number, and than as we were a Relief to him in carrying him out of the dismal Condition he was in, so he was equally a Relief to us, in being our Guide thro' the rest of the Country, our Interpreter with the Natives, and our Director how to manage with the Savages, and how to enrich our selves with the Wealth of the Country; that therefore we would put his Gold among our common Stock, and every one should give him as much as would make his up just as much as any single Share of our own, and for the future we would take our Lot together, taking his solemn Engagement to us, as we had before one to another, that we would not conceal the least Grain of Gold we found, one from another.

In the next Conference we acquainted him with the Adventures of the Golden River, and how we had shared what we got there; so that every Man had a larger Stock than he for his Share; that therefore instead of taking any from him, we had resolved every one to add a little to him. He appeared very glad that we had met with such good Success, but would not take a Grain from us, till at last pressing him very hard, he told us, that then he would take it thus: That when we came to get any more, he would have so much out of the first as should make him even, and then we would go on as equal Adventures; and thus we agreed.

He then told us, he thought it would not be an unprofitable Adventure, if before we set forward, and after we had got a Stock of Provisions, we should make a Journey North to the Edge of the Desart he had told us of, from whence our Negroes might bring every one a large Elephant's Tooth, and that he would get some more to assist; and that after a certain Length of Carriage, they might be conveyed by Canoes to the Coast, where they would yield a very great Profit.

I objected against this, on Account of our other Design we had of getting Gold Dust; and that our Negroes, who, we knew would be faithful to us, would get much more by searching the Rivers for Gold for us, than by lugging a great Tooth of an Hundred and fifty Pound Weight, a Hundred Mile, or more, which would be an unsufferable Labour to them after so hard a Journey, and would certainly kill them.

He acquiesced in the Justice of this Answer, but fain would have had us gone to see the woody Part of the Hills, and the Edge of the Desart, that we might see how the Elephants Teeth lay scattered up and down there; but when we told him the Story of what we had seen before, as is said above, he said no more.

We stay'd here twelve Days, during which Time the Natives were very obliging to us, and brought us Fruits, Pompions,[99] and a Root like Carrots, tho' of quite another Taste, but not unpleasant neither, and some *Guiney* Fowls whose Names we did not know. In short, they brought us Plenty of what they had, and we lived very well, and we gave them all such little Things as our Cutler had made, for he had now a whole Bag full of them.

On the thirteenth Day we set forward, taking our new Gentleman with us. At Parting, the Negroe King sent two Savages with a Present to him, of some dried Flesh, but I do not remember what it was, and he gave him again three Silver Birds which our Cutler help'd him to, which I assure you was a Present for a King.

We travelled now South, a little West, and here we found the first River for above 2000 Miles March, whose Water run South, all the rest running North or West. We followed this River, which was no bigger than a good large Brook in *England*, till it began to encrease its Water. Every now and then we found our *Englishman* went down as it were privately to the Water, which was to try the Land. At Length, after a Day's March upon this River, he came running up to us with his Hands full of Sand,[a] and saying *Look here*. Upon looking, we found that a good deal of Gold lay spangled[100] among the Sand of the River. Now, says he, I think we may begin to work; so he divided our Negroes into Couples, and set them to Work, to search and wash the Sand and Ooze in the Bottom of the Water where it was not deep.

In the first Day and a Quarter, our Men all together had gathered a Pound and two Ounces of Gold, or thereabouts; and as we found the Quantity encreased, the farther we went, we followed it about three Days, till another small Rivulet join'd the first, and then searching up the Stream, we found Gold there too; so we pitch'd our Camp in the Angle where the Rivers join'd, and we diverted our selves, as I may call it, in washing the Gold out of the Sand of the River, and in getting Provisions.

Here we stay'd thirteen Days more, in which time we had many pleasant Adventures with the Savages, too long to mention here, and some of them too homely to tell of;[b] for some of our Men had made something free with their Women, which, had not our new Guide made Peace for us with one of their Men, at the Price of seven fine Bits of Silver, which our Artificer had cut out into the Shapes of Lions, and Fishes, and Birds, and had punch'd Holes to hang them up by (an inestimable Treasure!) we must have gone to War with them and all their People.

All the while we were busy washing Gold Dust out of the Rivers, and our Negroes the like, our ingenious Cutler was hammering and cutting, and he was grown so dexterous by Use, that he formed all Manner of Images. He cut out Elephants, Tygers, Civet Cats, Ostriches, Eagles, Cranes, Fowls, Fishes, and indeed whatever he pleased, in thin Plates of hammer'd Gold, for his Silver and Iron was almost all gone.

At one of the Towns of these Savage Nations we were very friendly received by their King; and as he was very much taken with our Workman's Toys, he sold him an Elephant cut out of a Gold Plate as thin as a Six-pence, at an extravagant Rate. He was so much taken with it, that he would not be quiet till he had given him almost a Handful of Gold Dust, as they call it. I suppose it might weigh three Quarters of a Pound; the Piece of Gold that the Elephant was made of, might be about the Weight of a Pistole,[101] rather less than more. Our Artist was so honest, tho' the Labour and Art was all his own, that he brought all the Gold, and put it into our common Stock: But we had indeed no Manner of Reason in the least to be covetous; for, as our new Guide told us, we then were strong enough to defend our selves, and had Time enough to stay (for we were none of us in Haste) might in time get together what Quantity of Gold we pleased, even to an Hundred Pound Weight a Man, if we thought fit; and therefore he told us, tho' he had as much Reason to be sick of the Country as any of us, yet if we thought to turn our March a little to the South-East, and pitch upon a Place proper for our Head Quarters, we might find Provisions plenty enough, and extend our selves over the Country among the Rivers for two or three Year to the Right and Left, and we should soon find the Advantage of it.

The Proposal, however good as to the profitable Part of it, suited none of us; for we were all more desirous to get Home, than to be rich, being tired of the excessive Fatigue of above a Year's continual Wandring among Desarts and wild Beasts.

However, the Tongue of our new Acquaintance had a Kind of Charm in it, and used such Arguments, and had so much the Power of Perswasion, that there was no resisting him. He told us, it was preposterous not to take the Fruit of all our Labours, now we were come to the Harvest; that we might see the Hazard the *Europeans* run, with Ships and Men, and at great Expense, to fetch a little Gold; and that we that were in the Center of it, to go away empty handed, was unaccountable; that we were strong enough to fight our Way thro' whole Nations, and might make our Journey afterward to what Part of the Coast we pleased; and we should never forgive our selves when we came to our own Country, to see we had 500 Pistoles in Gold, and might as easily have had 5000, or 10000, or what we pleased; that he was no more covetous than we, but seeing it was in all our Powers to retrieve our Misfortunes at once, and to make our selves easy for all our Lives, he could not be faithful to us, or grateful for the Good we had done him, if he did not let us see the Advantage we had in our Hands; and he assured us, he would make it clear to our own Understanding, that we might in two Years time, by good Management, and by the Help of our Negroes, gather every Man a Hundred Pound Weight of Gold, and get together perhaps two Hundred Ton of Teeth: Whereas, if once we push'd on to the Coast, and separated, we should never be able to see that Place again with our Eyes, or do any more than Sinners did with Heaven, wish themselves there, but know they can never come at it.

Our Surgeon was the first Man that yielded to his Reasoning, and after him the Gunner; and they two indeed had a great Influence over us, but none of the rest had any Mind to stay, nor I neither, I must confess; for I had no Notion of a great deal of Money, or what to do with my self, or what to do with it if I had it. I thought I had enough already, and all the Thoughts I had about disposing of it, if I came to *Europe*, was only how to spend it as fast as I could, buy me some Clothes, and go to Sea again to be a Drudge for more.

However, he prevailed with us by his good Words at last, to stay but for six Months in the Country, and then, if we did resolve to go, he would submit: So at length we yielded to that, and he carry'd us about fifty *English* Miles South-East, where we found several Rivulets of Water, which seem'd to come all from a great Ridge of Mountains, which lay to the North-East, and which, by our Calculation, must be the Beginning that Way of the great Wast, which we had been forc'd Northward to avoid.

Here we found the Country barren enough, but yet we had, by his Direction, Plenty of Food; for the Savages round us, upon giving them some of our Toys, as I have so often mentioned, brought us in whatever they had: And here we found some Maise, or *Indian* Wheat, which the Negroe Women planted, as we sow Seeds in a Garden, and immediately our new Proveditor[102] ordered some of our Negroes to plant it, and it grew up presently, and by watering it often, we had a Crop in less than three Months Growth.

As soon as we were settled, and our Camp fix'd, we fell to the old Trade of Fishing for Gold in the Rivers mentioned above; and our *English* Gentleman so well knew how to direct our Search, that we scarce ever lost our Labour.

One time, having set us to Work, he asked, if we would give him Leave, with four or five Negroes, to go out for six or seven Days, to seek his Fortune, and see what he could discover in the Country, assuring us, whatever he got should be for the publick Stock. We all gave him our Consent, lent him a Gun; and two of our Men desiring to go with him, they took then six Negroes with them, and two of our Buffloes that came with us the whole Journey; they took about eight Days Provision of Bread with them, but no Flesh, except about as much dried Flesh as would serve them two Days.

They travelled up to the Top of the Mountains I mentioned just now, where they saw, (as our Men afterwards vouch'd it to be) the same Desart which we were so justly terrified at, when we were on the further Side, and which, by our Calculation, could not be less than 300 Miles broad, and above 600 Miles in Length, without knowing where it ended.

The Journal of their Travels is too long to enter upon here; they stayed out two and fifty Days, when they brought us seventeen Pound, and something more (for we had no exact Weight) of Gold Dust, some of it in much larger Pieces than any we found before; besides about fifteen Ton of Elephants Teeth, which he had, partly by good Usage, and partly by bad, obliged the Savages of the Country to fetch, and bring down to him from the Mountains, and which he made others bring with him quite down to our Camp. Indeed we wondered what was coming to us, when we saw him attended with above 200 Negroes; but he soon undeceived us, when he made them all throw down their Burthens on a Heap, at the Entrance of our Camp.

Besides this, they brought two Lions Skins, and five Leopards Skins, very large and very fine. He asked our Pardon for his long Stay, and that he had made no greater a Booty, but told us, he had one Excursion more to make, which he hop'd should turn to a better Account.

So having rested himself, and rewarded the Savages that brought the Teeth for him, with some Bits of Silver and Iron cut out Diamond Fashion, and with two shap'd like little Dogs, he sent them away mightily pleased.

The second Journey he went, some more of our Men desired to go with him, and they made a Troop of ten white Men, and ten Savages, and the two Buffloes to carry their Provisions and Ammunition. They took the same Course, only not exactly the same Tract, and they stay'd thirty two Days only, in which time they killed no less than fifteen Leopards, three Lions, and several other Creatures, and brought us Home four and twenty Pound, some Ounces of Gold Dust, and only six Elephants Teeth, but they were very great ones.

Our Friend the *Englishman* shewed us now, that our Time was well bestow'd; for in five Months which we had stayed here, we had gathered so much Gold Dust, that when we came to share it, we had five Pound and a Quarter to a Man, besides what we had before, and besides six or seven Pound Weight which we had at several times given our Artificer to make Baubles with; and now we talk'd of going forward to the Coast, to put an End to our Journey; but our Guide laught at us then: Nay you can't go now, *says he*; for the rainy Season begins next Month, and there will be no stirring then. This we found indeed reasonable, so we resolved to furnish our selves with Provisions that we might not be obliged to go abroad too much in the Rain, and we spread our selves some one Way, some another, as far as we cared to venture, to get Provisions, and our Negroes killed us some Deer which we cured as well as we could, in the Sun, for we had now no Salt.

By this time the rainy Months were set in, and we could scarce, for above two Months, look out of our Hutts. But that was not all, for the Rivers were so swelled with the Land Floods that we scarce knew the little Brooks and Rivulets from the great navigable Rivers. This had been a very good Opportunity for to have convey'd by Water, upon Rafts, our Elephants Teeth, of which we had a very great Pile; for as we always gave the Savages some Reward for their Labour, the very Women would bring us Teeth upon every Opportunity, and sometimes a great Tooth carried between two; so that our Quantity was encreased to about two and twenty Ton of Teeth.

As soon as the Weather proved fair again, he told us he would not press us to any further Stay, since we did not care whether we got any more Gold or no; that we were indeed the first Men ever he met with in his Life, that said they had Gold enough, and of whom it might be truly said, that when it lay under our Feet, we would not stoop to take it up. But since he had made us a Promise, he would not break it, nor press us to make any farther Stay, only he thought he ought to tell us, that now was the Time, after the Land Flood, when the greatest Quantity of Gold was found; and that if we stayed but one Month, we should see Thousands of Savages spread themselves over the whole Country, to wash the Gold out of the Sand, for the *European* Ships who would come on the Coast; that they do it then, because the Rage of the Floods always works down a great deal of Gold out of the Hills; and if we took the Advantage to be there before them, we did not know what extraordinary things we might find.

This was so forcible, and so well argued, that it appeared in all our Faces we were prevailed upon; so we told him we would all stay: For tho' it was true we were all eager to be gone, yet the evident Prospect of so much Advantage, could not well be resisted: That he was greatly mistaken when he suggested, that we did not desire to encrease our Store of Gold, and in that we were resolved to make the utmost Use of the Advantage that was in our Hands, and would stay as long as any Gold was to be had, if it was another Year.

He could hardly express the Joy he was in on this Occasion, and the fair Weather coming on, we began just as he directed, to search about the Rivers for more Gold; at first we had but little Encouragement, and began to be doubtful, but it was very plain that the Reason was the Water was not fully fallen, or the Rivers reduced to their[a] usual Channel; but in a few Days we were fully requited, and found much more Gold than at first, and in bigger Lumps; and one of our Men washed out of the Sand a Piece of Gold as big as a small Nut, which weighed by our Estimation, for we had no small Weights, almost an Ounce and a half.

This Success made us extreamly diligent, and in little more than a Month, we had all together gotten near sixty Pound Weight of Gold; but after this, as he told us, we found Abundance of the Savages, both Men, Women and Children, hunting every River and Brook, and even the dry Land of the Hills for Gold, so that we could do nothing like then, compared to what we had done before.

But our Artificer found a Way to make other People find us in[103] Gold without our own Labour; for when these People began to appear, he had a considerable Quantity of his Toys, Birds, Beasts, &c. such as before, ready for them, and the *English* Gentleman being the Interpreter, he brought the Savages to admire them; so our Cutler had Trade enough; and to be sure sold his Goods at a monstrous Rate; for he would get an Ounce of Gold, sometimes two, for a Bit of Silver, perhaps of the Value of a Groat, nay if it were Iron; and if it was of Gold, they would not give the more for it; and it was incredible almost to think what a Quantity of Gold he got that Way.

In a Word, to bring this happy Journey to a Conclusion, we encreased our Stock of Gold here in three Months Stay more, to such a Degree, that bringing it all to a common Stock, in order to Share it, we divided almost four Pound Weight again to every Man, and then we set forward for the Gold Coast, to see what Method we could find out for our Passage into *Europe*.

There happened several very remarkable Incidents in this Part of our Journey, as to how we were, or were not, received friendly, by the several Nations of Savages through whom we past; how we delivered one Negroe King from Captivity, who had been a Benefactor to our new Guide; and how our Guide in Gratitude, by our Assistance, restored him to his Kingdom, which perhaps might contain about 300 Subjects; how he entertained us; and how he made his Subjects go with our *Englishman*, and fetch all our Elephants Teeth, which we had been obliged to leave behind us, and to carry them for us to the River, the Name of which I forgot, where we made Rafts, and in eleven Days more came down to one of the *Dutch* Settlements on the Gold Coast, where we arrived in perfect Health, and to our great Satisfaction. As for our Cargo of Teeth, we sold it to the *Dutch* Factory,[104] and received Clothes and other Necessaries for our selves, and such of our Negroes as we thought fit to keep with us; and it is to be observed, that we had four Pound of Gunpowder left when we ended our Journey. The *Negro Prince* we made perfectly free, clothed him out of our common Stock, and gave him a Pound and a half of Gold for himself, which he knew very well how to manage, and here we all parted after the most friendly Manner possible. Our *Englishman* remained in the *Dutch* Factory some time, and, as I heard afterwards, died there of Grief; for he having sent a Thousand Pound

Sterling over to *England* by the Way of *Holland*, for his Refuge, at his Return to his Friends, the Ship was taken by the *French*, and the Effects all lost.

The rest of my Comrades went away in a small Bark, to the two *Portuguese* Factories, near *Gambia*, in the Latitude of fourteen; and I with two Negroes which I kept with me, went away to *Cape Coast Castle*,[105] where I got Passage for *England*, and arrived there in *September*; and thus ended my first Harvest of *Wild Oats*, the rest were not sowed to so much Advantage.

I had neither Friend, Relation, nor Acquaintance in *England*, tho' it was my Native Country, I had consequently no Person to trust with what I had, or to counsel me to secure or save it; but falling into ill Company, and trusting the Keeper of a Publick House in *Rotherhith* with a great Part of my Money, and hastily squandering away the rest, all that great Sum, which I got with so much Pains and Hazard, was gone in little more than two Years Time; and as I even rage in my own Thoughts to reflect upon the Manner how it was wasted, so I need record no more; the rest Merits to be conceal'd with Blushes, for that it was spent in all Kinds of Folly and Wickedness; so this Scene of my Life may be said to have begun in Theft, and ended in Luxury; a sad Setting out, and a worse Coming home.

About the Year   I began to see the Bottom of my Stock, and that it was Time to think of farther Adventures, for my Spoilers, as I call them, began to let me know, that as my Money declined, their Respect would ebb with it, and that I had nothing to expect of them farther than as I might command it by the Force of my Money, which in short would not go an Inch the farther, for all that had been spent in their Favour before.

This shocked me very much, and I conceived a just Abhorrence of their Ingratitude; but it wore off; nor had I with it any Regret at the wasting so glorious a Sum of Money, as I brought to *England* with me.

I next shipped my self, in an evil Hour to be sure, on a Voyage to *Cadiz*, in a Ship called the   and in the Course of our Voyage, being on the Coast of *Spain*, was obliged to put in to the *Groyn*,[106] by a strong South-West Wind.

Here I fell into Company with some Masters of Mischief, and among them, one forwarder than the rest, began an intimate Confidence with me, so that we called one another Brothers, and communicated all our Circumstances to one another; his Name was *Harris*. This Fellow came to me one Morning, asking me if I would go on Shore, and I agreed; so we got the Captain's Leave for the Boat, and went together. When we were together, he asked me if I had a Mind for an Adventure that might make amends for all past Misfortunes; I told him yes, with all my Heart; for I did not care where I went, having nothing to lose, and no Body to leave behind me.

He then asked me if I would swear to be secret, and that if I did not agree to what he proposed, I would nevertheless never betray him; I readily bound my self to that, upon the most solemn Imprecations and Curses that the Devil and both of us could invent.

He told me then, there was a brave Fellow in the other Ship, pointing to another *English* Ship which rode in the Harbour, who in Concert with some of the Men had resolved to mutiny the next Morning, and run away with the Ship; and that if we could get Strength enough among our Ship's Company we might do the same. I liked the Proposal very well, and he got eight of us to join with him, and he told us, that as soon as his Friend had begun the Work, and was Master of the Ship, we should be ready to do the like; this was his Plot, and I without the least Hesitation, either at the Villainy of the Fact, or the Difficulty of performing it, came immediately into the wicked Conspiracy, and so it went on among us; but we could not bring our Part to Perfection.

Accordingly on the Day appointed, his Correspondent in the other Ship, whose Name was *Wilmot*, began the Work, and having seized the Captain's Mate, and other Officers, secured the Ship, and gave the Signal to us; we were but eleven in our Ship, who were in the Conspiracy, nor could we get any more that we could trust, so that leaving the Ship, we all took the Boat and went off to join the other.

Having thus left the Ship I was in, we were entertained with a great deal of Joy by Captain *Wilmot* and his new Gang; and being well prepared for all manner of Roguery, bold, desperate, I mean my self, without the least Checks of Conscience, for what I was entered upon, or for any Thing I might do, much less with any Apprehension of what might be the Consequence of it; I say, having thus embarked with this Crew, which at last brought me to consort with the most famous Pyrates of the Age, some of whom have ended their Journals at the Gallows: I think the giving an Account of some of my other Adventures may be an agreeable Piece of Story; and this I may venture to say before Hand, upon the Word of a PYRATE, that I shall not be able to recollect the full, no not by far, of the great Variety which has formed one of the most reprobate Schemes that ever Man was capable to present to the World.

I that was, as I have hinted before, an original Thief, and a Pyrate even by Inclination before, was now in my Element, and never undertook any Thing in my Life with more particular Satisfaction.

Captain *Wilmot*, for so we are now to call him, being thus possessed of a Ship, and in the Manner as you have heard, it may be easily concluded he had nothing to do to stay in the Port, or to wait either the Attempts which might be made from the Shore, or any Change which might happen among his Men. On the Contrary, we weighed Anchor the same Tide, and stood out to Sea, steering away for the *Canaries*. Our Ship had Twenty Two Guns, but was able to carry Thirty; and besides, as she was fitted out for a Merchant Ship only, she was not furnished either with Ammunition or small-Arms sufficient for our Design, or for the Occasion we might have in Case of a Fight; so we put into *Cadiz*, that is to say, we came to an Anchor in the Bay; and the Captain and one whom we call'd young Captain *Kid*,[107] who was the Gunner, and some of the Men who could best be trusted, among whom was my Comrade *Harris*, who was made second Mate, and my self who was made a Lieutenant; some Bales of *English* Goods were proposed to be carried on Shore with us for Sale; but my Comrade, who was a compleat Fellow at his Business, proposed a better Way for it; and having been in the Town before, told us in short, that he would buy what Powder and Bullet, small Arms, or any thing else we wanted, on his own Word, to be paid for when they came on Board, in such *English* Goods as we had there. This was by much the best Way, and accordingly he and the Captain went on Shore by themselves, and having made such a Bargain as they found for their Turn, came away again in two Hours time, and bringing only a Butt of Wine, and five Casks of Brandy with them, we all went on Board again.

The next Morning two Barco Longo's[108] came off to us deep loaden, with five *Spaniards* on board them, for Traffick. Our Captain sold them good Pennyworths, and they delivered us sixteen Barrels of Powder, twelve small Runlets[109] of fine Powder for our small Arms, sixty Musquets, and twelve Fuzees for the Officers; seventeen Ton of Cannon Ball, fifteen Barrels of Musquet Bullets, with some Swords, and twenty good Pair of Pistols. Besides this, they brought thirteen Butts of Wine (for we that were now all become Gentlemen scorn'd to drink the Ship's Beer) also sixteen Puncheons[110] of Brandy, with twelve Barrels of Raisins, and twenty Chests of Lemons: All which paid for in *English* Goods; and over and above, the Captain received 600 Pieces of Eight in Money. They would have come again, but we would stay no longer.

From hence we sailed to the *Canaries*, and from thence onward to the *West-Indies*, where we committed some Depredation upon the *Spaniards* for Provision, and took some Prizes, but none of any great Value, while I remained with them, which was not long at that Time; for having taken a *Spanish* Sloop on the Coast of *Cartagena*,[111] my Friend made a Motion to me, that we should desire Captain *Wilmot* to put us into the Sloop, with a Proportion of Arms and Ammunition, and let us try what we could do; she being much fitter for our Business than the great Ship, and a better Sailer. This he consented to, and we appointed our Rendezvous at *Tobago*, making an Agreement, that whatever was taken by either of our Ships, should be shared among the Ship's Company of both; all which we very punctually observed, and join'd our Ships again about fifteen Months after, at the Island of *Tobago*, as above.

We cruised near two Years in those Seas, chiefly upon the *Spaniards*; not that we made any Difficulty of taking *English* Ships, or *Dutch*, or *French*, if they came in our Way; and particularly Captain *Wilmot* attack'd a New-England Ship bound from the *Maderas* to *Jamaica*; and another bound from *New-York* to *Berbadoes*, with Provisions; which last was a very happy Supply to us. But the Reason why we meddled as little with *English* Vessels as we could, was, first, because, if they were Ships of any Force, we were sure of more Resistance from them; and secondly, because we found the *English* Ships had less Booty when taken; for the *Spaniards* generally had Money on board, and that was what we best knew what to do with. Captain *Wilmot* was indeed more particularly cruel when he took any *English* Vessel, that they might not too soon have Advice of him in *England*, and so the Men of War have Orders to look out for him. But this Part I bury in Silence for the present.

We encreased our Stock in these two Years considerably, having taken 60000 Pieces of Eight in one Vessel, and 100000 in another; and being thus first grown rich, we resolved to be strong too; for we had taken a Brigantine[112] built at *Virginia*, an excellent Sea Boat, and a good Sailer, and able to carry twelve Guns; and a large *Spanish* Frigat-built Ship,[113] that sailed incomparably well also, and which afterwards, by the Help of good Carpenters, we fitted up to carry twenty eight Guns. And now we wanted more Hands, so we put away for the Bay of *Campeachy*,[114] not doubting we should ship as many Men there as we pleased, and so we did.

Here we sold the Sloop that I was in; and Captain *Wilmot* keeping his own Ship, I took the Command of the *Spanish* Frigat, as Captain, and my Comrade *Harris* as eldest Lieutenant, and a bold enterprizing Fellow he was as any the World afforded. One *Culverdine*[115] was put into the Brigantine, so that we were now three stout Ships, well Mann'd, and Victualled for twelve Months; for we had taken two or three Sloops from *New-England* and *New-York*, loaden with Flour, Pease, and Barrell'd Beef, and Pork, going for *Jamaica* and *Berbadoes*; and for more Beef we went on Shore on the Isle of *Cuba*, where we killed as many black Cattel as we pleased, tho' we had very little Salt to cure them.

Out of all the Prizes we took here, we took their Powder and Bullet, their small Arms and Cutlasses; and as for their Men, we always took the Surgeon and the Carpenter, as Persons who were of particular Use to us upon many Occasions; nor were they always unwilling to go with us, tho' for their own Security, in Case of Accidents, they might easily pretend they were carried away by Force, of which I shall give a pleasant Account in the Course of my other Expeditions.

We had one very merry Fellow here, a Quaker, whose Name was *William Walters*, whom we took out of a Sloop bound from *Pensilvania* to *Berbadoes*. He was a Surgeon, and they called him Doctor; but he was not employed in the Sloop as a Surgeon, but was going to *Berbadoes* to get a *Birth*,[116] as the Sailors call it. However, he had all his Surgeon's Chest on board, and we made him go with us, and take all his Implements with him. He was a comick Fellow indeed, a Man of very good solid Sense, and an excellent Surgeon; but what was worth all, very good humour'd and pleasant in his Conversation, and a bold, stout, brave Fellow too, as any we had among us.

I found *William*, as I thought, not very averse to go along with us, and yet resolved to do it so, that it might be apparent he was taken away by Force; and to this Purpose he comes to me, Friend, says he, thou sayest I must go with thee, and it is not in my Power to resist thee, if I would; but I desire thou wilt oblige the Master of the Sloop which I am on board, to certify under his Hand that I was taken away by Force, and against my Will; and this he said with so much Satisfaction in his Face, that I could not but understand him. Ay, ay, *says I*, whether it be against your Will, or no, I'll make him and all the Men give you a Certificate of it, or I'll take them all along with us, and keep them till they do: So I drew up the Certificate my self, wherein I wrote that he was taken away by main Force, as a Prisoner, by a Pyrate Ship; that they carried away his Chest and Instruments first, and then bound his Hands behind him, and forced him into their Boat; and this was signed by the Master and all his Men.

Accordingly I fell a swearing at him, and called to my Men to tye his Hands behind him, and so we put him into our Boat, and carry'd him away. When I had him on board, I called him to me: Now, Friend, says I, I have brought you away by Force, it is true, but I am not of the Opinion I have brought you away so much against your Will as they imagine: Come, says I, you will be a useful Man to us, and you shall have very good Usage among us; so I unbound his Hands, and first ordered all things that belonged to him to be restored to him, and our Captain gave him a Dram.[117]

Thou hast dealt friendly by me, says he, and I'll be plain with thee, whether I came willingly to thee, or not: I shall make my self as useful to thee as I can; but thou knowest it is not my Business to meddle when thou art to fight. No, no, says the Captain, but you may meddle a little when we share the Money. Those things are useful to furnish a Surgeon's Chest, says *William*, and smiled; but I shall be moderate.

In short, *William* was a most agreeable Companion, but he had the better of us in this Part, that, if we were taken, we were sure to be hang'd, and he was sure to escape; and he knew it well enough: But in short he was a sprightly Fellow, and fitter to be Captain than any of us. I shall have often an Occasion to speak of him in the rest of the Story.

Our Cruising so long in these Seas began now to be so well known, that not in *England* only, but in *France* and *Spain*, Accounts had been made publick of our Adventures, and many Stories told how we murthered the People in cold Blood, tying them Back to Back, and throwing them into the Sea; one Half of which however was not true, tho' more was done than it is fit to speak of here.

The Consequence of this however was, that several *English* Men of War were sent to the *West Indies*, and were particularly instructed to cruize in the Bay of *Mexico*, and the Gulph of *Florida*, and among the *Bahama* Islands, if possible, to attack us.

We were not so ignorant of things, as not to expect this, after so long a Stay in that Part of the World; but the first certain Account we had of them, was at the *Honduras*, when a Vessel coming in from *Jamaica*, told us, that two *English* Men of War were coming directly from *Jamaica* thither, in Quest of us. We were indeed as it were embay'd,[118] and could not have made the least Shift to have got off, if they had come directly to us; but as it happen'd, some body had informed them that we were in the Bay of *Campeachy*, and they went directly thither, by which we were not only free of them, but were so much to the Windward of them, that they could not make any Attempt upon us, tho' they had known we were there.

We took this Advantage, and stood away for *Carthagena*, and from thence with great Difficulty beat it up at a Distance from under the Shore for St. *Martha*,[119] till we came to the *Dutch* Island of *Curasoe*, and from thence to the Island of *Tobago*; which, as before, was our Rendezvous; which being a deserted uninhabited Island, we at the same time made use of for a Retreat: Here the Captain of the *Brigantine* died, and Captain *Harris* at that time my Lieutenant, took the Command of the *Brigantine*.

Here we came to a Resolution, to go away to the Coast of *Brasil*, and from thence to the Cape of *Good Hope*, and so for the *East-Indies*: But Captain *Harris*, as I have said, being now Captain of the *Brigantine*, alledged that his Ship was too small for so long a Voyage; but that if Captain *Wilmot* would consent, he would take the Hazard of another Cruize, and he would follow us in the first Ship he could take: So we appointed our Rendezvous to be at *Madagascar*, which was done by my Recommendation of the Place, and the Plenty of Provisions to be had there.

Accordingly he went away from us *in an evil Hour*, for instead of taking a Ship to follow us, he was taken, as I heard afterwards, by an *English* Man of War, and being laid in Irons, died of meer Grief and Anger before he came to *England*: His Lieutenant, I have heard, was afterwards executed in *England* for a Pyrate, and this was the End of the Man who first brought me into this unhappy Trade.

We parted from *Tobago* three Days after, bending our Course for the Coast of *Brasil*, but had not been at Sea above Twenty Four Hours, when we were separated by a terrible Storm, which held three Days, with very little Abatement or Intermission. In this Juncture, Captain *Wilmot* happen'd unluckily to be on board my Ship, very much to his Mortification; for we not only lost Sight of his Ship, but never saw her more, till we came to *Madagascar*, where she was cast away. In short, after having in this Tempest lost our Fore-Top Mast, we were forced to put back to the Isle of *Tobago* for Shelter, and to repair our Damage, which brought us all very near our Destruction.

We were no sooner on Shore here, and all very busy looking out for a Piece of Timber for a Top-Mast, but we perceived standing in for the Shore, an *English* Man of War of Thirty six Guns: It was a great Surprize to us indeed, because we were disabled so much, but to our great good Fortune we lay pretty snug and close among the high Rocks, and the Man of War did not see us, but stood off again upon his Cruise; so we only observed which Way she went, and at Night leaving our Work, resolved to stand off to Sea, steering contrary Way from that which we observed she went. And this we found had the desired Success, for we saw him no more: We had gotten an old Mizen Top-Mast on board, which made us a Jury Fore-Top-Mast[120] for the present, and so we stood away for the Isle *Trinidad*, where, though there were *Spaniards* on Shore, yet we landed some Men with our Boat, and cut a very good Piece of Fir to make us a new Top-Mast, which we got fitted up effectually, and also we got some Cattle here to eke out our Provisions, and calling a Council of War among our selves, we resolved to quit those Seas for the present, and steer away for the Coast of *Brasil*.

The first thing we attempted here, was only getting fresh Water; but we learnt, that there lay the *Portuguese* Fleet at the Bay of *All-Saints*, bound for *Lisbon*, ready to sail, and only waited for a fair Wind; this made us lye by, wishing to see them put to Sea, and accordingly as they were, with, or without Convoy, to attack or avoid them.

It sprung up a fresh Gale in the Evening, at S. W. by W. which being fair for the *Portugal* Fleet, and the Weather pleasant and agreeable; we heard the Signal given to unmore,[121] and running in under the Island of *Si*—[122] we hauled our Main-Sail and Fore-Sail up in the Brails,[123] lower'd the Top-

Sail upon the Cap, and clewed them up[124] that we might lye as snug as we could, expecting their coming out; and the next Morning saw the whole Fleet come out accordingly; but not at all to our Satisfaction, for they consisted of Twenty six Sail, and most of them Ships of Force, as well as Burthen, both Merchant Men and Men of War; so seeing there was no meddling, we lay still where we was also, till the Fleet was out of Sight, and then stood off and on, in hopes of meeting with further Purchase.

It was not long before we saw a Sail, and immediately gave her Chase, but she proved an excellent Sailer, and standing out to Sea, we saw plainly she trusted to her Heels, that is to say, to her Sails; however, as we were a clean Ship we gained upon her, tho' slowly, and had we had a Day before us, we should certainly have come up with her, but it grew dark apace, and in that Case we knew we should lose Sight of her.

Our merry Quaker perceiving us to crowd[125] still after her in the Dark, wherein we could not see which way she went, come very drily to me; *Friend* Singleton, says he, *doest thee know what we are a doing?* Says I, *yes, why we are chasing yon Ship, are we not? And how dost thou know that*, says he very gravely still? *Nay, that is true*, says I again, *we cannot be sure. Yes Friend*, says he, *I think we may be sure that we are running away from her, not chasing her. I am afraid*, adds he, *thou art turned Quaker, and hast resolved not to use the Hand of Power, or art a Coward, and art flying from thy Enemy.*

What do you mean, says I, I think I swore at him; *what do ye sneer at now? you have always one dry Rub or another to give us.*

Nay, says he, *it's plain enough, the Ship stood off to Sea, due East on purpose to lose us, and thou may'st be sure her Business does not lie that Way; for what should she do at the Coast of* Africa *in this Latitude, which would be as far South as* Congo *or* Angola; *but as soon as it is dark, that we shall lose Sight of her, she will tack and stand away West again for the* Brasil *Coast, and for the Bay, where thou knowest she was going before; and are not we then a running away from her?* I am greatly in hopes, Friend, *Says the dry gibing Creature*, Thou wilt turn Quaker, for I see thou art not for Fighting.

Very well WILLIAM, says I, *then I shall make an excellent Pyrate.* However, *William* was in the right, and I apprehended what he meant immediately, and Captain *Wilmot*, who lay very sick in his Cabin, overhearing us, understood him as well as I, and called out to me, that *William* was right, and it was our best Way to change our Course, and stand away for the Bay, where it was Ten to one but we should snap her in the Morning.

Accordingly, we went about snip, got our Larboard Tacks[126] on board, set the Top-gallant Sails,[127] and crowded for the Bay of *All-Saints*, where we came to an Anchor, early in the Morning just out of Gun Shot of the Forts; we furl'd our Sails with Rope-Yarns,[128] that we might haul home the

Sheets without going up to loose them, and lowering our Main and Fore-Yards,[129] looked just as if we had lain there a good while.

In two Hours after, we saw our Game, standing in for the Bay with all the Sail she could make, and she came innocently into our very Mouths, for we lay still, till we saw her almost within Gun Shot; when our Fore Mast Geers[130] being stretched fore and aft, we first run up our Yards, and then hauled home the Top-Sail Sheets; the Rope-Yarns that furled them giving Way of themselves, the Sails were set in a few Minutes; at the same time slipping our Cable, we came upon her before she could get under Way upon 'tother Tack: They were so surprized, that they made little or no Resistance, but struck[131] after the first Broad-Side.

We were considering what to do with her, when *William* came to me. *Hark thee Friend*, says he, *thou hast made a fine Spot of Work of it now, hast thou not? To borrow thy Neighbour's Ship here, just at thy Neighbour's Door, and never ask him Leave; now dost thou not think there are some Men of War in the Port, thou hast given them the Alarm sufficiently; thou wilt have them upon thy Back before Night, depend upon it, to ask thee, wherefore, Thou dist so?*

Truly William, said I, *for ought I know, that may be true: What then shall we do next?* Says he, *thou hast but two Things to do, either go in and take all the rest, or else get thee gone before they come out, and take thee; for I see they are hoisting a Top-Mast[132] to yon great Ship, in order to put to Sea immediately, and they won't be long before they come to talk with thee; and what wilt thou say to them, when they ask thee why thou borrowedst their Ship without Leave?*

As *William* said, so it was, we could see by our Glasses that they were all in a Hurry, manning and fitting some Sloops they had there, and a large Man of War, and it was plain they would soon be with us; but we were not at a Loss what to do; we found the Ship we had taken was loaden with nothing considerable for our Purpose, except some Cocoa, some Sugar, and Twenty Barrels of Flower; the rest of her Loading was Hides; so we took out all we thought for our Turn, and among the rest all her Ammunition, great Shot, and small Arms, and turned her off; we also took a Cable and three Anchors she had, which were for our Purpose, and some of her Sails; she had enough left just to carry her into Port, and that was all.

Having done this, we stood on upon the *Brasil* Coast, Southward, till we came to the Mouth of the River *Janiero*: But as we had two Days the Wind blowing hard at S.E. and S.S.E. we were obliged to come to an Anchor under a little Island, and wait for a Wind. In this time the *Portuguese* had it seems given Notice over Land to the Governour there, that a Pyrate was upon the Coast; so that when we came in View of the Port, we saw two Men of War riding just without the Bar, whereof one we found was getting under Sail with all possible Speed, having slipt her Cable, on purpose to speak with us; the other was not so forward, but was preparing to follow: In less than an Hour they stood both fair after us, with all the Sail they could make.

Had not the Night come on, *William*'s Words had been made good; they would certainly have asked us the Question what we did there? for we found the foremost Ship gained upon us, especially upon one Tack; for we plied away from them to Windward, but in the Dark losing Sight of them, we resolved to change our Course, and stand away directly to Sea, not doubting but we should lose them in the Night.

Whether the *Portuguese* Commander guessed we would do so or no, I know not; but in the Morning when the Day-light appeared, instead of having lost him, we found him in Chase of us, about a League a-Stern; only to our great good Fortune we could see but one of the two; however this one was a great Ship, carried six and forty Guns, and an admirable Sailer, as appeared by her out-sailing us; for our Ship was an excellent Sailer too, as I have said before.

When I found this, I easily saw there was no Remedy, but we must engage; and as we knew we could expect no Quarters from those Scoundrels the *Portuguese*, a Nation I had an original Aversion to, I let Captain *Wilmot* know how it was. The Captain, sick as he was, jumped up in the Cabin, and would be led out upon the Deck, for he was very weak, to see how it was; well, *says he*; we'll fight them.

Our Men were all in good heart before, but to see the Captain so brisk who had lain ill of a Calenture[133] Ten or Eleven Days, gave them double Courage, and they went all Hands to work to make a clear Ship and be ready. *William* the Quaker comes to me with a kind of a Smile; Friend, says he, what does yon Ship follow us for? Why says I, to fight us you may be sure; Well, says he, and will he come up with us dost thou think? Yes, said I, you see she will. Why then, Friend, says the dry Wretch, why dost thou run from her still, when thou seest she will over-take thee? Will it be better for us to be over-taken further off than here? Much at one for that, says I; why what would you have us do? Do! says he, let us not give the poor Man more Trouble than needs must; let us stay for him, and hear what he has to say to us; he will talk to us in Powder and Ball said I: Very well then, says he if that be his Country Language, we must talk to him in the same, must we not? Or else how shall he understand us? Very well *William*, says I, we understand you; and the Captain as ill as he was, called to me, *William*'s right again, says he, as good here as a League further; so he gives a Word of Command, *Haul up the Main-Sail*, we'll shorten Sail for him.

Accordingly we shortened Sail; and as we expected her upon our Lee Side, we being then upon our Starboard Tack, brought 18 of our Guns to the Larboard Side, resolving to give him a Broad-Side that should warm him; it was about half an Hour before he came up with us, all which time we luffed up,[134] that we might keep the Wind of him, by which he was obliged to run up under our Lee,[135] as we designed him; when we got him upon our Quarter we edg'd down, and received the Fire of five or six of his Guns; by this time you may be sure all our Hands were at their Quarters, so we clapt our Helm hard *a Weather*,[136] let go the Lee Braces[137] of the Main Top-sail, and laid it a-back, and so our Ship fell athwart the *Portuguese* Ship's Hawse;[138] then we immediately poured in our Broad-Side, raking them fore and aft, and killed them a great many Men.

The *Portuguese*, we could see were in the utmost Confusion; and not being aware of our Design, their Ship having fresh Way, run their Boltsprit[139] into the fore Part of our main Shrouds,[140] as that they could not easily get clear of us, and so we lay locked after that Manner, the Enemy could not bring above five or six Guns, besides their Small-Arms, to bear upon us, while we played our whole Broadside upon him.

In the middle of the Heat of this Fight, as I was very busy upon the Quarter Deck, the Captain calls to me, for he never stirred from us, what the Devil is Friend *William* a-doing yonder, says the Captain, has he any Business upon Deck? I stept forward, and there was Friend *William* with two or three stout Fellows lashing the Ships Boltsprit fast to our Main-Mast, for fear they should get away from us; and every now and then he pulled a Bottle out of his Pocket and gave the Men a Dram to encourage them. The Shot flew about his Ears as thick as may be supposed in such an Action, where the *Portuguese*, to give them their due, fought very briskly, believing at first they were sure of their Game, and trusting to their Superiority; but there was *William*, as composed, and in as perfect Tranquillity as to Danger, as if he had been over a Bowl of Punch, only very busy securing the Matter, that a Ship of Fourty six Guns should not run away from a Ship of Eight and Twenty.

This Work was too hot to hold long; our Men behaved bravely; our Gunner, a gallant Man, shouted below, pouring in his Shot at such a Rate, that the *Portuguese* began to slacken their Fire; we had dismounted several of their Guns by firing in at their Forecastle, and raking them, as I said, fore and aft; and presently comes *William* up to me; *Friend* says he, very calmly, *What doest thou mean? Why dost thou not visit thy Neighbour in the Ship, the Door being open for thee?* I understood him immediately, for our Guns had so tore their Hull, that we had beat two Port Holes into one, and the Bulk Head of their Steerage[141] was split to Pieces, that they could not retire to their close Quarters; so I gave the Word immediately to board them. Our Second Lieutenant, with about Thirty Men, entered in an Instant over the

Forecastle,[142] followed by some more, with the Boat-swain, and cutting in Pieces about Twenty five Men that they found upon the Deck, and then throwing some Grenadoes[143] into the Steerage, they entered there also; upon which the *Portuguese* cried Quarter presently, and we mastered the Ship, contrary indeed to our own Expectation; for we would have compounded with them, if they would have sheered off, but laying them athwart the Hawse at first, and following our Fire furiously, without giving them any time to get clear of us, and work their Ship; by this means, tho' they had six and forty Guns, they were not able to Fight above five or six, as I said above, for we beat them immediately from their Guns in the Forecastle, and killed them Abundance of Men between Decks, so that when we entered they had hardly sound Men enough to fight us Hand to Hand upon their Deck.

The Surprize of Joy, to hear the *Portuguese* cry Quarter, and see their Antient struck,[144] was so great to our Captain, who as I have said, was reduced very weak with a high Fever, that it gave him new Life; Nature conquered the Distemper, and the Fever abated that very Night: So that in two or three Days he was sensibly better, his Strength began to come, and he was able to give his Orders effectually in every thing that was material, and in about ten Days was entirely well, and about the Ship.

In the mean time, I took Possession of the *Portuguese* Man of War, and Captain *Wilmot* made me, or rather I made my self, Captain of her for the present; about Thirty of their Seamen took Service with us, some of which were *French*, some *Genoeses*, and we set the rest on Shore the next Day, on a little Island on the Coast of *Brasil*, except some wounded Men who were not in a Condition to be removed; and whom we were bound to keep on board, but we had an Occasion afterwards to dispose of them at the Cape, where at their own Request we set them on Shore.

Captain *Wilmot*, as soon as the Ship was taken, and the Prisoners stowed, was for standing in for the River *Janiero* again, not doubting but we should meet with the other Man of War, who not having been able to find us, and having lost the Company of her Comrade, would certainly be returned, and might be surprized by the Ship we had taken, if we carryed *Portuguese* Colours, and our Men were all for it.

But our Friend *William* gave us better Counsel; for he came to me; Friend, says he, I understand the Captain is for sailing back to the *Rio Janiero*, in Hopes to meet with the other Ship that was in Chase of thee yesterday; is it true, dost thou intend it? Why, yes, says I, *William*, pray why not? Nay, *says he*, thou mayst do so if thou wilt. Well, I know that too, *William*, said I; but the Captain is a Man will be ruled by Reason, what have you to say to it? Why, says *William* gravely, I only ask what is thy

Business, and the Business of all the People thou hast with thee? Is it not to get Money? Yes, *William*, it is so, in our honest Way: And wouldst thou, says he, rather have Money without Fighting, or Fighting without Money? I mean, which wouldst thou have by Choice, suppose it to be left to thee? O *William*, *says I*, the first of the two, to be sure. Why then, *says he*, what great Gain hast thou made of the Prize thou hast taken now, tho' it has cost the Lives of thirteen of thy Men, besides some hurt? It is true, thou hast got the Ship and some Prisoners, but thou wouldst have had twice the Booty in a Merchant Ship, with nor one Quarter of the Fighting; and how dost thou know either what Force, or what Number of Men may be in the other Ship, and what Loss thou mayst suffer, and what Gain it shall be to thee, if thou take her? I think indeed thou mayst much better let her alone.

Why, *William*, it is true said I, and I'll go tell the Captain what your Opinion is, and bring you Word what he says. Accordingly I went to the Captain, and told him *William*'s Reasons, and the Captain was of his Mind, that our Business was indeed Fighting when we could not help it, but that our main Affair was Money, and that with as few Blows as we could; so that Adventure was laid aside, and we stood along Shore again South, for the River *de la Plata*, expecting some Purchase thereabouts; especially we had our Eyes upon some of the *Spanish* Ships from the *Buenos Ayres*, which are generally very rich in Silver, and one such Prize would have done our Business. We ply'd about here in the Latitude of   South for near a Month, and nothing offer'd; and here we began to consult what we should do next, for we had come to no Resolution yet. Indeed my Design was always for the *Cape de Bona Speranza*, and so to the *East Indies*. I had heard some flaming Stories of Captain *Avery*,[145] and the fine things he had done in the *Indies*, which were doubled and doubled even Ten Thousand-fold, and from taking a great Prize in the Bay of *Bengal*, where he took a Lady said to be the *Great Mogul*'s Daughter, with a great Quantity of Jewels about her. We had a Story told us, that he took a *Mogul* Ship, so the foolish Sailors called it, loaden with Diamonds.

I would fain have had Friend *William*'s Advice, whither we should go, but he always put it off with some *Quaking* Quibble or other. In short, he did not care for directing us neither; whether he made a Piece of Conscience of it, or whether he did not care to venture having it come against him afterwards, or no, this I know not; but we concluded at last without him.

We were however pretty long in resolving, and hanker'd[146] about the *Rio de la Plata* a long time; at last we spy'd a Sail to Windward, and it was such a Sail as I believe had not been seen in that Part of the World a great while; it wanted not that we should give it Chase, for it stood directly towards us, as well as they that steer'd could make it; and even that was more Accident of Weather than any thing else: For if the Wind had chopt about[147] any where, they must have gone with it. I leave any Man that is a Sailor, or understands any thing of a Ship, to judge what a Figure this Ship made when we first saw her, and what we could imagine was the Matter with her. Her Main Top-Mast was come by the Board, about six Foot above the Cap, and fell forward, the Head of the Top-gallant Mast, hanging in the Fore Shrouds by the Stay; at the same time the Pareil[148] of the Mizen Topsail Yard, by some Accident, giving Way, the Mizen Topsail Braces (the standing Part of which being fast to the Main Topsail Shrouds) brought the Mizen Topsail, Yard and all, down with it, which spread over Part of the Quarter Deck like an Awning: The Fore-Topsail was hoisted up two Thirds of the Mast, but the Sheets were flown.[149] The Fore Yard was lower'd down upon the Forecastle, the Sail loose, and Part of it hanging over-board. In this Manner she came down upon us with the Wind quartering:[150] In a Word, the Figure the whole Ship made, was the most confounding to Men that understood the Sea, that ever was seen; she had no Boat, neither had she any Colours out.

When we came near to her, we fired a Gun to bring her to. She took no Notice of it, nor of us, but came on just as she did before. We fired again, but 'twas all one: At length we came within Pistol Shot of one another, but no body answered nor appeared; so we began to think that it was a Ship gone ashore somewhere in Distress, and the Men having forsaken her, the high Tide had floated her off to Sea. Coming nearer to her, we run up along Side of her so close, that we could hear a Noise within her, and see the Motion of several People thro' her Ports.

Upon this we Mann'd our two Boats full of Men, and very well armed, and ordered them to board her at the same Minute, as near as they could, and to enter one at her Fore-chains[151] on one Side, and the other a Midship on the other Side. As soon as they came to the Ship's Side, a surprizing Multitude of black Sailors, *such as they were*, appeared upon Deck, and in short, terrify'd our Men so much, that the Boat which was to enter her Men in the Waste,[152] stood off again, and durst not board her; and the Men that enter'd out of the other Boat, finding the first Boat, as they thought, beaten off, and seeing the Ship full of Men, jump'd all back again into their Boat, and put off, not knowing what the Matter was. Upon this we prepared to pour in a Broadside upon her. But our Friend *William* set us to Rights again here; for it seems he guess'd how it was sooner than we did, and coming up to me (for it was our Ship that came up with her) Friend, says he, I am of Opinion thou art wrong in this Matter, and thy Men have been wrong also in their Conduct: I'll tell thee how thou shalt take this

Ship, without making use of those things call'd Guns. How can that be, *William*, said I? Why, said he, thou mayst take her with thy Helm; thou seest they keep no Steerage, and thou seest the Condition they are in; board her with thy Ship upon her Lee Quarter, and so enter her from the Ship: I am perswaded thou wilt take her without Fighting, for there is some Mischief has befallen the Ship, which we know nothing of.

In a Word, it being a smooth Sea, and little Wind, I took his Advice, and lay'd her aboard.[153] Immediately our Men entred the Ship, where we found a large Ship with upwards of 600 Negroes, Men and Women, Boys and Girls, and not one Christian, or white Man, on board.

I was struck with Horror at the Sight, for immediately I concluded, as was partly the Case, that these black Devils had got loose, had murthered all the white Men, and thrown them into the Sea; and I had no sooner told my Mind to the Men, but the Thought of it so enraged them, that I had much ado to keep my Men from cutting them all in Pieces. But *William*, with many Perswasions prevailed upon them, by telling of them, that it was nothing but what, if they were in the Negroes Condition, they would do, if they could; and that the Negroes had really the highest Injustice done them, to be sold for Slaves without their Consent; and that the Law of Nature dictated it to them; that they ought not to kill them, and that it would be wilful Murder to do it.

This prevailed with them, and cooled their first Heat; so they only knock'd down twenty or thirty of them, and the rest run all down between Decks, to their first Places, believing, as we fancy'd, that we were their first Masters come again.

It was a most unaccountable Difficulty we had next, for we could not make them understand one Word we said, nor could we understand one Word our selves that they said. We endeavoured by Signs to ask them whence they came, but they could make nothing of it; we pointed to the Great Cabin, to the Round-house, to the Cook-room, then to our Faces, to ask if they had no white Men on board, and where they were gone? But they could not understand what we meant: On the other Hand, they pointed to our Boat, and to their Ship, asking Questions as well as they could, and said a Thousand things, and expressed themselves with great Earnestness, but we could not understand a Word of it all, or know what they meant by any of their Signs.

We knew very well they must have been taken on board the Ship as Slaves, and that it must be by some *European* People too. We could easily see that the Ship was a *Dutch*-built Ship, but very much alter'd, having been built upon, and as we suppose, in *France*; for we found two or three *French* Books on board, and afterwards we found Clothes, Linnen, Lace, some old Shoes, and several other things: We found among the Provisions, some Barrels of *Irish* Beef, some *Newfoundland* Fish, and several other Evidences that there had been Christians on board, but saw no Remains of them. We found not a Sword, Gun, Pistol, or Weapon of any kind, except some Cutlasses; and the Negroes had hid them below where they lay. We ask'd them what was become of all the small Arms, pointing to our own, and to the Places where those belonging to the Ship had hung: One of the Negroes understood me presently, and beckon'd to me to come up upon the Deck, where taking my Fuzee, which I never let go out of my Hand for some time after we had master'd the Ship; I say, offering to take hold of it, he made the proper Motion of throwing it into the Sea, by which I understood, as I did afterwards, that they had thrown all the small Arms, Powder, Shot, Swords, &c. into the Sea, believing, as I supposed, those things would kill them, tho' the Men were gone.

After we understood this, we made no Question but that the Ship's Crew having been surprized by these desperate Rogues, had gone the same Way, and had been thrown over-board also. We look'd all over the Ship, to see if we could find any Blood, and we thought we did perceive some in several Places; but the Heat of the Sun melting the Pitch and Tar upon the Decks, made it impossible for us to discern it exactly, except in the Round-house,[154] where we plainly saw that there had been much Blood. We found the Skuttle open, by which we supposed the Captain and those that were with him had made their Retreat into the Great Cabin, or those in the Cabin had made their Escape up into the Round-house.

But that which confirmed us most of all in what had happen'd, was, that upon farther Enquiry we found that there were seven or eight of the Negroes very much wounded, two or three of them with Shot; whereof one had his Leg broke, and lay in a miserable Condition, the Flesh being mortified, and, as our Friend *William* said, in two Days more he would have died. *William* was a most dexterous Surgeon, and he shew'd it in this Cure; for tho' all the Surgeons we had on board both our Ships (and we had no less than five that called themselves bred Surgeons, besides two or three who were Pretenders or Assistants) and all these gave their Opinion that the Negroe's Leg must be cut off, and that his Life could not be saved without it; that the Mortification had touch'd the Marrow in the Bone, that the Tendons were mortified, and that he could never have the Use of his Leg, if it should be cured. *William* said nothing in general, but that his Opinion was otherwise, and that he desired the Wound might be search'd, and that he would then tell them farther. Accordingly he went to Work with the Leg, and, as he desired he might have some of the Surgeons to assist him, we appointed him two of the ablest of them to help, and all of them to look on, if they thought fit.

William went to Work his own Way, and some of them pretended to find Fault at first. However, he proceeded, and search'd every Part of the Leg where he suspected the Mortification had touch'd it: In a Word, he cut off a great deal of mortified Flesh; in all which the poor Fellow felt no Pain. *William* proceeded till he brought the Vessels which he had cut to bleed, and the Man to cry out: Then he reduced the Splinters of the Bone, and calling for Help, *set it, as we call it*, and bound it up, and laid the Man to Rest, who found himself much easier than before.

At the first Opening, the Surgeons began to triumph, the Mortification seem'd to spread, and a long red Streak of Blood appeared from the Wound upwards to the Middle of the Man's Thigh, and the Surgeons told me the Man would die in a few Hours. I went to look at it, and found *William* himself under some Surprize; but when I ask'd him how long he thought the poor Fellow could live, he look'd gravely up at me, and said, *As long as thou canst*: I am not at all apprehensive of his Life, said he, but I would cure him if I could, without making a Cripple of him. I found he was not just then upon the Operation, as to his Leg, but was mixing up something to give the poor Creature, to repel, as I thought, the spreading Contagion, and to abate or prevent any feverish Temper that might happen in the Blood: After which he went to Work again, and open'd the Leg in two Places above the Wound, cutting out a great deal of mortified Flesh, which it seems was occasioned by the Bandage which had press'd the Parts too much, and withal, the Blood being at that time in a more than common Disposition to mortify, might assist to spread it.

Well, our Friend *William* conquer'd all this, clear'd the spreading Mortification, that the red Streak went off again, the Flesh began to heal, and Matter to run; and in a few Days the Man's Spirits began to recover, his Pulse beat regular, he had no Fever, and gathered Strength daily; and in a Word he was a perfect sound Man in about ten Weeks, and we kept him amongst us, and made him an able Seaman., But to return to the Ship, we never could come at a certain Information about it, till some of the Negroes which we kept on board, and whom we taught to speak *English*, gave the Account of it afterwards, and this maim'd Man in particular.

We enquired by all the Signs and Motions we could imagine, what was become of the People, and yet we could get nothing from them. Our Lieutenant was for torturing some of them to make them confess; but *William* opposed that vehemently; and when he heard it was under Consideration, he came to me, Friend, says he, I make a Request to thee, not to put any of these poor Wretches to Torment. Why, *William*, said I, why not? You see they will not give any Account of what is become of the white Men. Nay, says *William*, do not say so; I suppose they have given thee a full Account of every Particular of it. How so, says I, pray what are we the wiser for all their Jabbering? Nay, says *William*, that may be thy Fault, for ought I know; thou wilt not punish the poor Men because they cannot speak *English*, and perhaps they never heard a Word of *English* before. Now I may very well suppose, that they have given thee a large Account of every thing; for thou seest with what Earnestness, and how long some of them have talk'd to thee, and if thou canst not understand their Language, nor they thine, how can they help that; at the best thou doest but suppose that they have not told thee the whole Truth of the Story, and on the contrary I suppose they have, and how wilt thou decide the Question, whether thou art right, or whether I am right? Besides, what can they say to thee, when thou askest them a Question upon the Torture, and at the same time they do not understand the Question, and thou doest not know whether they say *Ay* or *No*?

It is no Complement to my Moderation, to say I was convinc'd by these Reasons; and yet we had all much ado to keep our second Lieutenant from murthering some of them to make them tell what, if[a] they had told, he did not understand one Word of it; but he would not be perswaded but that the Negroes must needs understand him, when he ask'd them, whether the Ship had any Boat or no, like ours, and what was become of it?

But there was no Remedy but to wait till we made these People understand *English*; and to adjourn the Story till that time. The Case was thus. Where they were taken on board the Ship, that we could never understand, because they never knew the *English* Names which we give to those Coasts, or what Nation they were who belong'd to the Ship, because they knew not one Tongue from another; but thus far the Negroe I examin'd, who was the same whose Leg *William* had cured, told us, that they did not speak the same Language we spoke, nor the same our *Portugueze* spoke; so that in all Probability they must be *French* or *Dutch*.

Then he told us, that the white Men used them barbarously; that they beat them unmercifully; that one of the Negroe Men had a Wife, and two Negroe Children, one a Daughter about sixteen Years old; that a White Man abused the Negroe Man's Wife, and afterwards his Daughter, which, as he said, made all the Negroe Men mad; and that the Woman's Husband was in a great Rage, at which the White Man was so provoked, that he threaten'd to kill him; but in the Night, the Negroe Man being loose, got a great Club, by which he made us understand he meant a Handspike, and that when the same *Frenchman* (*if it was a* Frenchman) came among them again, he began again to abuse the Negroe Man's Wife; at which the

Negroe taking up the Handspike, knock'd his Brains out at one Blow; and then taking the Key from him with which he usually unlock'd the Hand-cuffs which the Negroes were fetter'd with, he set about a Hundred of them at Liberty, who getting up upon the Deck by the same Skuttle that the White Man came down; and taking the Man's Cutlass who was killed, and laying hold of what came next them, they fell upon the Men that were upon the Deck, and killed them all, and afterwards those they found upon the Forecastle; that the Captain and his other Men, who were in the Cabin and the Round-house, defended themselves with great Courage, and shot out at the Loopholes at them, by which he and several other Men were wounded, and some killed, but that they broke into the Round house after a long Dispute, where they killed two of the white Men, but own'd that the two white Men killed eleven of their Men before they could break in; and then the rest having got down the Skuttle into the Great Cabin, wounded three more of them.

That after this, the Gunner of the Ship having secured himself in the Gun-room, one of his Men haul'd up the Long-Boat close under the Stern, and putting into her all the Arms and Ammunition they could come at, got all into the Boat, and afterwards took in the Captain, and those that were with him, out of the Great Cabin. When they were all thus embark'd, they resolved to lay the Ship aboard again, and try to recover it; that they boarded the Ship in a desperate Manner, and killed at first all that stood in their Way; but the Negroes being by this time all loose, and having gotten some Arms, tho' they understood nothing of Power and Bullet, or Guns; yet the Men could never master them. However, they lay under the Ship's Bow, and got out all the Men they had left in the Cook-room; who had maintained themselves there, notwithstanding all the Negroes could do, and with their small Arms killed between thirty and forty of the Negroes, but were at last forc'd to leave them.

They could give me no Account whereabouts this was, whether near the Coast of *Africk*, or far off, or how long it was before the Ship fell into our Hands; only in general, it was a great while ago, *as they called it*, and by all we could learn, it was within two or three Days after they had set Sail from the Coast. They told us, that they had killed about thirty of the white Men, having knock'd them on the Head with Crows[155] and Hand-spikes, and such things as they could get; and one strong Negroe killed three of them with an Iron Crow, after he was shot twice thro' the Body, and that he was afterwards shot thro' the Head by the Captain himself at the Door of the Round-house, which he had split open with the Crow; and this we suppose was the Occasion of the great Quantity of Blood which we saw at the Round-house Door.

139

The same Negroe told us, that they threw all the Powder and Shot they could find, into the Sea, and they would have thrown the great Guns into the Sea, if they could have lifted them. Being ask'd how they came to have their Sails in such a Condition, his Answer was, *they no understand, they no know what the Sails do*; that was, they did not so much as know that it was the Sails that made the Ship go; or understand what they meant, or what to do with them. When we asked him whither they were going; he said, they did not know, but believed they should go Home to their own Country again. I asked him in particular, what he thought we were, when we came first up with them? He said, they were terribly frighted, believing we were the same white Men that had gone away in their Boats, and were come again in a great Ship, with the two Boats with them, and expected they would kill them all.

This was the Account we got out of them, after we had taught them to speak *English*, and to understand the Names and Use of the things belonging to the Ship, which they had Occasion to speak of, and we observed that the Fellows were too innocent to dissemble in their Relation, and that they all agreed in the Particulars, and were always in the same Story, which confirm'd very much the Truth of what they said.

Having taken this Ship, our next Difficulty was, what to do with the Negroes. The *Portugueze* in the *Brasils* would have bought them all of us, and been glad of the Purchase, if we had not shew'd our selves Enemies there, and been known for Pyrates; but as it was, we durst not go on Shore any where thereabouts, or treat with any of the Planters, because we should raise the whole Country upon us; and if there were any such things as Men of War in any of their Ports, we should be assured to be attack'd by them, and by all the Force they had by Land or Sea.

Nor could we think of any better Success, if we went Northward to our own Plantations. One while we determined to carry them all away to the *Buenos Ayres*, and sell them there to the *Spaniards*; but they were really too many for them to make Use of; and to carry them round to the South-Seas, which was the only Remedy that was left, was so far, that we should be no Way able to subsist them for so long a Voyage.

At last, our old never-failing Friend *William* help'd us out again, as he had often done, at a Dead-lift.[156] His Proposal was this, that he should go as Master of the Ship, and about twenty Men such as we could best trust, and attempt to trade privately upon the Coast of *Brasil*, with the Planters, not at the principal Ports, because that would not be admitted.

We all agreed to this, and appointed to go away our selves towards the *Rio de la Plata*, where we had Thought of going before, and to wait for him not there, but at *Port St. Pedro*, as the *Spaniards* call it, lying at the Mouth of the River which they call *Rio Grande*, and where the *Spaniards* had a small Fort, and a few People, but we believe there was no Body in it.

Here we took up our Station, cruising off and on, to see if we could meet any Ships going to, or coming from the *Buenos Ayres*, or the *Rio de la Plata*; but we met with nothing worth Notice. However, we employed our selves in things necessary for our going off to Sea; for we filled all our Water Casks, and got some Fish for our present Use, to spare as much as possible our Ship's Stores.

William in the mean time went away to the North, and made the Land about the *Cape de St. Thomas*,[157] and betwixt that and the Isles *de Tuberon*,[158] he found Means to trade with the Planters for all his Negroes, as well the Women as the Men, and at a very good Price too; for *William*, who spoke *Portuguese* pretty well, told them a fair Story enough, that the Ship was in Scarcity of Provisions, that they were driven a great Way out of their Way, and indeed, *as we say*, out of their Knowledge, and that they must go up to the Northward as far as *Jamaica*, or sell there upon the Coast. This was a very plausible Tale, and was easily believed; and if you observe the Manner of the Negroes Sailing, and what happened in their Voyage, was every Word of it true.

By this Method, and being true to one another, *William* past for what he was; I mean, for a very honest Fellow, and by Assistance of one Planter, who sent to some of his Neighbour Planters, and managed the Trade among themselves, he got a quick Market; for in less than five Weeks, *William* sold all his Negroes, and at last sold the Ship it self, and shipp'd himself and his twenty Men, and two Negroe Boys whom he had left, in a Sloop, one of those which the Planters used to send on board for the Negroes. With this Sloop Captain *William*, as we then called him, came away, and found us at *Port St. Pedro*, in the Latitude of 32 Degrees, 30 Minutes South.

Nothing was more surprizing to us, than to see a Sloop come along the Coast, carrying *Portugueze* Colours, and come in directly to us, after we were assured he had discovered both our Ships. We fired a Gun upon her nearer Approach, to bring her to an Anchor, but immediately she fired five Guns by Way of Salute, and spread her *English* Antient: Then we began to guess it was Friend *William*, but wondered what was the Meaning of his being in a Sloop, whereas we sent him away in a Ship of near 300 Tuns; but he soon let us into the whole History of his Management, with which we had a great deal of Reason to be very well satisfy'd. As soon as he had brought the Sloop to an Anchor, he came aboard of my Ship, and there he gave us an Account how he began to trade, by the Help of a *Portugueze* Planter, who lived near the Sea-side; how he went on Shore, and went up to the first House he could see, and asked the Man of the House to sell him some Hoggs, pretending at first he only stood in upon the Coast to take in fresh Water, and buy some Provisions; and the Man not only sold him seven fat Hoggs, but invited him in, and gave him and five Men he had with him, a very good Dinner, and he invited the Planter on board his Ship, and in Return for his Kindness, gave him a Negroe Girl for his Wife.

This so obliged the Planter, that the next Morning he sent him on board, in a great Luggage Boat, a Cow and two Sheep, with a Chest of Sweet-meats, and some Sugar, and a great Bag of Tobacco, and invited Captain *William* on Shore again: That after this, they grew from one Kindness to another, that they began to talk about Trading for some Negroes; and *William* pretending it was to do him Service, consented to sell him thirty Negroes for his private Use in his Plantation, for which he gave *William* ready Money in Gold, at the Rate of five and thirty Moydores *per* Head; but the Planter was obliged to use great Caution[159] in the bringing them on Shore: For which Purpose, he made *William* weigh[160] and stand out to Sea, and put in again, above fifty Miles farther North, where at a little Creek he took the Negroes on Shore at another Plantation, being a Friend's of his whom it seems he could trust.

This Remove brought *William* into a farther Intimacy, not only with the first Planter, but also with his Friends, who desired to have some of the Negroes also; so that from one to another, they bought so many, till one over-grown Planter took 100 Negroes, which was all *William* had left, and sharing them with another Planter, that other Planter chaffer'd with *William* for Ship and all, giving him in Exchange a very clean, large, well-built Sloop of near sixty Tons, very well furnish'd, carrying six Guns, but we made her afterwards carry twelve Guns. *William* had 300 Moydores of Gold, besides the Sloop, in Payment for the Ship, and with this Money, he stored the Sloop as full as she could hold with Provisions, especially Bread, some Pork, and about sixty Hoggs alive: Among the rest, *William* got eighty Barrels of good Gunpowder, which was very much for our Purpose, and all the Provisions which were in the *French* Ship he took out also.

This was a very agreeable Account to us, especially when we saw, that *William* had received in Gold coin'd, or by Weight, and some *Spanish* Silver, 60000 Pieces of Eight, besides a new Sloop, and a vast Quantity of Provisions.

We were very glad of the Sloop in particular, and began to consult what we should do, whether we had not best turn off our great *Portuguese* Ship, and stick to our first Ship and the Sloop, seeing we had scarce Men enough for all three, and that the biggest Ship was thought too big for our Business; however, another Dispute which was now decided, brought the first to a Conclusion. The first Dispute was, whither we should go? My Comrade, as I called him now, that is to say, he that was my Captain before we took this *Portuguese* Man of War, was for going to the South Seas, and coasting up the West Side of *America*, where we could not fail of making several good Prizes upon the *Spaniards* and that then if Occasion required, we might come home by the South-Seas to the *East-Indies* and so go round the Globe as others had done before us.

But my Head lay another Way, I had been in the *East-Indies*, and had entertained a Notion ever since that, that if we went thither we could not fail of making good Work of it, and that we might have a safe Retreat, and good Beef to Victual our Ship, among my old Friends the Natives of *Zamguebar*, on the Coast of *Mozambique*, or the Island of St. *Laurence*: I say, my Thoughts lay this Way and I read so many Lectures to them all, of the Advantages they would certainly make of their Strength, by the Prizes they would take in the Gulph of *Mocha* or the *Red-Sea*, and on the Coast of *Malabar* or the Bay of *Bengal*, that I amaz'd them.

With these Arguments I prevailed on them, and we all resolved to steer away S. E. for the Cape of *Good Hope*; and in Consequence of this Resolution, we concluded to keep the Sloop, and sail with all three, not doubting, as I assured them, but we should find Men there to make up the Number wanting, and if not, we might cast any of them off when we pleased.

We could do no less than make our Friend *William* Captain of the Sloop, which with such good Management he had brought us. He told us, tho' with much good Manners, he would not command her as a Fregat,[161] but if we would give her to him for his Share of the *Guinea* Ship, which we came very honestly by, he would keep us Company as a Victualler, if we commanded him, as long as he was under the same Force that took him away.

We understood him, so we gave him the Sloop, but upon Condition that he should not go from us, and should be entirely under our Command: However, *William* was not so easy as before; and indeed, as we afterwards wanted the Sloop, to cruise for Purchase,[162] and a Right thorow-paced Pyrate in her; so I was in such Pain for *William*, that I could not be without him, for he was my Privy-Counsellour and Companion upon all Occasions; so I put a *Scotsman*, a bold enterprizing gallant Fellow into her, named *Gordon*, and made her carry 12 Guns, and four Paterero's,[163] though indeed we wanted Men, for we were none of us Mann'd in Proportion to our Force.

We sailed away for the Cape of *Good Hope*, the Beginning of *October* 1706, and passed by in Sight of the Cape, the 12 of *November* following, having met with a great deal of bad Weather: We saw several Merchant Ships in the Road there, as well *English* as *Dutch*, whether outward bound or homeward we could not tell; *be it what it would*, we did not think fit to come to an Anchor, not knowing what they might be, or what they might attempt against us, when they knew what we were: However, as we wanted fresh Water, we sent the two Boats belonging to the *Portuguese* Man of War, with all *Portuguese* Seamen or *Negroes* in them, to the Watering Place, to take in Water: And in the mean time we hung out a *Portuguese* Antient at Sea, and lay by all that Night. They knew not what we was, but it seems we past for any thing but really what we was.

Our Boats returning the third time loaden, about five a Clock next Morning, we thought our selves sufficiently water'd, and stood away to the Eastward; but before our Men returned the last time, the Wind blowing an easy Gale at West, we perceived a Boat in the Grey of the Morning, under Sail, crowding to come up with us, as if they were afraid we should be gone. We soon found it was an *English* Long-Boat, and that it was pretty full of Men; we could not imagine what the Meaning of it should be; but as it was but a Boat, we thought there could be no great Harm in it to let them come on board: And if it appeared they came only to enquire who we were, we would give them a full Account of our Business, by taking them along with us, seeing we wanted Men as much as any thing; but they saved us the Labour of being in doubt how to dispose of them, for it seems our *Portuguese* Seamen who went for Water, had not been so silent at the Watering Place, as we thought they would have been. But the Case, in short was this. Captain —, *I forbear his Name at present, for a particular Reason*, Captain of an *East India* Merchant Ship, bound afterwards for *China*, had found some Reason to be very severe with his Men, and had handled some of them very roughly at St. *Helena*; insomuch, that they threaten'd among themselves to leave the Ship the first Opportunity, and had long wish'd for that Opportunity: Some of these Men, it seems, had met with our Boat at the Watering Place, and enquiring of one another who we were, and upon what Account; whether the *Portuguese* Seamen, by faultring in their Account, made them suspect that we were out upon the Cruise, or whether they told it in plain *English*, or no (for they all spoke *English* enough to be understood) but so it was, that as soon as ever the Men carried the News on board, that the Ships which lay by to the Eastward were *English*, and that they were going upon the *Account*,[164] which by the Way was a Sea Term for a Pyrate; I say, as soon as ever they heard it, they went to work, and getting all things ready in the Night, their Chests and Clothes, and whatever else they could, they came away before it was Day, and came up with us about seven a Clock.

When they came by the Ship's Side which I commanded, we hailed them in the usual Manner, to know what and who they were, and what their Business? They answered, they were *Englishmen*, and desired to come aboard: We told them they might lay the Ship on board, but ordered they should let only one Man enter the Ship, till the Captain knew their Business, and that he should come without any Arms: They said Ay, with all their Hearts.

We presently found their Business, and that they desired to go with us; and as for their Arms, they desired we would send Men on board the Boat, and that they would deliver them all to us, which was done. The Fellow that came up to me, told me how they had been used by their Captain, how he had starved the Men, and used them like Dogs; and that if the rest of the Men knew they should be admitted, he was satisfied two Thirds of them would leave the Ship. We found the Fellows were very hearty in their Resolution, and jolly brisk Sailors they were; so I told them I would do nothing without our Admiral, that was, the Captain of the other Ship: So I sent my Pinnace on board Captain *Wilmot*, to desire him to come on board; but he was indisposed, and being to Leeward, excused his coming, but left it all to me: But before my Boat was returned, Captain *Wilmot* called to me by his Speaking Trumpet, which all the Men might hear as well as I, thus, calling me by my Name, *I hear they are honest Fellows, pray tell them they are all welcome, and make them a Bowl of Punch.*

As the Men heard it as well as I, there was no need to tell them what the Captain said; and as soon as the Trumpet had done, they set up a Huzza that shewed us they were very hearty in their coming to us; but we bound them to us by a stronger Obligation still, after this: For when we came to *Madagascar*, Captain *Wilmot*, with Consent of all the Ship's Company, ordered that these Men should have as much Money given them out of the Stock, as was due to them for their Pay in the Ship they had left; and after that, we allowed them Twenty Pieces of Eight a Man Bounty Money: And thus we entred them upon Shares, as we were all, and brave stout Fellows they were, being Eighteen in Number, whereof two were Midship-Men, and one a Carpenter.

It was the 28th of *November*, when having had some bad Weather, we came to an Anchor in the Road off of St. *Augustine* Bay, at the South West End of my old Acquaintance the Isle of *Madagascar*: We lay here a while, and traffick'd with the Natives for some good Beef, tho' the Weather was so hot, that we could not promise our selves to salt any of it up to keep; but I shewed them the Way which we practised before, to salt it first with *Salt-Petre*, then cure it, by drying it in the Sun, which made it eat very agreeably, tho' not so wholesome for our Men, that not agreeing with our Way of Cooking, *viz.* Boiling with Pudding, Brewes,[165] &c. and particularly this Way would be too salt, and the Fat of the Meat be resty, or dry'd away, so as not to be eaten.

This however we could not help, and made our selves amends by feeding heartily on the fresh Beef while we were there, which was excellent good and fat, every Way as tender, and as well relished as in *England*, and thought to be much better to us who had not tasted any in *England* for so long a Time.

Having now for some time remained here, we began to consider that this was not a Place for our Business; and I that had some Views, a particular Way of my own, told them, that this was not a Station for those that look'd for Purchase; that there were two Parts of the Island which were particularly proper for our Purposes; first the Bay on the East Side of the Island, and from thence to the Island *Mauritius*, which was the usual Way which Ships that came from the *Malabar* Coast, or the Coast of *Coromandel*, Fort *St. George*,[166] &c. used to take, and where, if we waited for them, we ought to take our Station.

But on the other Hand, as we did not resolve to fall upon the *European* Traders, who were generally Ships of Force, and well Manned, and where Blows must be looked for; so I had another Prospect, which I promised my self would yield equal Profit, or perhaps greater, without any of the Hazard and Difficulty of the former, and this was the Gulph of *Mocha* or the *Red Sea*.

I told them that the Trade here was great, the Ships rich, and the Streight of *Babelmandel*[167] narrow; so that there was no doubt but we might cruise so as to let nothing slip our Hands, having the Seas open from the *Red Sea* along the Coast of *Arabia*, to the *Persian* Gulph, and the *Malabar* Side of the *Indies*.

I told them, what I had observed when I sailed round the Island, in my former Progress, how that on the Northmost Point of the Island were several very good Harbours, and Roads for our Ships: That the Natives were even more civil, and tractable, if possible, than those where we were, not having been so often ill treated by *European* Sailors, as those had in the South and East Sides; and that we might always be sure of a Retreat, if we were driven to put in by any Necessity, either of Enemies or of Weather.

They were easily convinced of the Reasonableness of my Scheme, and Captain *Wilmot*, whom I now called our Admiral, tho' he was at first of the Mind to go and lye at the Island *Mauritius*, and wait for some of the *European* Merchant Ships from the Road of *Coromandel*, or the Bay of *Bengal*, was now of my Mind. It is true, we were strong enough to have attacked an *English East India* Ship of the greatest Force, though some of them were said to carry fifty Guns; but I represented to him, that we were sure to have Blows, and Blood if we took them, and after we had done, their Loading was not of equal Value to us, because we had no room to dispose of their Merchandize: And as our Circumstances stood, we had rather have taken one outward bound *East India* Ship, with her ready Cash on board, perhaps to the Vallue of forty or fifty Thousand Pound, than three homeward bound, though their Loading would at *London* be worth three times the Money; because, we knew not whither to go to dispose of the Cargo; whereas the Ships from *London* had Abundance of things we knew how to make use of, besides their Money; such as their Stores of Provisions, and Liquors, and great Quantities of the like sent to the Governours and Factories at the *English* Settlements, for their Use: So that if we resolved to look for our own Country Ships, it should be those that were outward bound, not the *London* Ships homeward.

All these things considered, brought the Admiral to be of my Mind entirely; so after taking in Water, and some fresh Provisions where we lay, which was near *Cape St. Mary*, on the South-West Corner of the Island, we weighed, and stood away South, and afterwards S.S.E. to round the Island, and in about six Days Sail, got out of the Wake of the Island, and steer'd away North, till we came off of *Port Dauphin*,[168] and then North by East, to the Latitude of 13 Degrees, 40 Minutes, which was, in short, just at the farthest Part of the Island; and the Admiral keeping a-head, made the open Sea fair to the West, clear of the whole Island; upon which he brought to, and we sent the Sloop to stand in round the farthest Point North, and coast along the Shore, and see for a Harbour to put into, which they did, and soon brought us an Account, that there was a deep Bay, with a very good Road, and several little Islands under which they found good Riding, in 10 to 17 Fathom Water, and accordingly there we put in.

However, we afterwards found Occasion to remove our Station, as you shall hear presently. We had now nothing to do, but go on Shore, and acquaint our selves a little with the Natives, take in fresh Water, and some fresh Provisions, and then to Sea again. We found the People very easy to deal with, and some Cattel they had; but it being at the Extremity of the Island, they had not such Quantities of Cattle here. However, for the present, we resolved to appoint this for our Place of Rendezvous, and go and look out. This was about the latter End of *April*.

Accordingly we put to Sea, and cruised away to the Northward, for the *Arabian* Coast: It was a long Run; but as the Winds generally blow Trade from the South, and S.S.E. from *May* to *September*, we had good Weather, and in about twenty Days we made the Island of *Saccatia*, lying South from the *Arabian* Coast, and E.S.E. from the Mouth of the Gulph of *Mocha*, or the Red Sea.

Here we took in Water, and stood off and on upon the *Arabian* Shore. We had not cruised here above three Days, or thereabouts, but I spy'd a

Sail, and gave her Chase; but when we came up with her, never was such a poor Prize chased by Pyrates that look'd for Booty; for we found nothing in her, but poor, half-naked *Turks* going a Pilgrimage to *Mecca*, to the Tomb of their Prophet *Mahomet*; the Jonk[169] that carry'd them had no one thing worth taking away, but a little Rice, and some Coffee, which was all the poor Wretches had for their Subsistence; so we let them go, for indeed we knew not what to do with them.

The same Evening we chased another Jonk with two Masts, and in something better Plight to look at than the former. When we came on board, we found them upon the same Errand, but only that they were People of some better Fashion than the other; and here we got some Plunder, some *Turkish* Stores, a few Diamonds in the Ear-drops of five or six Persons, some fine *Persian* Carpets, of which they made their Saffra's[170] to lye upon, and some Money; so we let them go also.

We continued here eleven Days longer, and saw nothing but now and then a Fishing-Boat; but the twelfth Day of our Cruise, we spy'd a Ship: Indeed I thought at first it had been an *English* Ship, but it appeared to be an *European* freighted for a Voyage from *Goa*, on the Coast of *Malabar*, to the Red Sea, and was very rich. We chased her, and took her, without any Fight, tho' they had some Guns on board too, but not many. We found her Manned with *Portuguese* Seamen, but under the Direction of five Merchant *Turks*, who had hired her on the Coast of *Malabar*, of some *Portugal* Merchants, and had loaden her with Pepper, Salt-petre, some Spices, and the rest of the Loading was chiefly Callicoes and wrought Silks, some of them very rich.

We took her, and carried her to *Saccatia*, but we really knew not what to do with her, for the same Reasons as before; for all their Goods were of little or no Value to us. After some Days we found Means to let one of the *Turkish* Merchants know, that if he would ransom the Ship, we would take a Sum of Money, and let them go. He told me, if I would let one of them go on Shore for the Money, they would do it: So we adjusted the Value of the Cargo at 30000 Ducats. Upon this Agreement we allowed the Sloop to carry him on Shore at *Dofar* in *Arabia*,[171] where a rich Merchant laid down the Money for them, and came off with our Sloop; and on Payment of the Money, we very fairly and honestly let them go.

Some Days after this, we took an *Arabian* Jonk going from the Gulph of *Persia* to *Mocha*, with a good Quantity of Pearl on board; we gutted him of the Pearl, which, it seems, was belonging to some Merchants at *Mocha*,[172] and let him go, for there was nothing else worth our taking.

We continued cruising up and down here, till we began to find our Provisions grow low, when Captain *Wilmot* our Admiral told us, 'twas time to

148

think of going back to the Rendezvous, and the rest of the Men said the same, being a little weary of beating about for above three Months together, and meeting with little or nothing compar'd to our great Expectations. But I was very loath to part with the Red Sea at so cheap a Rate, and press'd them to tarry a little longer, which at my Instance we did; but three Days afterwards, to our great Misfortune, understood, that by Landing the *Turkish* Merchants at *Dofar*, we had alarmed the Coast as far as the Gulph of *Persia*, so that no Vessel would stir that Way, and consequently nothing was to be expected on that Side.

I was greatly mortify'd at this News, and could no longer withstand the Importunities of the Men, to return to *Madagascar*. However, as the Winds continued still to blow at S.S.E. to E. by S. we were obliged to stand away towards the Coast of *Africa*, and the *Cape Guarde Foy*,[173] the Winds being more variable under the Shore, than in the open Sea.

Here we chopp'd[174] upon a Booty which we did not look for, and which made Amends for all our Waiting; for the very same Hour that we made Land, we spy'd a large Vessel sailing along the Shore, to the Southward. The Ship was of *Bengal*, belonging to the Great *Mogul*'s Country, but had on board a *Dutch* Pilot, whose Name, if I remember right, was *Vanderdiest*, and several *European* Seamen, whereof three were *English*. She was in no Condition to resist us; the rest of her Seamen were *Indians* of the *Mogul*'s Subjects, some *Malabars*, and some others. There were five *Indian* Merchants on board, and some *Armenian*: It seems they had been at *Mocha* with Spices, Silks, Diamonds, Pearls, Callicoe, &c. such Goods as the Country afforded, and had little on board now but Money in Pieces of Eight, which, by the Way, was just what we wanted; and the three *English* Seamen came along with us, and the *Dutch* Pilot would have done so too; but the two *Armenian* Merchants entreated us not to take him; for that he being their Pilot, there was none of the Men knew how to guide the Ship: So, at their Request, we refused him; but we made them promise he should not be used ill for being willing to go with us.

We got near 200000 Pieces of Eight in this Vessel; and if they said true, there was a *Jew* of *Goa* who intended to have embark'd with them, who had 200000 Pieces of Eight with him, all his own; but his good Fortune springing out of his ill Fortune, hinder'd him, for he fell sick at *Mocha*, and could not be ready to travel, which was the Saving of his Money.

There was none with me at the Taking this Prize, but the Sloop; for Captain *Wilmot*'s Ship proving leaky, he went away for the Rendezvous before us, and arrived there the Middle of *December*; but not liking the Port, he left a great Cross on Shore, with Directions written on a Plate of Lead fixt to it, for us to come after him to the great Bay of *Mangahelly*,[175] where he found a very good Harbour; but we learnt a Piece of News here, that kept us from him a great while, which the Admiral took Offence at; but we stopt his Mouth with his Share of 200000 Pieces of Eight to him and his Ship's Crew. But the Story which interrupted our coming to him was this. Between *Mangahelly* and another Point called *Cape St. Sebastian*, there came on Shore in the Night, an *European* Ship; and whether by Stress of Weather, or Want of a Pilot, I know not, but the Ship stranded, and could not be got off.

We lay in the Cove, or Harbour, where, as I have said, our Rendezvous was appointed, and had not yet been on Shore, so we had not seen the Directions our Admiral had left for us.

Our Friend *William*, of whom I have said nothing a great while, had a great Mind one Day to go on Shore, and importuned me to let him have a little Troop to go with him, for Safety, that they might see the Country. I was mightily against it for many Reasons; but particularly I told him, he knew the Natives were but Savages, and they were very treacherous, and I desired him that he would not go; and had he gone on much farther, I believe I should have downright refused him, and commanded him not to go.

But in order to perswade me to let him go, he told me, he would give me an Account of the Reason why he was so importunate. He told me, the last Night he had a Dream, which was so forcible, and made such an Impression upon his Mind, that he could not be quiet till he had made the Proposal to me to go, and if I refused him, then he thought his Dream was significant, and if not, then his Dream was at an End.

His Dream was, he said, that he went on Shore with 30 Men, of which the Cockswain he said was one, upon the Island, and that they found a Mine of Gold, and enrich'd them all; but this was not the main thing he said, but that the same Morning he had dreamt so, the Cockswain came to him just then, and told him, that he dreamt he went on Shore on the Island of *Madagascar*, and that some Men came to him and told him, they would shew him where he should get a Prize would make them all rich.

These two things put together began to weigh with me a little, tho' I was never inclined to give any Heed to Dreams; but *William*'s Importunity turn'd me effectually, for I always put a great deal of Stress upon his Judgment: So that in short, I gave them Leave to go; but I charged them not to go far off from the Sea Coast, that if they were forced down to the Sea-Side upon any Occasion, we might perhaps see them, and fetch them off with our Boats.

They went away early in the Morning, one and thirty Men of them in Number, very well arm'd, and very stout Fellows; they travell'd all the

Day, and at Night made us a Signal that all was well, from the Top of a Hill, which we had agreed on, by making a great Fire.

Next Day they march'd down the Hill on the other Side, inclining towards the Sea-Side, as they had promised, and saw a very pleasant Valley before them with a River in the Middle of it, which a little farther below them seemed to be big enough to bear small Ships: They marched a-pace towards this River, and were surprized with the Noise of a Piece going off, which by the Sound could not be far off; they listened long, but could hear no more, so they went on to the River Side, which was a very fine fresh Stream, but widened a-pace, and they kept on by the Banks of it, till almost at once it opened or widened into a good large Creek, or Harbour, about five Miles from the Sea; and that which was still more surprizing, as they marched forward, they plainly saw in the Mouth of the Harbour, or Creek, the Wreck of a Ship.

The Tide was up, as we call it, so that it[a] did not appear very much above the Water, but as they made downwards, they found it grew bigger, and bigger, and the Tide soon after ebbing out, they found it lay dry upon the Sands, and appeared to be the Wreck of a considerable Vessel, larger than could be expected in that Country.

After some time, *William* taking out his Glass to look at it more nearly, was surprized with hearing a Musquet Shot whistle by him, and immediately after that, he heard the Gun, and saw the Smoke from the other Side; upon which our Men immediately fired three Musquets to discover, if possible, what or who they were. Upon the Noise of these Guns, Abundance of Men came running down to the Shore, from among some Trees, and our Men could easily perceive that they were *Europeans*, tho' they knew not of what Nation: However, our Men halloo'd to them, as loud as they could, and by and by they got a long Pole, and set it up, and hung a white Shirt upon it for a Flag of Truce. They on the other Side saw it, by the help of their Glasses too, and quickly after, our Men see a Boat launch off from the Shore, as they thought, but it was from another Creek it seems, and immediately they came rowing over the Creek to our Men, carrying also a white Flag as a Token of Truce.

It is not easy to describe the Surprize of joy and Satisfaction that appeared on both Sides, to see not only white Men, but *English* Men, in a Place so remote; but what then must it be, when they came to know one another, and to find that they were not only Country Men, but Comrades, and that this was the very Ship that Captain *Wilmot*, our Admiral, commanded, and whose Company we had lost in the Storm at *Tobago*, after making an Agreement to Rendezvous at *Madagascar*?

They had, it seems, got Intelligence of us, when they came to the South Part of the Island, and had been a roving as far as the Gulph of *Bengal,* when they met Captain *Avery,*[176] with whom they joined, took several rich Prizes, and amongst the rest, one Ship with the great *Mogul's* Daughter, and an immense Treasure in Money and Jewels, and from thence they came about the Coast of *Coromandel,* and afterwards that of *Malabar,* into the Gulph of *Persia,* where they also took some Prize, and then designed for the South Part of *Madagascar;* but the Winds blowing hard at S.E. and S.E. by E. they came to the Northward of the Isle, and being after that separated by a furious Tempest from the N.W. they were forced into the Mouth of that Creek, where they lost their Ship. And they told us also, that they heard that Captain *Avery* himself had lost his Ship also, not far off.

When they had thus acquainted one another with their Fortunes, the poor over-joyed Men were in Haste to go back to communicate their Joy to their Comrades; and leaving some of their Men with ours, the rest went back; and *William* was so earnest to see them, that he and two more went back with them, and there he came to their little Camp where they lived. There were about a hundred and sixty Men of them in all; they had got their Guns on Shore, and some Ammunition, but a good deal of their Powder was spoil'd. However they had raised a fair Platform, and mounted twelve Pieces of Cannon upon it, which was a sufficient Defence to them on that Side of the Sea; and just at the End of the Platform they had made a Launch,[177] and a little Yard, and were all hard at Work building another little Ship, as I may call it, to go to Sea in, but they put a Stop to this Work upon the News they had of our being come in.

When our Men went into their Hutts, it was surprizing indeed to see the vast Stock of Wealth they had got, in Gold, and Silver, and Jewels, which however they told was a Trifle to what Captain *Avery,* had wherever he was gone.

It was five Days we had waited for our Men, and no News of them, and indeed, I gave them over for lost; but was surprized, after five Days waiting, to see a Ship's Boat come rowing towards us along Shore; what to make of it, I could not tell, but was at last better satisfied, when our Men told me they heard them halloo, and saw them wave their Caps to us.

In a little time they came quite up to us, and I saw Friend *William* stand up in the Boat and make Signs to us; so they came on Board: But when I saw there was but fifteen of our one and thirty Men, I asked him what was become of their Fellows? *O!* says William, *they are all very well, and my Dream is fully made good, and the Cockswain's too.*

This made me very impatient to know how the Case stood; so he told us the whole Story, which indeed surprized us all. The next Day we weighed, and stood away Southerly to join Captain *Wilmot* and his Ship at *Manga-helly*, where we found him, as I said, a little chagrin at our Stay; but we pacified him afterwards with telling him the History of *William*'s Dream, and the Consequence of it.

In the mean time, the Camp of our Comrades was so near *Mangahelly*, that our Admiral, and I, Friend *William*, and some of the Men, resolved to take the Sloop, and go and see them, and fetch them all, and their Goods, Bag and Baggage, on board our Ship, which accordingly we did; and found their Camp, their Fortifications, the Battery of Guns they had erected, their Treasure, and all the Men, just as *William* had related it; so after some Stay, we took all the Men into the Sloop, and brought them away with us.

It was some time before we knew what was become of Captain *Avery*; but after about a Month, by the Direction of the Men who had lost their Ship, we sent the Sloop to cruise along the Shore, to find out, if possible, where they were, and in about a Week's Cruise our Men found them; and particularly, that they had lost their Ship, as well as our Men had lost theirs, and that they were every Way in as bad a Condition as ours.

It was about ten Days before the Sloop returned, and Captain *Avery* with them; and this was the whole Force that, as I remember, Captain *Avery* ever had with him; for now we joined all our Companies together, and it stood thus: We had two Ships and a Sloop, in which, we had three Hundred and twenty Men, but much too few to Man them as they ought to be, the great *Portuguese* Ship requiring of her self near 400 Men to Man her compleatly: As for our lost, *but now found* Comrade, her Compliment of Men was 180, or there abouts, and Captain *Avery* had about three Hundred Men with him, whereof, he had ten Carpenters with him, most of which were taken aboard the Prize they had taken; so that, in a Word, all the Force *Avery* had at *Madagascar* in the Year 1699, or thereabouts, amounted to our three Ships, for his own was lost, as you have heard, and never had any more than about twelve Hundred Men in all.

It was about a Month after this, that all our Crews got together, and as *Avery* was unshipt, we all agreed to bring our own Company into the *Portu-guese* Man of War and the Sloop, and give Captain *Avery* the *Spanish* Frigate, with all the Tackles, and Furniture, Guns, and Ammunition for his Crew by themselves; for which they being full of Wealth, agreed to give us Forty Thousand Pieces of Eight.

It was next considered, what Course we should take: Captain *Avery*, to give him his due, proposed our building a little City here, establishing our selves on Shore, with a good Fortification, and Works proper to defend our selves; and that, as we had Wealth enough, and could encrease it to what Degree we pleased, we should content our selves to retire here, and bid

Defiance to the World. But I soon convinc'd him that this Place would be no Security to us, if we pretended to carry on our cruising Trade: For that then all the Nations of *Europe*, and indeed of that Part of the World, would be engaged to root us out. But if we resolved to live there, as in a Retirement, and plant in the Country, as private Men, and give over our Trade of Pyrating, then indeed we might Plant, and settle our selves where we pleased; but then I told him, the best Way would be to treat with the Natives, and buy a Tract of Land of them, farther up the Country, seated upon some navigable River, where Boats might go up and down for Pleasure, but not Ships to endanger us: That thus Planting the high Ground with Cattle, such as Cows and Goats, of which the Country also was full, to be sure we might live here as well as any Men in the World; and I owned to him, I thought it was a good Retreat for those that were willing to leave off, and lay down, and yet did not care to venture home and be hanged; that is to say, to run the Risque of it.

Captain *Avery*, however he made no positive Discovery of his Intentions, seemed to me to decline my Notion of going up into the Country to Plant; on the contrary, it was apparent he was of Captain *Wilmot*'s Opinion, that they might maintain themselves on Shore, and yet carry on their cruising Trade too; and upon this they resolved: But as I afterwards understood, about fifty of their Men went up the Country, and settled themselves in an Inland Place, as a Colony; whether they are there still or not, I cannot tell, or how many of them are left alive; but it's my Opinion, they are there still, and that they are considerably encreased, for as I hear, they have got some Women among them, tho' not many; for it seems five *Dutch* Women, and three or four little Girls were taken by them in a *Dutch* Ship which they afterwards took going to *Mocha*, and three of those Women marrying some of these Men, went with them to live in their new Plantation; but of this I only speak by Hear-say.

As we lay here some time, I found our People mightily divided in their Notions; some were for going this Way, and some that, till at last I began to foresee they would part Company, and perhaps we should not have Men enough to keep together, to Man the great Ship, so I took Captain *Wilmot* aside, and began to talk to him about it; but soon perceived that he enclined himself to stay at *Madagascar*, and having got a vast Wealth for his own Share, had secret Designs of getting Home some Way or other.

I argued the Impossibility of it, and the Hazard he would run, either of falling into the Hands of Thieves and Murtherers in the *Red Sea*, who would never let such a Treasure as his was pass their Hands, or of his falling into the Hands of the *English*, *Dutch*, or *French*, who would certainly hang him for a Pyrate. I gave him an Account of the Voyage I had made from this very Place to the Continent of *Africk*, and what a Journey it was to travel on Foot.

In short, nothing could perswade him, but he would go into the *Red Sea* with the Sloop, and where the Children of *Israel* past through the Sea dry-shod, and landing there, would travel to *Grand Cairo* by Land, which is not above eighty Miles, and from thence he said he could Ship himself by the Way of *Alexandria*, to any Part of the World.

I represented the Hazard, and indeed the Impossibility of his passing by *Mocha*, and *Judda*,[178] without being attack'd, if he offered it by Force; or plundered, if he went to get Leave, and explained the Reasons of it so much, and so effectually, that tho' at last he would not hearken to it himself, none of his Men would go with him. They told him, they would go any where with him, to serve him, but that this was running himself and them into certain Destruction, without any Possibility of avoiding it, or Probability of answering his End. The Captain took what I said to him quite wrong, and pretended to resent it, and gave me some Buccanier Words[179] upon it; but I gave him no Return to it, but this, that I advised him for his Advantage, that if he did not understand it so, it was his Fault, not mine; that I did not forbid him to go, nor had I offered to perswade any of the Men not to go with him, tho' it was to their apparent Destruction.

However, warm Heads are not easily cooled; the Captain was so eager, that he quitted our Company, and with most Part of his Crew, went over to Captain *Avery*, and sorted with[180] his People, taking all the Treasure with him, which, by the Way, was not very fair in him, we having agreed to share all our Gains, whether more or less, whether absent or present.

Our Men mutter'd a little at it, but I pacified them as well as I could, and told them, it was easy for us to get as much, if we minded our Hits;[181] and Captain *Wilmot* had set us a very good Example: For by the same Rule, the Agreement of any farther Sharing of Profits with them, was at an End. I took this Occasion to put into their Heads, some Part of my farther Designs, which were, to range over the Eastern Sea, and see if we could not make our selves as rich as Mr. *Avery*, who, it was true, had gotten a prodigious deal of Money, tho' not one Half of what was said of it in *Europe*.

Our Men were so pleased with my forward, enterprizing Temper, that they assured me that they would go with me, one and all, over the whole Globe, wherever I would carry them; and as for Captain *Wilmot*, they would have nothing more to do with him. This came to his Ears, and put him into a great Rage; so that he threaten'd, if I came on Shore, he would cut my Throat.

Defoe: Novels, Volume 5

I had Information of it privately, but took no Notice of it at all, only I took Care not to go unprovided for him, and seldom walked about but in very good Company. However, at last Captain *Wilmot* and I met, and talked over the Matter very seriously, and I offered him the Sloop to go where he pleased: Or, if he was not satisfied with that, I offered to take the Sloop, and leave him the great Ship. But he declined both, and only desired that I would leave him six Carpenters, which I had in our Ship, more than I had need of, to help his Men to finish the Sloop that was begun before we came thither, by the Men that lost his Ship. This I consented readily to, and lent him several other Hands that were useful to them, and in a little time they built a stout Brigantine able to carry fourteen Guns, and two Hundred Men.

What Measures they took, and how Captain *Avery* managed afterwards, is too long a Story to meddle with here; nor is it any of my Business, having my own Story still upon my Hands.

We lay here about these several simple[182] Disputes almost five Months, when about the latter End of *March* I set Sail with the great Ship, having in her forty four Guns, and four hundred Men, and the Sloop, carrying eighty Men. We did not steer to the *Malabar* Coast, and so to the Gulph of *Persia*, as was at first intended, the East Monsoons blowing yet too strong, but we kept more under the *African* Coast, where we had the Wind variable till we pass'd the Line, and made the Cape *Bassa* in the Latitude of four Degrees 10 Minutes; from thence, the Monsoons beginning to change to the N. E. and N. N. E. we led it away, with the Wind large, to the *Maldivies*, a famous Ledge of Islands, well known by all the Sailors who have gone into those Parts of the World; and, leaving these Islands a little to the South, we made Cape *Comerin*, the Southermost Land of the Coast of *Malabar*, and went round the Isle of *Ceylon*. Here we lay by a while, to wait for Purchase; and here we saw three large *English East-India* Ships going from *Bengal*, or from Fort St. *George*, homeward for *England*, or rather for *Bombay* and *Surat*, till the Trade[183] set in.

We brought to, and hoisting an *English* Ancient and Pendant,[184] lay by for them, as if we intended to attack them. They could not tell what to make of us a good while, though they saw our Colours; and, I believe, at first they thought us to be *French*; but as they came nearer to us, we let them soon see what we were, for we hoisted a black Flag with two cross Daggers[185] in it, on our Main Top-mast Head, which let them see what they were to expect.

We soon found the Effect of this; for, at first they spread their Antients, and made up to us in a Line as if they would fight us, having the Wind off Shore fair enough, to have brought them on board us; but when they saw what Force we were of, and found we were Cruisers of another kind, they stood away from us again, with all the Sail they could make. If they had come up, we should have given them an unexpect Welcome, but as it was, we had no Mind to follow them, so we let them go for the same Reasons which I mentioned before.

But though we let them pass, we did not design to let others go, at so easy a Price: It was but the next Morning that we saw a Sail, standing round Cape *Comerin*, and steering, as we thought, the same Course with us. We knew not at first what to do with her, because she had the Shore on her Larboard Quarter, and if we offered to chase her, she might put into any Port or Creek, and escape us; but to prevent this, we sent the Sloop, to get in between her and the Land; as soon as she saw that, she haled in to keep the Land aboard, and when the Sloop stood towards her, she made right ashore with all the Canvas she could spread.

The Sloop however came up with her, and engaged her, and found she was a Vessel of ten Guns, *Portuguese* built, but in the *Dutch* Traders Hands, and manned by *Dutchmen*, who were bound from the Gulph of *Persia*, to *Batavia*,[186] to fetch Spices and other Goods from thence. The Sloop's Men took her, and had the Rummaging of her before we came up. She had in her some *European* Goods, and a good round Sum of Money, and some Pearl; so that tho' we did not go to the Gulph or the Pearl, the Pearl came to us out of the Gulph, and we had our Share of it. This was a rich Ship, and the Goods were of very considerable Value, besides the Money and the Pearl.

We had a long Consultation here, what we should do with the Men; for, to give them the Ship, and let them pursue their Voyage to *Java*, would be to alarm the *Dutch* Factory there, who are by far the strongest in the *Indies*, and to make our Passage that Way impracticable; whereas we resolved to visit that Part of the World, in our Way, but were not willing to pass the great Bay of *Bengal*, where we hoped for a great deal of Purchase; and therefore it behoved us not to be Way-laid before we came there, because they knew we must pass by the Straights of *Malacca*, or those of *Sundy*,[187] and either Way it was very easy to prevent us.

While we were consulting this in the great Cabin, the Men had had the same Debate before the Mast, and it seems the Majority there were for pickling up the poor *Dutchmen* among the Herrings; in a Word, they were for throwing them all into the Sea. Poor *William* the Quaker was in great Concern about this, and comes directly to me, to talk about it. *Hark thee*, says William, *what wilt thou do with these* Dutchmen *thou hast on board, thou wilt not let them go I suppose*, says he? *Why* says I, William, *would you advise me to let them go? No*, says William, *I cannot say it is fit for thee to let them go; that is to say, to go on with their Voyage to* Batavia, *because it is not for thy Turn, that the* Dutch *at* Batavia *should have any Knowledge of thy being in these Seas. Well then*, says I, *to him, I know no Remedy but to throw them Overboard. You know* William, says I, *a* Dutchman *swims like a Fish, and all our People here are of the same Opinion as well as I; at the same time I resolved it should not be done, but wanted to hear what* William *would say: But he gravely replyed, if all the Men in the Ship were of that Mind, I will never believe that thou wilt be of that Mind thy self; for I have heard thee protest against Cruelty in all other Cases. Well* William says I, *that is true, but what then shall we do with them? Why*, says William, *is there no way but to murther them? I am perswaded thou canst not be in earnest; no indeed* William, says I, *I am not in earnest, but they shall not go to* Iava, *no nor to* Ceylon, *that is certain. But*, says William, *the Men have done thee no Injury at all, Thou hast taken a great Treasure from them, what canst thou pretend to hurt them for? Nay*, William, says I, *do not talk of that, I have Pretence enough if that be all: My Pretence is to prevent doing me hurt, and that is as necessary a Piece of the Law of Self-Preservation as any you can name; but the main Thing is, I know not what to do with them to prevent their prating.*

While *William* and I was talking, the poor *Dutchmen* were openly condemned to die as it may be called, by the whole Ship's Company; and so warm were the Men upon it, that they grew very clamorous; and when they heard that *William* was against it, some of them swore they should die, and if *William* opposed it, he should drown along with them.

But, as I was resolved to put an End to their cruel Project, so I found it was time to take upon me a little, or the bloody Humour might grow too strong; so I called the *Dutchmen* up, and talked a little with them. First, I asked them if they were willing to go with us; two of them offered it presently, but the rest, which were fourteen, declined it. Well then, said I, where would you go? They desired they should go to *Ceylon*. No, I told them, I could not allow them to go to any *Dutch* Factory, and told them very plainly the Reasons of it, which they could not deny to be just. I let them know also the cruel bloody Measures of our Men, but that I had resolved to save them, if possible, and therefore I told them, I would set them on Shore at some *English* factory in the Bay of *Bengal*, or put them on board any *English* Ship I met, after I was past the Streights of *Sundy* or of *Malacca*, but not before; for as to my coming back again, I told them, I would run the venture of their *Dutch* Power from *Batavia*, but I would not have the News come there before me, because it would make all their Merchant Ships lay up, and keep out of our Way.

It come next into our Consideration, what we should do with their Ship? but this was not long resolving; for there were but two Ways, either to set her on Fire, or to run her on Shore, and we chose the last; so we set her

Fore-Sail with the Tack at the Cat-head,[188] and leasht her Helm a little to Starboard, to answer her Head-Sail, and so set her a-going, with neither Cat or Dog in her, and it was not above two Hours before we saw her run right ashore upon the Coast, a little beyond the Cape *Comerin*, and away we went round about *Ceylon*, for the Coast of *Coromandel*.

We sailed along there, not in Sight of the Shore, only, but so near, as to see the Ships in the Road at *Fort St. David*,[189] *Fort St. George*, and at the other Factories along that Shore, as well as along the Coast of *Galconda*, carying our *English* Antient when we came near the *Dutch* Factories, and *Dutch* Colours when we past by the *English* Factories. We met with little Purchase upon this Coast, except two small Vessels of *Golconda*, bound cross the Bay with Bales of Callicoes and Muslins, and wrought Silks, and fifteen Bales of Romalls,[190] from the Bottom of the Bay, which were going, on whose Account we knew not, to *Achin*, and to other Ports on the Coast of *Malacca*; we did not enquire to what Place in particular, but we let the Vessels go, having none but *Indians* on board.

In the Bottom of the Bay, we met with a great *Jonk* belonging to the *Mogul*'s Court, with a great many People, Passengers as we supposed them to be; it seems they were bound for the River *Hugely*,[191] or *Ganges* and came from *Sumatra*; this was a Prize worth taking indeed, and we got so much Gold in her, besides other Goods which we did not meddle with, Peper in particular, that it had like to have put an End to our Cruise; for almost all my Men said we were rich enough, and desired to go back again to *Madagascar*; but I had other things in my Head still, and when I came to talk to them, and set Friend *William* to talk with them, we put such further Golden Hopes into their Heads, that we soon prevailed with them to let us go on.

My next Design was, to leave all the dangerous Streights of *Malacca*, *Sincapore*, and *Sundy*, where we could expect no great Booty, but what we might light on in *European* Ships, which we must fight for; and tho' we were able to fight, and wanted no Courage, even to Desperation; yet we were rich too, and resolved to be richer, and took this for our Maxim: That while we were sure the Wealth we sought was to be had without fighting, we had no Occasion to put our selves to the Necessity of fighting for that which would come upon easy Terms.

We left therefore the Bay of *Bengal*, and coming to the Coast of *Sumatra*, we put in at a small Port, where there was a Town, inhabited only by *Mallayans*, and here we took in fresh Water, and a large Quantity of good Pork pickled up, and well salted, notwithstanding the Heat of the Climate, being in the very Middle of the *Torrid Zone*, viz. In three Degrees, fifteen Minutes North Latitude. We also took on board both our Vessels, forty

159

Hogs alive, which served us for fresh Provisions, having Abundance of Food for them such as the Country produced; such as Guams,[192] Potatoes, and a sort of coarse Rice good for nothing else, but to feed the Swine. We killed one of these Hogs every Day, and found them to be excellent Meat. We took in also a monstrous Quantity of Ducks, and Cocks and Hens, the same kind as we have in *England*, which we kept for Change of Provisions, and if I remember right, we had no less than two Thousand of them; so that at first we were pestered with them very much, but we soon lessened them by boiling, roasting, stewing, &c. for we never wanted while we had them.

My long projected Design now lay open to me, which was, to fall in amongst the *Dutch* Spice Islands, and see what Mischief I could do there; accordingly we put out to Sea, the 12th of *August*, and passing the Line the 17th, we stood away due South leaving the Straits of *Sundy*, and the Isle of *Iava* on the East, till we came to the Latitude of eleven Degrees, twenty Minutes, when we steered East and E.N.E. having easy Gales from the W.S.W. till we came among the *Moluccas*, or Spice Islands.

We passed those Seas with less Difficulty than in other Places, the Winds to the South of *Iava*, being more variable, and the Weather good, tho' sometimes we met with Squauly Weather, and short Storms; but when we came in among the Spice Islands themselves, we had a Share of the Monsoones, or Trade Winds, and made use of them accordingly.

The infinite Number of Islands which lye in these Seas, embarrast us strangely, and it was with great Difficulty that we worked our Way thro' them; then we steered for the North Side of the *Phillipines*, where we had a double Chance for Purchase, *viz.* either to meet with the *Spanish* Ships from *Acapulco* on the Coast of *New-Spain*, or we were certain not to fail of finding some Ships or Jonks of *China*, who, if they came from *China*, would have a great Quantity of Goods of Value on Board, as well as Money; or if we took them going back, we should find them loaden with Nutmegs and Cloves from *Banda* and *Ternate*, or from some of the other Islands.

We were right in our Guesses here to a tittle, and we steered directly through a large Out-let, which they call a Streight, tho' it be fifteen Miles broad, and to an Island they call *Daurma*, and from thence N.N.E. to *Banda*; between these Islands we met with a *Dutch* Jonque, or Vessel going to *Amboyna*.[193] We took her without much Trouble, and I had much ado to prevent our Men murthering all the Men, as soon as they heard them say, they belonged to *Amboyna*, the Reason I suppose any one will guess.

We took out of her about sixteen Ton of Nutmegs, some Provisions, and their small Arms, for they had no great Guns, and let the Ship go: From thence we sailed directly to the *Banda* Island or Islands,[194] where we were sure to get more Nutmegs, if we thought fit; for my Part: I would willingly have got more Nutmegs, tho' I had paid for them, but our People abhorred paying for any thing; so we got about twelve Ton more at several times, most of them from Shore, and only a few in a small Boat of the Natives, which was going to *Gilolo*. We would have traded openly, but the *Dutch*, who have made themselves Masters of all those Islands, forbid the People dealing with us, or any Strangers whatever, and keep them so in Awe, that they durst not do it; so we could indeed have made nothing of it, if we had stay'd longer, and therefore resolved to be gone for *Ternate*,[195] and see if we could make up our Loading with Cloves.

Accordingly we stood away North, but found our selves so intangled among innumerable Islands, and without any Pilot that understood the Channel and Races between them, that we were obliged to give it over, and resolved to go back again to *Banda*, and see what we could get among the other Islands thereabouts.

The first Adventure we made here, had like to have been fatal to us all, for the Sloop being ahead, made the Signal to us for seeing a Sail, and afterwards another, and a third, by which we understood she saw three Sail, whereupon we made more Sail to come up with her, but on a sudden was gotten among some Rocks, falling foul upon them in such a Manner as frighted us all very heartily; for having it seems but just Water enough as it were to an Inch, our Rudder struck upon the Top of a Rock, which gave us a terrible Shock, and split a great Piece off of the Rudder, and indeed disabled it so, that our Ship would not steer at all; at least not so as to be depended upon, and we were glad to Hand[196] all our Sails, except our Foresail and Main-top-sail, and with them we stood away to the East, to see if we could find any Creek or Harbour, where we might lay the Ship on Shore, and repair our Rudder; besides, we found the Ship her self had received some Damage, for she had some little Leak near her Stern Post, but a great Way under Water.

By this Mischance we lost the Advantages, whatever they were, of the three Sail of Ships which we afterward came to hear, were small *Dutch* Ships from *Batavia*, going to *Banda* and *Amboyna*, to load Spice, and no doubt had a good Quantity of Money on board.

Upon the Disaster I have been speaking of, you may very well suppose that we came to an Anchor as soon as we could, which was upon a small Island not far from *Banda*, where tho' the *Dutch* keep no Factory, yet they come at the Season to buy Nutmegs and Mace. We stay'd there thirteen Days; but there being no Place where we could lay the Ship on Shore, we sent the Sloop to cruise among the Islands, to look out for a Place fit for us. In the mean time we got very good Water here, some Provisions, Roots, and Fruits, and a good Quantity of Nutmegs and Mace, which we found Ways to trade with the Natives for, without the Knowledge of their Masters the *Dutch*.

At length our Sloop return'd, having found another Island where there was a very good Harbour, we run in, and came to an Anchor. We immediately unbent[197] all our Sails, sent them ashore upon the Island, and set up seven or eight Tents with them: Then we unrigged our Top-masts, and cut them down, hoisted all our Guns out, our Provisions and Loading, and put them ashore in the Tents. With the Guns we made two small Batteries, for fear of a Surprize, and kept a Look out upon the Hill. When we were all ready, we laid the Ship a-ground upon a hard Sand, the upper End of the Harbour, and shor'd her up on each Side. At low Water she lay almost dry, so we mended her Bottom, and stopt the Leak which was occasioned by straining some of the Rudder Irons with the Shock which the Ship had against the Rock.

Having done this, we also took Occasion to clean her Bottom, which, having been at Sea so long, was very foul. The Sloop Wash'd and Tallow'd[198] also, but was ready before us, and cruised eight or ten Days among the Islands, but met with no Purchase; so that we began to be tired of the Place, having little to divert us, but the most furious Claps of Thunder that ever were read or heard of in the World.

We were in Hopes to have met with some Purchase here among the *Chinese*, who we had been told came to *Ternate* to trade for Cloves, and to the *Banda* Isles, for Nutmegs, and we could have been very glad to have loaded our Galleon, or great Ship, with these two Sorts of Spice, and have thought it a glorious Voyage; but we found nothing stirring more than what I have said, except *Dutchmen*, who by what Means we could not imagine, had either a Jealousy[199] of us, or Intelligence of us, and kept themselves close in their Ports.

I was once resolved to have made a Descent at the Island of *Dumas*,[200] the Place most famous for the best Nutmegs; but Friend *William*, who was always for doing our Business without Fighting, disswaded me from it, and gave such Reasons for it, that we could not resist; particularly the great Heats of the Season, and of the Place, for we were now in the Latitude of just half a Degree South; but while we were disputing this Point, we were soon determined by the following Accident. We had a strong Gale of Wind at S. W. by W. and the Ship had fresh Way, but a great Sea rolling in upon us from the N.E. which we afterwards found was the Pouring in of the Great Ocean East of *New Guinea*. However, as I said, we stood away large,[201] and made fresh Way, when on the sudden, from a dark Cloud which hover'd over our Heads, came a Flash, or rather Blast of Lightning, which was so terrible, and quiver'd so long among us, that not I only, but all our Men thought the Ship was on Fire. The Heat of the Flash or Fire was so sensibly felt in our Faces, that some of our Men had Blisters raised by it on their Skins, not immediately perhaps by the Heat, but by the poisonous or noxious Particles, which mix'd themselves with the Matter inflam'd. But this was not all; the Shock of the Air which the Fracture in the Clouds made, was such, that our Ship shook as when a Broadside is fired, and her Motion being check'd as it were at once by a Repulse superior to the Force that gave her Way before, the Sails all flew back in a Moment, and the Ship lay, as we might truly say, Thunder-struck. As the Blast from the Cloud was so very near us, it was but a few Moments after the Flash, that the terriblest Clap of Thunder followed that was ever heard by Mortals. I firmly believe a Blast of a Hundred Thousand Barrels of gunpowder could not have been greater to our Hearing; nay indeed, to some of our Men it took away their Hearing.

It is not possible for me to describe, or any one to conceive the Terrour of that Minute. Our Men were in such a Consternation, that not a Man on board the Ship had Presence of Mind to apply to the proper Duty of a Sailor, except Friend *William*; and had not he run very nimbly, and with a Composure that I am sure I was not Master of, to let go the Fore-sheet,[202] set in the Weather Brace of the Fore-yard, and haul'd down the Topsails, we had certainly brought all our Masts by the Board, and perhaps have been overwhelm'd in the Sea.

As for my self, I must confess my Eyes were open to my Danger, tho' not the least to any thing of Application for Remedy. I was all Amazement and Confusion, and this was the first Time that I can say I began to feel the Effects of that Horrour which I know since much more of, upon the just Reflection on my former Life. I thought my self doom'd by Heaven to sink that Moment into eternal Destruction; and with this peculiar Mark of Terror, *viz.* That the Vengeance was not executed in the ordinary Way of human Justice, but that God had taken me into his immediate Disposing, and had resolved to be the Executer of his own Vengeance.

Let them alone describe the Confusion I was in, who know what was the Case of — *Child of Shadwell*, or *Francis Spira*.[203] It is impossible to describe. My Soul was all Amazement and Surprize; I thought my self just sinking into Eternity, owning the divine Justice of my Punishment, but not at all feeling any of the moving, softning Tokens of a sincere Penitent, afflicted at the Punishment, but not at the Crime, alarmed at the Vengeance, but not terrify'd at the Guilt, having the same Gust to the Crime, tho' terrified to the last Degree at the Thought of the Punishment, which I concluded I was just now going to receive.

But perhaps many that read this will be sensible of the Thunder and Lighting, that may think nothing of the rest, or rather may make a Jest of it all, so I say no more of it at this time, but proceed to the Story of the Voyage. When the Amazement was over, and the Men began to come to themselves, they fell a calling for one another, every one for his Friend, or for those he had most Respect for; and it was a singular Satisfaction to find that no body was hurt. The next thing was to enquire if the Ship had received no Damage, when the Boatswain stepping forward, found that Part of the Head[204] was gone, but not so as as to endanger the Bolt-sprit; so we hoisted our Topsails again, hauled aft the Fore-sheet, brac'd the Yards, and went our Course as before: Nor can I deny but that we were all somewhat like the Ship, our first Astonishment being a little over, and that we found the Ship swim again, we were soon the same irreligious hardned Crew that we were before, and I among the rest.

As we now steer'd, our Course lay N.N.E. and we passed thus with a fair Wind, thro' the Streight or Channel between the Island of *Gilolo*,[205] and the Land of *Nova Guinea*, when we were soon in the open Sea or Ocean, on the South East of the *Philippines*, being the great Pacifick, or South Sea, where it may be said to join it self with the vast *Indian* Ocean.

As we passed into these Seas steering due North, so we soon cross'd the Line to the North Side, and so sailed on towards *Mindanoa* and *Manilla*, the chief of the *Philippine* Islands, without meeting with any Purchase, till we came to the Northward of *Manilla*, and then our Trade began; for here we took three *Japonese* Vessels, tho' at some Distance from *Manilla*. Two of them had made their Market, and were going Home with Nutmegs, Cinnamon, Cloves, &c. besides all Sorts of *European* Goods brought with the *Spanish* Ships from *Acapulco*. They had together eight and thirty Ton of Cloves, and five or six Ton of Nutmegs, and as much Cinnamon. We took the Spice, but meddled with very little of the *European* Goods, they being, as we thought, not worth our while, but we were very sorry for it soon after, and therefore grew wiser upon the next Occasion.

The third *Japonese* was the best Prize to us, for he came with Money, and a great deal of Gold uncoin'd, to buy such Goods as we mentioned above: We eased him of his Gold, and did him no other Harm, and having no Intention to stay long here, we stood away for *China*.

We were at Sea above two Months upon this Voyage, beating it up against the Wind, which blew steadily from the North East, and within a Point or two one Way or other; and this indeed was the Reason why we met with the more Prizes in our Voyage.

We were just gotten clear of the *Philippines*, and as we purposed to go to the Isle of *Formosa*,[206] when the Wind blew so fresh at N.N.E. that there was no making any thing of it, and we were forced to put back to *Laconia*,[207] the most Northerly of those Islands. We rode here very secure, and shifted our Situation not in View of any Danger, for there was none, but for a better Supply of Provisions, which we found the People very willing to supply us with.

There lay while we remained here, three very great Galleons or *Spanish* Ships, from the South Seas, whether newly come in, or ready to sail, we could not understand at first; but as we found the *China* Traders began to load and set forward to the North, we concluded the *Spanish* Ships had newly unloaded their Cargo, and these had been buying; so we doubted not but we should meet with Purchase in the rest of our Voyage, neither indeed could we well miss of it.

We stay'd here till the beginning of *May*, when we were told the *Chinese* Traders would set forward, for the Northern Monsoons end about the latter End of *March*, or the Beginning of *April*; so that they are sure of fair Winds Home. Accordingly we hired some of the Country Boats, which are very swift Sailers, to go and bring us Word how Affairs stood at *Manilla*, and when the *China* Jonks would sail, and by this Intelligence we ordered our Matters so well, that three Days after we set Sail, we fell in with no less than eleven of them, out of which however having by Misfortune of discovering our selves, taken but three, we contented our selves, and pursued our Voyage to *Formosa*. In these three Vessels we took in short such a Quantity of Cloves, Nutmegs, Cinnamon, and Mace, besides Silver, that our Men began to be of my Opinion, *That we were rich enough*; and in short, we had nothing to do now, but to consider by what Methods to secure the immense Treasure we had got.

I was secretly glad to hear, that they were of this Opinion; for I had long before resolved, if it was possible, to perswade them to think of returning, having fully perfected my first projected Design, of Rummaging among the Spice Islands, and all those Prizes, which were exceeding rich at *Manilla*, was quite beyond my Design.

But now I had heard what the Men said, and how they thought we were very well. I let them know by Friend *William*, that I intended only to sail to the Island *Formosa*, where I should find Opportunity to turn our Spices and *European* Goods into ready Money, and that then I would tack about for the South, the Northern Monsoons being perhaps by that time also ready to set in. They all approved of my Design, and willingly went forward, because, besides the Winds, which would not permit until *October*, to go to the South: I say, besides this, we were now a very deep Ship, having near two Hundred Ton of Goods on board, and particularly some very valuable. The Sloop also had a Proportion.

With this Resolution we went on chearfully, when within about twelve Days Sail more, we made the Island *Formosa*, at a great Distance, but were our selves shot beyond the Southermost Part of the Island, being to Leeward, and almost upon the Coast of *China*. Here we were a little at a Loss; for the *English* Factories were not far off, and we might be obliged to fight some of their Ships, if we met with them; which tho' we were able enough to do, yet we did not desire it on many Accounts; and particularly because we did not think it was our business to have it known who we were, or that such a kind of People as we had been seen on the Coast. However, we were obliged to keep up to the Northward, keeping as good an Offing as we could, with respect to the Coast of *China*. We had not sailed long, but we chased a small *Chinese* Jonk; and having taken her, we found she was bound to the Island of *Formosa*, having no Goods on board but some Rice, and a small Quantity of Tea; but she had three *Chinese* Merchants in her, and they told us they were going to meet a large Vessel of their Country, which came from *Tonquin*, and lay in a River in *Formosa* whose Name I forget, and they were going to the *Philippine* Islands, with Silks, Muslins, Callicoes, and such Goods as are the Product of *China*, and some Gold; that their Business was to sell their Cargo, and buy Spices and *European* Goods.

This suited very well with our Purpose; so I resolved now that we would leave off being Pyrates, and turn Merchants; so we told them what Goods we had on board, and that if they would bring their Super-Cargoes or Merchants on board, we would trade with them. They were very willing to trade with us, but terribly afraid to trust us; nor was it an unjust Fear, for we had plundered them already of what they had. On the other Hand, we were as diffident as they, and very uncertain what to do; but *William* the Quaker put this Matter into a Way of Barter. He came to me, and told me he really thought the Merchants look'd like fair Men, that meant honestly; and besides, says *William*, it is their Interest to be honest now; for as they know upon what Terms we got the Goods we are to truck with them, so they know we can afford good Pennyworths; and in the next Place, it saves them going the whole Voyage: So that the Southerly Monsoons yet holding, if they traded with us, they could immediately return with their Cargo to *China, tho' by the Way we afterwards found they intended for* Japan. But that was all one, for by this Means they sav'd at least eight Months Voyage. Upon these Foundations *William* said he was satisfied we might trust them: For, says *William*, I would as soon trust a Man whose Interest binds him to be just to me, as a Man whose Principle binds himself. Upon the whole, *William* proposed that two of the Merchants should be left on board our Ship as Hostages, and that Part of our Goods should be loaded in their Vessel, and let the third go with it into the Port where their Ship lay; and when he had delivered the Spices, he should bring back such things as it was agreed should be exchanged. This was concluded on, and *William* the Quaker ventured to go along with them, which upon my Word I should not have cared to have done, nor was I willing that he should; but he went still upon the Notion, that it was their Interest to treat him friendly.

In the mean time we came to an Anchor under a little Island, in the Latitude of 23 Degrees, 28 Minutes, being just under the Northern Tropick, and about twenty Leagues from the Island. Here we lay thirteen Days, and I began to be very uneasy for my Friend *William*, for they had promised to be back again in four Days, which they might very easily have done. However, at the End of thirteen Days we saw three Sail coming directly to us, which a little surprized us all at first, not knowing what might be the Case, and we began to put our selves in a Posture of Defence; but as they came nearer us, we were soon satisfy'd: For the first Vessel was that which *William* went in, who carried a Flag of Truce, and in a few Hours they all came to an Anchor, and *William* came on board us with a little Boat, with the *Chinese* Merchant in his Company, and two other Merchants, which seem'd to be a kind of Brokers for the rest.

Here he gave us an Account, how civilly he had been used, how they had treated him with all imaginable Frankness and Openness, that they had not only given him the full Value of his Spices and other Goods which he carry'd, in Gold, by good Weight, but had loaded the Vessel again with such Goods as he knew we were willing to trade for; and that afterwards they had resolved to bring the great Ship out of the Harbour, to lye where we were, that so we might make what Bargain we thought fit; only *William* said he had promised in our Name, that we should use no Violence with them, nor detain any of the Vessels after we had done trading with them. I told him, we would strive to outdo them in Civility, and that we would make good every Part of his Agreement. In Token whereof I caused a white Flag likewise to be spread at the Poop[208] of our great Ship, which was the Signal agreed on.

As to the third Vessel which came with them, it was a kind of Bark of the Country, who having Intelligence of our Design to traffick, came off to deal with us, bringing a great deal of Gold, and some Provisions, which at that time we were very glad of.

In short, we traded upon the high Seas with these Men, and indeed we made a very good Market, and yet sold Thieves Pennyworths too. We sold here above sixty Ton of Spice, chiefly Cloves and Nutmegs, and above two Hundred Bales of *European* Goods; such as Linnen and Wollen Manufactures. We considered we should have Occasion for some such things our selves, and so we kept a good Quantity of *English* Stuffs, Cloaths, Bays, &c.

for our selves. I shall not take up any of the little Room I have left here, with the further Particulars of our Trade; 'tis enough to mention, that except a Parcel of Tea, and twelve Bales of fine *China* wrought Silks, we took nothing in Exchange for our Goods but Gold: So that the Sum we took here in that glittering Commodity, amounted to above Fifty Thousand Ounces good Weight.

When we had finished our Barter, we restored the Hostages, and gave the three Merchants about the Quantity of Twelve Hundred Weight of Nutmegs, and as many of Cloves, with a handsom Present of *European* Linnen and Stuff for themselves, as a Recompence for what we had taken from them; and so we sent them away exceedingly well satisfy'd.

Here it was that *William* gave me an Account, that while he was on board the *Japonese* Vessel, he met with a kind of Religious, or *Japan* Priest, who spoke some Words of *English* to him; and being very inquisitive to know how he came to learn any of those Words, he told him, that there was in his Country *thirteen Englishmen*; he called them *Englishmen* very articulately and distinctly, for he had conversed with them very frequently and freely: He said they were all that were left of two and thirty Men, who came on Shore on the North Side of *Japan*, being driven upon a great Rock in a stormy Night, where they lost their Ship, and the rest of their Men were drowned: That he had perswaded the King of his Country to send Boats off to the Rock or Island, where the Ship was lost, to save the rest of the Men, and to bring them on Shore; which was done, and they were used very kindly; and had Houses built for them, and Land given them to plant for Provision, and that they lived by themselves.

He said he went frequently among them, to perswade them to worship their God, an Idol, I suppose, of their own making, which he said they ungratefully refused; and that therefore the King had once or twice ordered them to be all put to Death; but that, *as he said*, he had prevailed upon the King to spare them, and let them live their own Way, as long as they were quiet and peaceable, and did not go about to withdraw others from the Worship of the Country.

I ask'd *William*, why he did not enquire from whence they came? I did, *said William*, for how could I but think it strange, said he, to hear him talk of *English* Men on the North Side of *Japan*. Well, said I, what Account did he give of it? An Account, said *William*, that will surprize thee, and all the World after thee, that shall hear of it, and which makes me wish thou wouldst go up to *Japan*, and find them out. What do ye mean, said I? Whence could they come? Why, says *William*, he pull'd out a little Book, and in it a Piece of Paper, where it was written in an *English* Man's Hand, and in plain *English* Words, thus; and says *William*, I read it my self: *We came from Greenland*, and from the *North Pole*. This indeed was amazing to us all, and more to those Seamen among us who knew any thing of the infinite Attempts which had been made from *Europe*, as well by the *English* as the *Dutch*, to discover a Passage that Way into those Parts of the World; and as *William* press'd us earnestly to go on to the North, to rescue those poor Men, so the Ship's Company began to incline to it; and in a Word, we all came to this, that we would stand in to the Shore of *Formosa*, to find this Priest again, and have a farther Account of it all from him. Accordingly the Sloop went over, but when they came there, the Vessels were very unhappily sail'd and this put an End to our Enquiry after them, and perhaps may have disappointed Mankind of one of the most noble Discoveries that ever was made, or will again be made in the World, for the Good of Mankind in general: But so much for that.

William was so uneasy at losing this Opportunity, that he press'd us earnestly to go up to *Japan*, to find out these Men. He told us, that if it was nothing but to recover Thirteen honest poor Men from a kind of Captivity, which they would otherwise never be redeemed from, and where perhaps they might some time or other be murdered by the barbarous People, in Defence of their Idolatry; it were very well worth our while, and it would be in some Measure making amends for the Mischiefs we had done in the World: But we that had no Concern upon us for the Mischiefs we had done, had much less about any Satisfaction to be made for it; so he found that kind of Discourse would weigh very little with us. Then he press'd us very earnestly to let him have the Sloop to go by himself, and I told him I would not oppose it; but when he came to the Sloop, none of the Men would go with him; for the Case was plain, they had all a Share in the Cargo of the great Ship, as well as in that of the Sloop, and the Richness of the Cargo was such, that they would not leave it by any means: So poor *William*, much to his Mortification, was obliged to give it over. What became of those thirteen Men, or whether they are not there still, I can give no Account of.

We were now at the End of our Cruise; what we had taken was indeed so considerable, that it was not only enough to satisfy the most covetous and the most ambitious Minds in the World, but it did indeed satisfy us; and our Men declared they did not desire any more. The next Motion therefore was about going back, and the Way by which we should perform the Voyage, so as not to be attack'd by the *Dutch* in the Straits of *Sundy*.[209]

We had pretty well stored our selves here with Provisions, and it being now near the Return of the Monsoons, we resolved to stand away to the Southward; and not only to keep without the *Philippine* Islands, that is to say, to the Eastward of them, but to keep on to the Southward, and see if we could not leave, not only the *Molucco's*, or Spice Islands, behind us, but even *Nova Guinea* and *Nova Hollandia* also; and so getting into the variable Winds, to the South of the Tropick of *Capricorn*, steer away to the West, over the great *Indian* Ocean.

This was indeed at first a monstrous Voyage in its Appearance, and the Want of Provisions threaten'd us. *William* told us in so many Words, that it was impossible we could carry Provisions enough to subsist us for such a Voyage, and especially fresh Water; and that as there would be no Land for us to touch at, where we could get any Supply, it was a Madness to undertake it.

But I undertook to remedy this Evil, and therefore desired them not to be uneasy at that, for I knew we might supply our selves at *Mindanao*, the most Southerly Island of the *Philippines*. Accordingly, we set Sail, having taken all the Provisions here that we could get, the 28th of *September*, the Wind veering a little at first from the N.N.W. to the N.E. by E. but afterwards settled about the N.E. and the E.N.E. We were nine Weeks in this Voyage, having met with several Interruptions by the Weather, and put in under the Lee of a small Island in the Latitude of 16 Degrees, 12 Minutes, of which we never knew the Name, none of our Charts having given any Account of it: I say, we put in here, by reason of a strange *Tornado* or Hurricane, which brought us into a great deal of Danger. Here we rode about sixteen Days, the Winds being very tempestuous, and the Weather uncertain. However, we got some Provisions on Shore, such as Plants and Roots, and a few Hoggs. We believed there were Inhabitants on the Island, but we saw none of them.

From hence, the Weather settling again, we went on, and came to the Southmost Part of *Mindanao*, where we took in fresh Water, and some Cows; but the Climate was so hot, that we did not attempt to salt up any more, than so as to keep a Fortnight or three Weeks, and away we stood South ward crossing the Line, and leaving *Gillolo* on the Starboard Side, we coasted the Country they call *New Guiney*, where, in the Latitude of eight Degrees South, we put in again for Provisions and Water, and where we found Inhabitants, but they fled from us, and were altogether inconversable. From thence, sailing still Southward, we left all behind us that any of our Charts or Maps take any Notice of, and went on till we came to the Latitude of 17 Degrees, the Wind continuing still N.E.

Here we made Land to the Westward, which when we had kept in Sight for three Days, coasting along the Shore, for the Distance of about four Leagues, we began to fear we should find no Outlet West, and so should be obliged to go back again, and put in among the *Molucco's* at last; but at length we found the Land break off, and go trending away to the West Sea, seeming to be all open to the South and S. W. and a great Sea came rowling out of the South, which gave us to understand, that there was no Land that Way for a great Way.

In a Word, we kept on our Course to the South, a little Westerly, till we pass'd the South Tropick, where we found the Winds variable; and now we stood away fair West, and held it out for about twenty Days, when we discovered Land right-a-head, and on our Larboard Bow, we made directly to the Shore, being willing to take all Advantages now for supplying our selves with fresh Provisions and Water, knowing we were now entering on that vast unknown *Indian* Ocean, perhaps the greatest Sea on the Globe, having with very little Interruption of Islands, a continued Sea quite round the Globe.

We found a good Road here, and some People on Shore; but when we landed, they fled up the Country, nor would they hold any Correspondence with us, or come near us, but shot at us several Times with Arrows as long as Launces. We set up white Flags for a Truce, but they either did not, or would not, understand it: On the contrary, they shot our Flag of Truce thro' several times with their Arrows; so that, in a Word, we never came near any of them.

We found good Water here, tho' it was something difficult to get at it, but for living Creatures we could see none; for the People, if they had any Cattle, drove them all away, and shew'd us nothing but themselves, and that sometimes in a threatening Posture, and in Number so great, that made us suppose the Island to be greater than we at first imagined. It is true, they would not come near enough for us to engage with them, at least, not openly; but they came near enough for us to see them, and by the Help of our Glasses, to see that they were clothed and arm'd, but their Clothes were only about their lower and middle Parts; that they had long Launces, like Half Pikes, in their Hands, besides Bows and Arrows; that they had great high Things on their Heads, made, as we believed, of Feathers, and which look'd something like our Grenadiers Caps in *England*.

When we saw them so shye, that they would not come near us, our Men began to range over the Island, *if it was such, for we never surrounded it*, to search for Cattel, and for any of the *Indians* Plantations, for Fruits or Plants; but they soon found, to their Cost, that they were to use more Caution than that came to, and that they were to discover perfectly every Bush and every Tree, before they ventured abroad in the Country; for, about fourteen of our Men going further than the rest, into a Part of the Country which seemed to be planted, as they thought, for it did but seem so, only I think it was overgrown with Canes, such as we make our Cane Chairs with: I say, venturing too far, they were suddenly attack'd with a Shower of

Arrows from almost every Side of them, as they thought, out of the Tops of the Trees.

They had nothing to do, but to fly for it, which however they could not resolve on, till five of them were wounded; nor had they escaped so, if one of them had not been so much wiser, or thoughtfuller than the rest, as to consider, that tho' they could not see the Enemy, so as to shoot at them, yet perhaps the Noise of their Shot might terrify them, and that they should rather fire at a Venture. Accordingly Ten of them faced about, and fired at random any where among the Canes.

The Noise and the Fire not only terrify'd the Enemy, but, as they believed, their Shot had luckily hit some of them; for they found not only that the Arrows which came thick among them before, ceased, but they heard the *Indians* halloo, after their Way, to one another, and make a strange Noise more uncouth and inimitably strange, than any they had ever heard, more like the Howling and Barking of wild Creatures in the Woods, than like the Voice of Men, only that sometimes they seemed to speak Words.

They observ'd also, that this Noise of the *Indians* went farther and farther off, so that they were satisfied the *Indians* fled away, except on one Side, where they heard a doleful Groaning and Howling, and where it continued a good while, which they supposed was from some or other of them being wounded, and howling by reason of their Wounds; or kill'd, and others howling over them: But our Men had enough of making Discoveries; so they did not trouble themselves to look farther, but resolved to take this Opportunity to retreat. But the worst of their Adventure was to come; for as they came back, they pass'd by a prodigious great Trunk of an old Tree, what Tree it was they said they did not know, but it stood like an old decay'd Oak in a Park, where the Keepers in *England* take *a Stand* as they call it, to shoot a Deer, and it stood just under the steep Side of a great Rock or Hill, that our People could not see what was beyond it.

As they came by this Tree, they were of a sudden shot at from the Top of the Tree, with seven Arrows and three Launces, which, to our great Grief, kill'd two of our Men, and wounded three more. This was the more surprizing, because being without any Defence, and so near the Trees, they expected more Launces and Arrows every Moment; nor would flying do them any Service, the *Indians* being, as appeared, very good Marksmen. In this Extremity they had happily this Presence of Mind, *viz.* to run close to the Tree, and stand, as it were under it; so that those above could not come at, or see them, to throw their Launces at them. This succeeded, and gave them Time to consider what to do: They knew their Enemies and Murtherers were above, for they heard them talk, and those above knew those were below; but they below were obliged to keep close for fear of their Launces from above. At length, one of our Men looking a little more strictly than the rest, thought he saw the Head of one of the *Indians*, just over a dead Limb of the Tree, which, it seems, the Creature sat upon. One Man immediately fired, and levell'd his Piece so true, that the Shot went thro' the Fellow's Head, and down he fell out of the Tree immediately, and came upon the Ground with such Force, with the Height of his Fall, that if he had not been killed with the Shot, he would certainly have been killed with dashing his Body against the Ground.

This so frighted themselves, that besides the howling Noise they made in the Tree, our Men heard a strange Clutter[210] of them in the Body of the Tree, from whence they concluded they had made the Tree hollow, and were got to hide themselves there. Now, had this been the Case, they were secure enough from our Men; for it was impossible any of our Men could get up the Tree on the Out-side, there being no Branches to climb by; and, to shoot at the Tree, that they tried several times to no Purpose, for the Tree was so thick, that no Shot would enter it. They made no Doubt however, but that they had their Enemies in a Trap, and that a small Siege would either bring them down Tree and all, or starve them out: So they resolved to keep their Post, and send to us for Help. Accordingly two of them came away to us for more Hands, and particularly desired, that some of our Carpenters might come with Tools, to help cut down the Tree, or at least to cut down other Wood, and set Fire to it; and That they concluded would not fail to bring them out.

Accordingly our Men went like a little Army, and with mighty Preparations for an Enterprize, the like of which has scarce been ever heard, to form the Siege of a great Tree. However, when they came there, they found the Task difficult enough, for the old Trunk was indeed a very great one, and very tall, being at least Two and Twenty Foot high, with seven old Limbs standing out every Way on the Top, but decay'd and very few Leaves, if any, left on it.

William the Quaker, whose Curiosity led him to go among the rest, proposed, that they should make a Ladder, and get up upon the Top, and then throw Wild-fire into the Tree, and smoke them out. Others proposed going back, and getting a great Gun out of the Ship, which should split the Tree in Pieces with the Iron Bullets: Others, that they should cut down a great deal of Wood, and pile it up round the Tree, and set it on Fire, and to burn the Tree, and the *Indians* in it.

These Consultations took up our People no less than two or three Days, in all which Time they heard nothing of the supposed Garrison within this wooden Castle, nor any Noise within. *William*'s Project was first gone about, and a large strong Ladder was made, to scale this wooden Tower; and in two or three Hours time, it would have been ready to mount: When, on a sudden, they heard the Noise of the *Indians* in the Body of the Tree again, and a little after, several of them appeared in the Top of the Tree, and threw some Launces down at our Men; one of which struck one of our Seamen a-top of the Shoulder, and gave him such a desperate Wound, that the Surgeons not only had a great deal of Difficulty to cure him, but the poor Man endured such horrible Tortures, that we all said they had better have killed him outright. However, he was cured at last, tho' he never recover'd the perfect Use of his Arm, the Launce having cut some of the Tendons on the Top of the Arm, near the Shoulder, which, as I suppose, performed the Office of Motion to the Limb before; so that the poor Man was a Criple all the Days of his life. But to return to the desperate Rogues in the Tree; our Men shot at them, but did not find they had hit them, or any of them; but as soon as ever they shot at them, they could hear them huddle down into the Trunk of the Tree again, and there to be sure they were safe.

Well, however, it was this which put by the Project of *William's* Ladder; for when it was done, who would venture up among such a Troop of bold Creatures as were there? And who, they supposed, were desperate by their Circumstances: And as but one Man at a time could go up, they began to think that it would not do; and indeed I was of the Opinion, *for about this time I was come to their Assistance*, that the going up the Ladder would not do unless it was thus, that a Man should, as it were run just up to the Top, and throw some Fire-works into the Tree, and so come down again; and this we did two or three Times, but found no Effect of it. At last, one of our Gunners made a Stink-pot, as we called it, being a Composition which only smokes, but does not flame or burn; but withal the Smoke of it is so thick, and the Smell of it so intolerably nauseous, that it is not to be suffered. This he threw into the Tree himself, and we waited for the Effect of it, but heard or saw nothing all that Night, or the next Day; so we concluded the Men within were all smother'd: When, on a sudden, the next Night, we heard them upon the Top of the Tree again, shouting and hallooing like Madmen.

We concluded, as any body would, that this was to call for Help, and we resolved to continue our Siege; for we were all enraged to see our selves so baulk'd by a few wild People whom we thought we had safe in our Clutches; and indeed never was there so many concurring Circumstances to delude Men, in any Case we had met with. We resolved however to try another Stink-pot the next Night, and our Engineer and Gunner had got it ready, when hearing a Noise of the Enemy, on the Top of the Tree, and in the Body of the Tree, I was not willing to let the Gunner go up the Ladder, which, I said, would be but to be certain of being murthered. However, he found a *Medium*[211] for it, and that was to go up a few Steps, and with a long Pole in his Hand, to throw it in upon the Top of the Tree, the Ladder being standing all this while against the Top of the Tree; but when the Gunner, with his Machine at the Top of his Pole, came to the Tree with three other Men to help him, behold the Ladder was gone.

This perfectly confounded us, and we now concluded the *Indians* in the Tree had by this Piece of Negligence taken the Opportunity, and come all down the Ladder, made their Escape, and had carried away the Ladder with them. I laugh'd most heartily at my Friend *William*, who, as I said, had the Direction of the Siege, and had set up a Ladder, for the Garrison, *as we called them*, to get down upon, and run away. But when Day-Light came, we were all set to rights again; for there stood our Ladder haul'd up on the Top of the Tree, with about Half of it in the Hollow of the Tree, and the other Half upright in the Air. Then we began to laugh at the *Indians* for Fools, that they could not as well have found their Way down by the Ladder, and have made their Escape, as to have pull'd it up by main Strength into the Tree.

We then resolved upon Fire, and so to put an End to the Work at once, and burn the Tree and its Inhabitants together; and accordingly we went to Work to cut Wood, and in a few Hours time we got enough, as we thought, together; and piling it up round the Bottom of the Tree, we set it on Fire: So waiting at a Distance, to see when the Gentlemens Quarters being too hot for them, they would come flying out at the Top. But we were quite confounded, when, on a sudden, we found the Fire all put out by a great Quantity of Water thrown upon it. We then thought the Devil must be in them to be sure. Says *William*, this is certainly the cunningest Piece of *Indian* Engineering that ever was heard of, and there can be but one thing more to guess at, besides Witchcraft and Dealing with the Devil, *which I believe not one Word of, says he*; and that must be, that this is an artificial Tree, or a natural Tree artificially made hollow down into the Earth, thro' Root and all; and that these Creatures have an artificial Cavity underneath it, quite into the Hill, or a Way to go thro', and under the Hill, to some other Place, and where that other Place is, we know not; but if it be not our own Fault, I'll find the Place, and follow them into it, before I am two Days older. He then called the Carpenters to know of them, if they had any large Saws that would cut thro' the Body, and they told him they had not any Saws that were long enough, nor could Men work into such a monstrous old Stump in a great while; but that they would go to Work with it with their Axes, and undertake to cut it down in two Days, and stock up the Root of it in two more. But *William* was for another Way, which proved much better than all this; for he was for silent Work, that, if possible, he might catch some of the Fellows in it; so he sets twelve Men to it with large Augurs, to bore great Holes into the Side of the Tree, to go almost thro', but not quite thro'; which Holes were bored without Noise, and when they were done, he filled them all with Gun-Powder, stopping strong Plugs bolted cross-ways into the Holes, and then boring a slanting Hole of a less Size down into the greater Hole, all which were fill'd with Powder, and at once blown up. When they took Fire, they made such a Noise, and tore and split the Tree in so many Places, and in such a Manner, that we could see plainly, such another Blast would demolish it, and so it did. Thus at the second time we could at two or three Places put our Hands into them, and discovered the Cheat, namely, that there was a Cave or Hole dug into the Earth, from, or thro' the Bottom of the hollow, and that it had Communication with another Cave further in, where we heard the Voices of several of the wild Folks calling and talking to one another.

When we came thus far we had a great Mind to get at them, and *William* desired, that three Men might be given him with Hand-Grenadoes, and he promised to go down first, and boldly he did so; for *William*, give him his due, had the Heart of a Lion.

They had Pistols in their Hands, and Swords by their Sides; but, as they had taught the *Indians* before, by their Stink-Pots, the *Indians* returned them in their own Kind, for they made such a Smoke come up out of the Entrance into the Cave or Hollow, that *William* and his three Men, were glad to come running out of the Cave, and out of the Tree too, for mere want of Breath, and indeed they were almost stifled.

Never was a Fortification so well defended, or Assailants so many ways defeated; we were now for giving it over, and particularly I called *William*, and told him, I could not but laugh to see us spinning out our Time here for nothing; that I could not imagine what we were doing, that it was certain the Rogues that were in it were cunning to the last Degree, and it would vex any Body to be so baulked by a few naked ignorant Fellows; but still it was not worth our while to push it any further, nor was there any thing that I knew of to be got by the Conquest when it was made, so that I thought it high time to give it over.

William acknowledged, that what I said was just, and that there was nothing but our Curiosity to be gratified in this Attempt; and tho', as *he said*, he was very desirous to have searched into the Thing, yet he would not insist upon it, so we resolved to quit it, and come away, which we did. However, *William* said, before we went, he would have this Satisfaction of them, *viz.* that he burnt down the Tree and stop up the Entrance into the

Cave. While he was doing this, the Gunner told him, he would have one Satisfaction of the Rogues, and this was, that he would make a Mine of it, and see which way it had Vent: Upon this he fetches two Barrels of Powder out of the Ships, and placed them in the Inside of the hollow Cave, as far in as he durst go to carry them, and then filling up the Mouth of the Cave where the Tree stood, and ramming it sufficiently hard, leaving only a Pipe or Touch-hole, he gave Fire to it, and stood at a Distance to see which way it would operate, when, on the sudden, he found the Force of the Powder burst its way out among some Bushes on the other Side the little Hill I mentioned, and that it came roaring out there as out of the Mouth of a Cannon; immediately running thither we saw the Effects of the Powder.

First, we saw that *there* was the other Mouth of the Cave, which the Powder had so torn and open'd, that the loose Earth was so fallen in again, that nothing of Shape could be discerned; but there we saw what was become of the Garrison of *Indians* too, who had given us all this Trouble; for some of them had no Arms, some no Legs, some no Head, some lay half buried in the Rubbish of the Mine, that is to say, in the loose Earth that fell in; and, in short, there was a miserable havock made of them all, for we had good Reason to believe, not one of them that were in the Inside could escape, but rather were shot out of the Mouth of the Cave like a Bullet out of a Gun.

We had now our full Satisfaction of the *Indians*, but, in short, this was a losing Voyage, for we had two Men killed, one quite crippled, five more wounded; we spent two Barrels of Powder, and eleven Days Time, and all to get the Understanding how to make an *Indian* Mine, or how to keep Garrison in a hollow Tree, and with this Wit bought at this dear Price, we came away, having taken in some fresh Water, but got no fresh Provisions.

We then considered what we should do to get back again to *Madagascar*; we were much about the Latitude of the *Cape of Good Hope*, but had such a very long Run, and were neither sure of meeting with fair Winds, or with any Land in the Way, that we knew not what to think of it. *William* was our last Resort in this Case again, and he was very plain with us. Friend, *said he*, to me,[a] what Occasion hast thou to run the Venture of starving, merely for the Pleasure of saying, thou hast been where no Body ever was before; there are a great many Places nearer home, of which thou mayest say the same thing, at a less Expence; I see no Occasion thou hast of keeping thus far South, any longer than till you are sure you are to the West End of *Iava* and *Sumatra*, and then thou may'st stand away North towards *Ceylon*, and the Coast of *Coromandel* and *Maderas*, where thou may'st get both fresh Water, and fresh Provisions, and to that Part it's likely we may hold out well enough with the Stores that we have already.

177

This was wholesome Advice, and such as was not to be slighted, so we stood away to the West, keeping between the Latitude of 31, and 35, and had very good Weather and fair Winds for about ten Days Sail, by which Time, by our Reckoning we were clear of the Isles, and might run away to the North; and, if we did not fall in with *Ceylon*, we should at least go into the great deep Bay of *Bengal*.

But we were out in our Reckoning a great deal, for when we had stood due North for about fifteen or sixteen Degrees, we met with Land again on our Star-board Bow, about three Leagues Distance, so we came to an Anchor about half a League from it, and Manned out our Boats to see what sort of a Country it was: We found it a very good one, fresh Water easy to come at, but no Cattle, that we could see, or Inhabitants, and we were very shye of searching too far after them, lest we should make such another Journey as we did last; so that we let rambling alone, and chose rather to take what we could find, which was only a few wild Mangoes, and some Plants of several Kinds, which we knew not the Names of.

We made no Stay here, but put to Sea again N.W. by N. but had little Wind for a Fortnight more, when we made Land again, and standing in with the Shore, we were surprized to find our selves on the South Shore of *Iava*; and just as we were coming to an Anchor, we saw a Boat carrying *Dutch* Colours, sailing along Shore. We were not sollicitous to speak with them, or any other of their Nation, but left it indifferent to our People, when they went on Shore, to see the *Dutchmen*, or not to see them; our Business was to get Provisions, which indeed by this time were very short with us.

We resolved to go on Shore with our Boats in the most convenient Place we could find, and to look out a proper Harbour to bring the Ship into, leaving it to our Fate, whether we should meet with Friends or Enemies, resolving however, not to stay any considerable Time, at least, not long enough to have Expresses sent cross the Island to *Batavia*, and for Ships to come round from thence to attack us.

We found, according to our Desire, a very good Harbour, where we rode in seven Fathom Water; well defended from the Weather, whatever might happen, and here we got fresh Provisions, such as good Hogs, and some Cows; and that we might lay in a little Store, we kill'd sixteen Cows, and pickled and barrelled up the Flesh as well as we could be supposed to do in the Latitude of eight Degrees from the Line.

We did all this in about five Days, and filled our Casks with Water, and the last Boat was coming off with Herbs and Roots, we being unmoor'd and our Fore Top-Sail loose for sailing, when we spy'd a large Ship to the Northward, bearing down directly upon us; we knew not what she might be, but concluded the worst, and made all possible Haste to get our Anchor up, and get under Sail, that we might be in a Readiness to see what she had to say to us, for we were under no great Concern for one Ship; but our Notion was, that we should be attack'd by three or four together.

By the time we had got up our Anchor, and the Boat was stow'd, the Ship was within a League of us, and, as we thought, bore down to engage us; so we spread our black Flag or Ancient on the Poop, and the bloody Flag[212] at the Top-mast Head, and having made a clear Ship,[213] we stretcht away to the Westward, to get the Wind of him.

They had, it seems, quite mistaken us before, expecting nothing of an Enemy or a Pyrate in those Seas, and not doubting but we had been one of their own Ships, they seem'd to be in some confusion when they found their Mistake so they immediately haul'd up on a-Wind on t'other Tack, and stood edging in for the Shore, towards the Eastermost Part of the Island. Upon this we tack'd, and stood after him with all the Sail we could, and in two Hours came almost within Gun Shot. Tho' they crowded all the Sail they could lay on, there was no Remedy but to engage us and they soon saw their Inequality of Force: We fired a Gun for them to bring to, so they Mann'd out their Boat, and sent to us with a Flag of Truce. We sent back the Boat, but with this Answer to the Captain, that he had nothing to do, but to strike, and bring his Ship to an Anchor under our Stern, and come on board us himself, when he should know our Demands; but that however, since he had not yet put us to the Trouble of forcing him, which we saw we were able to do, we assured them, that the Captain should return again in Safety, and all his Men; and that supplying us with such things as we should demand, his Ship should not be plundered. They went back with this Message, and it was some time after they were on board, before they struck,[214] which made us begin to think they refused it; so we fired a Shot, and in a few Minutes more we perceived their Boat put off; and as soon as the Boat put off, the Ship struck, and came to an Anchor, as was directed.

When the Captain came on board, we demanded an Account of their Cargo, which was chiefly Bales of Goods from *Bengal* for *Bantam*.[215] We told them our present Want was Provisions, which they had no need of, being just at the End of their Voyage; and that if they would send their Boat on Shore with ours, and procure us six and twenty Head of black Cattel, threescore Hogs, a Quantity of Brandy and Arrack, and three Hundred Bushels of Rice, we would let them go free.

As to the Rice, they gave us six Hundred Bushels, which they had actually on board, together with a Parcel Shipt upon Freight. Also they gave us thirty middling Casks of very good Arrack, but Beef and Pork they had none. However, they went on Shore with our Men, and bought eleven Bullocks and fifty Hogs, which were pickled up for our Occasion, and upon the Supplies of Provision from Shore, we dismiss'd them and their Ship.

We lay here seven Days before we could furnish our selves with the Provisions agreed for, and some of the Men fancied the *Dutchmen* were contriving our Destruction; but they were very honest, and did what they could to furnish the Black Cattel, but found it impossible to supply so many. So they came and told us ingenuously, that unless we could stay a while longer, they could get no more Oxen or Cows than those Eleven, with which we were obliged to be satisfied, taking the Value of them in other things rather than stay longer there. On our Side we were punctual with them in observing the Conditions we had agreed on, nor would we let any of our Men so much as go on board them, or suffer any of their Men to come on board us; for had any of our Men gone on board, no body could have answer'd for their Behaviour, any more than if they had been on Shore in an Enemy's Country.

We were now Victualled for our Voyage, and as we matter'd not Purchase, we went merrily on for the Coast of *Ceylon*, where we intended to touch to get fresh Water again, and more Provisions; and we had nothing material offer'd in this Part of the Voyage, only that we met with contrary Winds, and were above a Month in the Passage.

We put in upon the South Coast of the Island desiring to have as little to do with the *Dutch* as we could; and as the *Dutch* were Lords of the Country as to Commerce, so they are more so of the Sea Coast, where they have several Forts, and in particular, have all the Cinnamon, which is the Trade of that Island.

We took in fresh Water here, and some Provisions, but did not much trouble our selves about laying in any Stores, our Beef and Hogs which we got at *Iava* being not yet all gone by a good deal. We had a little Skirmish on Shore here with some of the People of the Island, some of our Men having been a little too familiar with the *Homely Ladies* of the Country; for Homely indeed they were, to such a Degree, that if our Men had not had good Stomachs that Way, they would scarce have touch'd any of them.

I could never fully get it out of our Men what they did, they were so true to one another in their Wickedness; but I understood in the main, that it was some barbarous thing they had done, and that they had like to have paid dear for it; for the Men resented it to the last Degree, and gathered in such Numbers about them, that had not sixteen more of our Men, in another Boat, come all in the Nick of Time, just to rescue our first Men, who were but Eleven, and so fetch them off by main Force, they had been all cut off, the Inhabitants being no less than two or three Hundred, armed with Darts and Launces, the usual Weapons of the Country, and which they are very dexterous at the throwing, even so dexterous, that it was scarce credible: And had our Men stood to fight them, as some of them were bold enough to talk of, they had been all overwhelmed and kill'd. As it was, seventeen of our Men were wounded, and some of them very dangerously. But they were more frighted than hurt too; for every one of them gave themselves over for dead Men, believing the Launces were poisoned. But *William* was our Comfort here too; for when two of our Surgeons were of the same Opinion, and told the Men foolishly enough, that they would die, *William* chearfully went to Work with them, and cured them all but one, who rather died by drinking some Arrack Punch, than of his Wound, the Excess of Drinking throwing him into a Fever.

We had enough of *Ceylon*, tho' some of our People were for going ashore again, sixty or seventy Men together, to be revenged; but *William* perswaded them against it, and his Reputation was so great among the Men, as well as with us that were Commanders, that he could influence them more than any of us.

They were mighty warm upon their Revenge, and they would go on Shore, and destroy five Hundred of them. Well, says *William*, and suppose you do, what are you the better? Why then, says one of them, speaking for the rest, we shall have our Satisfaction. Well, and what will you be the better for that, says *William*? They could then say nothing to that. Then, says *William*, if I mistake not, your Business is Money: Now I desire to know, if you conquer and kill two or three Thousand of these poor Creatures, they have no Money, pray what will you get? They are poor naked Wretches, what shall you gain by them? But then said *William*, perhaps, in doing this, you may chance to lose Half a Score of your own Company, as 'tis very probable you may, pray, what Gain is in it, and what Account can you give the Captain for his lost Men? In short, *William* argued so effectually, that he convinc'd them that it was mere Murther, to do so; and that the Men had a Right to their own, and that they had no Right to take them away: That it was destroying innocent Men, who had acted no otherwise than as the Laws of Nature dictated; and that it would be as much Murther to do so, as to meet a Man on the High-way, and kill him, for the mere sake of it, in cold Blood, not regarding whether he had done any Wrong to us or no.

These Reasons prevailed with them at last, and they were content to go away, and leave them as they found them. In the first Skirmish they killed between sixty and seventy Men, and wounded a great many more, but they had nothing, and our People got nothing by it, but the Loss of one Man's Life, and the Wounding sixteen more, as above.

But another Accident brought us to a Necessity of further Business with these People, and indeed we had like to have put an End to our Lives and Adventures all at once among them; for, about three Days after our Putting out to Sea, from the Place where we had that Skirmish, we were attack'd by a violent Storm of Wind from the South, or rather a Hurricane of Wind from all the Points Southward, for it blew in a most desperate and furious Manner, from the S.E. to the S.W. one Minute at one Point, and then instantly turning about again to another Point, but with the same Violence; nor were we able to work the Ship in that Condition: So that the Ship I was in split three Topsails, and at last brought the Main Top-mast by the Board; and in a Word, we were once or twice driven right ashore; and one time, had not the Wind shifted the very Moment it did, we had been dash'd in a Thousand Pieces upon a great Ledge of Rocks, which lay off about Half a League from the Shore; but, as I have said, the Wind shifting very often, and at that time coming to the E.S.E. we stretch off, and got above a League more Sea-room in Half an Hour. After that, it blew with some Fury S.W. by S. then S.W. by W. and put us back again a great Way to the Eastward of the Ledge of Rocks, where we found a fair Opening between the Rocks and the Land, and endeavoured to come to an Anchor there; but we found there was no Ground fit to Anchor in, and that we should lose our Anchors, there being nothing but Rocks. We stood thro' the Opening, which held about four Leagues; the Storm continued, and now we found a dreadful foul Shore, and knew not what Course to take. We look'd out very narrowly for some River, or Creek, or Bay, where we might run in, and come to an Anchor, but found none a great while. At length we saw a great Head-Land lye out far South into the Sea, and that to such a Length, that, in short, we saw plainly, that if the Wind held where it was, we could not Weather it; so we run in as much under the Lee of the Point as we could and came to an Anchor in about twelve Fathom Water.

But the Wind veering again in the Night, and blowing exceeding hard, our Anchors came home,[216] and the Ship drove till the Rudder struck against the Ground; and had the Ship gone Half her Length further, she had been lost, and every one of us with her. But our Sheet Anchor[217] held its own, and we heaved in some of the Cable, to get clear of the Ground we had struck upon. It was by this only Cable that we rode it out all Night and towards Morning we thoughts the Wind abated a little, and it was well for us that it was so for in spite of what our Sheet Anchor did for us we found the Ship fast a-ground in the Morning to our very great Surprize and Amazement.

When the Tide was out, tho' the Water here ebb'd away, the Ship lay almost dry upon a Bank of hard Sand, which never, I suppose, had any Ship upon it before; the People of the Country came down in great Numbers, to look at us and gaze, not knowing what we were, but gaping at us as at a great Sight or Wonder, at which they were surpriz'd, and knew not what to do.

I have Reason to believe, that upon the Sight they immediately sent an Account of a Ship being there, and of the Condition we were in; for the next Day there appeared a great Man, whether it was their King or no, I knew not, but he had Abundance of Men with him, and some with long Javelins in their Hands, as long as Half Pikes; and these came all down to the Water's Edge, and drew up in very good Order just in our View. They stood near an Hour without making any Motion, and then there came near twenty of them with a Man before them, carrying a white Flag before them. They came forward into the Water as high as their Wastes, the Sea not going so high as before, for the Wind was abated, and blew off Shore.

The Man made a long Oration to us, as we could see by his Gestures, and we sometimes heard his Voice, but knew not a Word he said. *William*, who was always useful to us, I believe, was here again the Saving of all our Lives. The Case was this. The Fellow, or what I might call him, when his Speech was done, gave three great Screams, for I know not what else to say they were, then lower'd his white Flag three times, and then made three Motions to us with his Arm, to come to him.

I acknowledge, that I was for Manning out the Boat, and going to them; but *William* would by no means allow me: He told me, we ought to trust no Body; that if they were the Barbarians, and under their own Government, we might be sure to be all murthered; and if they were Christians, we should not fare much better, if they knew who we were; that it was the Custom of the *Malabars*, to betray all People that they could get into their Hands; and that these were some of the same People; and that if we had any Regard to our own Safety, we should not go to them by any means. I opposed him a great while, and told him, I thought he used to be always right, but that now I thought he was not; that I was no more for running needless Risques, than he, or any one else; but I thought all Nations in the World, even the most savage People, when they held out a Flag of Peace, kept the Offer of Peace made by that Signal, very sacredly, and I gave him several Examples of it in my History of my *African* Travels, which I have here gone thro' in the Beginning of this Work; and that I could not think these People worse than some of them. And besides, I told him, our Case seem'd to be such, that we must fall into some body's Hands or other, and that we had better fall into their Hands by a friendly Treaty, than by a forced Submission; nay, tho' they had indeed a treacherous Design; and therefore I was for a Parley with them.

Well, Friend, says *William* very gravely, if thou wilt go, I cannot help it; I shall only desire to take my last Leave of thee at Parting, for depend upon it, thou wilt never see us again: Whether we in the Ship may come off any better at last, I cannot resolve thee; but this I will answer for, that we will not give up our Lives idly, and in cool Blood, as thou art going to do; we will at least preserve our selves as long as we can, and die at last like Men, not like Fools trapann'd by the Wiles of a few Barbarians.

William spoke this with so much Warmth, and yet with so much Assurance of our Fate, that I began to think a little of the Risque I was going to run. I had no more Mind to be murthered than he; and yet I could not for my Life be so faint-hearted in the thing, as he. Upon which I asked him, if he had any Knowledge of the Place, or had ever been here? He said, *No*. Then I asked him, if he had heard or read any thing about the People of this Island, and of their Way of treating any Christians that had fallen into their Hands? And he told me, he had heard of one, and he would tell me the Story afterward. His Name, he said, was *Knox*,[218] Commander of an *East India* Ship, who was driven on Shore, just as we were, upon this Island of *Ceylon*, tho' he could not say it was at the same Place, or whereabouts: That he was beguiled by the Barbarians, and inticed to come on Shore, just as we were invited to do at that time; and that when they had him, they surrounded him and eighteen or twenty of his Men, and never suffered them to return, but kept them Prisoners, or murthered them, he could not well tell which; but they were carried away up into the Country, separated from one another; and never heard of afterwards, except the Captain's Son, who miraculously made his Escape after twenty Years Slavery.

I had no Time then to ask him to give the full Story of this *Knox*, much less to hear him tell it me; but as it is usual in such Cases, when one begins to be a little touch'd,[219] I turn'd short with[220] him, Why then, Friend *William*, said I, what would you have us do? You see what Condition we are in, and what is before us; something must be done, and that immediately. Why, says *William*, I'll tell thee what thou shalt do: First cause a white Flag to be hang'd out, as they do to us, and Man out the Long-Boat and Pinnace with as many Men as they can well stow, to handle their Arms, and let me go with them, and thou shalt see what we will do. If I miscarry, thou may'st be safe; and I will also tell thee, that if I do miscarry, it shall be my own Fault, and thou shalt learn Wit by my Folly.

I knew not what to reply to him at first; but after some Pause, I said, *William, William*, I am as loath you should be lost, as you are that I should; and if there be any Danger, I desire you may no more fall into it than I.

Therefore, if you will, let us all keep in the Ship, fare alike, and take our Fate together.

No, no, says *William*, there's no Danger in the Method I propose; thou shalt go with me, if thou thinkest fit. If thou pleasest but to follow the Measures that I shall resolve on, depend upon it, tho' we will go off from the Ships, we will not a Man of us go any nearer them than within Call to talk with them. Thou seest they have no Boats to come off to us; but, says he, I rather desire thou wouldst take my Advice, and manage the Ship, as I shall give the Signal from the Boat and let us concert that Matter together before we go off.

Well, I found *William* had his Measures in his Head all laid before-hand, and was not at a Loss what to do at all; so I told him he should be Captain for this Voyage, and we would be all of us under his Orders, which I would see observed to a Tittle.

Upon this Conclusion of our Debates, he ordered four and Twenty Men into the Long-Boat, and twelve Men into the Pinnace, and the Sea being now pretty smooth, they went off, being all very well arm'd. Also he ordered, that all the Guns of the great Ship, on the Side which lay next the Shore, should be loaded with Musquet Balls, old Nails, Stubbs,[221] and such like Pieces of old Iron, Lead, and any thing that came to Hand; and that we should prepare to fire as soon as ever he saw us lower the white Flag, and hoist up a red one in the Pinnace.

With these Measures fix'd between us, they went off towards the Shore, *William* in the Pinnace with twelve Men, and the Long-Boat coming after him with four and twenty more, all stout, resolute Fellows, and very well arm'd. They row'd so near the Shore, as that they might speak to one another, carrying a white Flag as the other did, and offering a *Parle*. The Brutes, for such they were, shewed themselves very courteous, but finding we could not understand them, they fetch'd an old *Dutchman*, who had been their Prisoner many Years, and set him to speak to us. The Sum and Substance of his Speech was, That the King of the Country had sent his General down to know who we were, and what our Business was? *William* stood up in the Stern of the Pinnace, and told him, That as to that, he that was an *European* by his Language and Voice, might easily know what we were, and our Condition; the Ship being a-ground upon the Sand, would also tell him; that our Business there was that of a Ship in Distress; so *William* desired to know what they came down for with such a Multitude, and with Arms and Weapons, as if they came to War with us.

He answered, they might have good Reason to come down to the Shore, the Country being alarmed with the Appearance of Ships of Strangers upon the Coast; and as our Vessels were full of Men, and that we had Guns and

Weapons, the King had sent Part of his military Men, that, in Case of any Invasion upon the Country, they might be ready to defend themselves, whatsoever might be the Occasion.

But, says he, as you are Men in Distress, the King has ordered his General who is here also, to give you all the Assistance he can, and to invite you on Shore, to receive you with all possible Courtesy. Says *William* very quick upon him, before I give thee an Answer to that, I desire thee to tell me what thou art; for by thy Speech thou art an *European*. He answered presently, he was a *Dutchman*. That I know well, says *William*, by thy Speech; but art thou a Native *Dutchman* of *Holland*, or a Native of this Country, that has learnt *Dutch* by conversing among the *Hollanders*, who we know are settled upon this Island.

No, *says the Old Man*, I am a Native of *Delft* in the Province of *Holland* in *Europe*.

Well, says *William* immediately, but art thou a Christian or a Heathen, or what we call a Renegado?

I am, *says he*, a Christian, and so they went on in a short Dialogue, as follows.

Will. Thou art a *Dutchman*, and a Christian, thou sayest; pray, art thou a Freeman or a Servant?

Dutchm. I am a Servant to the King here, and in his Army.

Will. But art thou a Voluntier, or a Prisoner?

Dutchm. Indeed I was a Prisoner at first, but am at Liberty now, and so am a Voluntier.

Will. That is to say, being first a Prisoner thou hast Liberty to serve them; but art thou so at Liberty, that thou mayest go away, if thou pleasest, to thine own Countrymen?

Dutchm. No, I do not say so; my Countrymen live a great Way off, on the North and East Parts of the Island, and there is no going to them, without the King's express Licence.

Will. Well, and why dost not thou get a Licence to go away?

Dutchm. I have never ask'd for it.

Will. And I suppose, if thou didst, thou knowst thou couldst not obtain it.

Dutchm. I cannot say much as to that, but why do you ask me all these Questions?

Will. Why, my Reason is good; if thou art a Christian and a Prisoner, how canst thou consent to be made an Instrument to these Barbarians, to betray us into their Hands, who are thy Countrymen and Fellow-Christians? Is it not a barbarous thing in thee to do so?

Dutchm. How do I go about to betray you? Do I not give you an Account, how the King invites you to come on Shore, and has ordered you to be treated courteously, and assisted?

Will. As thou art a Christian, tho' I doubt it much, dost thou believe the King or the General, as thou callest it, means one Word of what he says?

Dutchm. He promises you by the Mouth of his Great General.

Will. I don't ask thee what he promises, or by whom; but I ask thee this: Canst thou say, that thou believest he intends to perform it?

Dutchm. How can I answer that? How can I tell what he intends?

Will. Thou canst tell what thou believest.

Dutchm. I cannot say but he will perform it; I believe he may.

Will. Thou art but a double-tongu'd Christian, I doubt: Come, I'll ask thee another Question: Wilt thou say, that thou believest it; and that thou wouldst advise me to believe it, and put our Lives into their Hands upon these Promises?

Dutchm. I am not to be your Adviser.

Will. Thou art perhaps afraid to speak thy Mind, because thou art in their Power: Pray, do any of them understand what thou and I say? Can they speak *Dutch*?

Dutchm. No, not one of them, I have no Apprehensions upon that Account at all.

Will. Why then answer me plainly, if thou art a Christian: Is it safe for us to venture upon their Words, to put our selves into their Hands, and come on Shore?

Dutchm. You put it very home to me: Pray let me ask you another Question: Are you in any Likelihood of getting your Ship off, if you refuse it?

Will. Yes, yes, we shall get off the Ship, now the Storm is over, we don't fear it.

Dutchm. Then I cannot say it is best for you to trust them.

Will. Well; it is honestly said.

Dutchm. But what shall I say to them?

Will. Give them good Words, as they give us.

Dutchm. What good Words?

Will. Why let them tell the King, that we are Strangers, who were driven on his Coast by a great Storm; that we thank him very kindly for his Offer of Civility to us, which, if we are farther distress'd, we will accept thankfully; but that at present we have no Occasion to come on Shore: And besides, that we cannot safely leave the Ship in the present Condition she is in, but that we are obliged to take Care of her, in order to get her off, and expect in a Tide or two more, to get her quite clear, and at an Anchor.

Dutchm. But he will expect you to come on Shore then to visit him, and make him some Present for his Civility.

Will. When we have got our Ship clear, and stopp'd the Leaks, we will pay our Respects to him.

Dutchm. Nay, you may as well come to him now as then.

Will. Nay, hold Friend, I did not say we would come to him then: You talk'd of making him a Present; that is, to pay our Respects to him, is it not?

Dutchm. Well, but I will tell him, that you will come on Shore to him when your Ship is got off?

Will. I have nothing to say to that, you may tell him what you think fit.

Dutchm. But he will be in a great Rage, if I do not.

Will. Who will he be in a great Rage at?

Dutchm. At you.

Will. What Occasion have we to value that?

Dutchm. Why, he will send all his Army down against you.

Will. And what if they were all here just now? What dost thou suppose they could do to us?

Dutchm. He would expect they should burn your Ships, and bring you all to him.

Will. Tell him, if he try, he may catch a *Tartar*.

Dutchm. He has a World of Men.

Will. Has he any Ships?

Dutchm. No, he has no Ships.

Will. Nor Boats?

Dutchm. No, nor Boats.

Will. Why, what then do you think we care for his Men? What canst thou do now to us, if thou hadst a Hundred Thousand with thee?

Dutchm. O! they might set you on Fire.

Will. *Set us a Firing* thou mean'st: That they might indeed; but *Set us on Fire*, they shall not; they may try at their Peril, and we shall make mad Work with your Hundred Thousand Men, if they come within Reach of our Guns, I assure thee.

Dutchm. But what if the King give you Hostages for your Safety?

Will. Whom can he give but mere Slaves and Servants like thy self, whose Lives he no more values, than we an *English* Hound?

Dutchm. Whom do you demand for Hostages?

Will. Himself and your Worship.

Dutchm. What would you do with him?

Will. Do with him, as he would do with us, cut his Head off.

Dutchm. And what would you do to me?

Will. Do with thee? We would carry thee home into thine own Country; and tho' thou deservest the Gallows, we would make a Man and a Christian of thee again, and not do by thee as thou wouldst have done by us, betray thee to a Parcel of merciless, savage Pagans, that know no God, nor how to shew Mercy to Man.

Dutchm. You put a Thought in my Head that I will speak to you about to Morrow.

Thus they went away, and *William* came on board, and gave us a full Account of his Parley with the Old *Dutchman*, which was very diverting, and to me instructing, for I had Abundance of Reason to acknowledge *William* had made a better Judgment of things than I.

It was our good Fortune to get our Ship off that very Night, and to bring her to an Anchor at about a Mile and a Half further out, and in deep Water, to our great Satisfaction; so that we had no need to fear the *Dutchman's* King with his Hundred Thousand Men; and indeed we had some Sport with them the next Day, when they came down, a vast prodigious Multitude of them, very few less in Number, in out Imagination, than a Hundred Thousand, with some Elephants; tho' if it had been an Army of Elephants, they could have done us no Harm, for we were fairly at our Anchor now, and out of their Reach; and indeed we thought our selves more out of their Reach, than we really were; and it was ten Thousand to One, that we had not been fast a-ground again; for the Wind blowing off Shore, tho' it made the Water smooth where we lay, yet it blew the Ebb further out than usual, and we could easily perceive the Sand which we touch'd upon before, lay in the Shape of a Half Moon, and surrounded us with two Horns of it; so that we lay in the Middle or Center of it, as in a round Bay, safe just as we were, and in deep Water; but present Death, as it were, on the right Hand, and on the left, for the two Horns, or Points of the Sand, reach'd out beyond where our Ship lay near two Miles.

On that Part of the Sand which lay on our East Side, this misguided Multitude extended themselves; and being most of them not above their Knees, or most of them not above Ancle deep in the Water, they, as it were, surrounded us on that Side, and on the Side of the main Land, and a little Way on the other Side of the Sand, standing in a Half Circle, or rather three Fifths of a Circle, for about six Miles in Length; the other Horn, or Point of the Sand which lay on our West Side being not quite so shallow, they could not extend themselves upon it so far.

They little thought what Service they had done us, and how unwillingly, and by the greatest Ignorance, they had made themselves Pilots to us, while we having not sounded the Place, might have been lost, before we were aware. It is true we might have sounded our new Harbour, before we had ventured out; but I cannot say for certain, whether we should or not; for I, for my Part, had not the least Suspicion of what our real Case was. However, I say, perhaps before we had weigh'd, we should have look'd about us a little. I am sure we ought to have done it; for besides these Armies of human Furies, we had a very leaky Ship, and all our Pumps could hardly keep the Water from growing upon us, and our Carpenters were over-board working to find out, and stop the Wounds we had received, heeling her first on one Side, and then on the other; and it was very diverting to see how, when our Men heel'd the Ship over to the Side next the wild Army that stood on the East Horn of the Sand, they were so amazed between Fright and Joy that it put them into a kind of Confusion, calling to one another, hallooing and skreeking in a Manner as it is impossible to describe.

While we were doing this, for we were in a great Hurry, you may be sure, and all Hands at Work, as well at the stopping our Leaks, as repairing our Rigging and Sails, which had receiv'd a great deal of Damage, and also in rigging a new Main-Top-Mast, and the like: I say, while we were doing all this, we perceived a Body of Men, of near a Thousand, move from that Part of the Army of the Barbarians, that lay at the Bottom of the sandy Bay, and came all along the Water's Edge, round the Sand, till they stood just on our Broadside *East*, and were within about Half a Mile of us. Then we saw the *Dutchman* come forward nearer to us, and all alone, with his white Flag and all his Motions, just as before, and there he stood.

Our Men had but just brought the Ship to Rights again, as they came up to our Broadside, and we had very happily found out and stopp'd the worst and most dangerous Leak that we had, to our very great Satisfaction; so I ordered the Boats to be haul'd up, and Mann'd as they were the Day before, and *William* to go as Plenipotentiary. I would have gone my self, if I had understood *Dutch*; but as I did not, it was to no Purpose, for I should be able to know nothing of what was said, but from him at second Hand, which might be done as well afterwards. All the Instructions I pretended to give *William*, was, if possible, to get the old *Dutchman* away, and, if he could, to make him come on board.

Well, *William* went just as before; and when he came within about sixty or seventy Yards of the Shore, he held up his white Flag, as the *Dutchman* did, and turning the Boat's Broadside to the Shore, and his Men lying upon their Oars, the Parley or Dialogue began again thus.

Will. Well, Friend, what do'st thou say to us now?
Dutchm. I come of the same mild Errand as I did yesterday.

Will. What do'st thou pretend to come of a mild Errand, with all these People at thy Back, and all the foolish Weapons of War they bring with them? Prithee, what dost thou mean?

Dutchm. The King hastens us to invite the Captain and all his Men, to come on Shore, and has ordered all his Men to shew them all the Civility they can.

Will. Well, and are all those Men come to invite us ashore?

Dutchm. They will do you no Hurt, if you will come on Shore peaceably.

Will. Well, and what dost thou think they can do to us, if we will not?

Dutchm. I would not have them do you any Hurt then neither.

Will. But prithee, Friend, do not make thy self Fool and Knave too: Do'st not thou know that we are out of Fear of all thy Army, and out of Danger of all that they can do? What makes thee act so simply as well as so knavishly?

Dutchm. Why you may think your selves safer than you are: You do not know what they may do to you. I can assure you they are able to do you a great deal of Harm, and perhaps burn your Ship.

Will. Suppose that were true, as I am sure it is false, you see we have more Ships to carry us off,* *pointing to the Sloop.*

Dutchm. We do not value that, if you had ten Ships, you dare not come on Shore with all the Men you have, in a hostile Way; we are too many for you.

Will. Thou dost not even in that speak as thou meanest; and we may give thee a Tryal of our Hands, when our Friends come up to us; for thou hearest they have discovered us.†

Dutchm. Yes, I hear they fire, but I hope your Ship will not fire again; for if they do, our General will take it for breaking the Truce, and will make the Army let fly a Shower of Arrows at you in the Boat.

Will. Thou mayest be sure the Ship will fire, that the other Ship may hear them, but not with Ball. If thy General knows no better, he may begin when he will; but thou mayest be sure we will return it to his Cost.

Dutchm. What must I do then?

Will. Do, why go to him, and tell him of it before-hand then; and let him know, that the Ship firing is not at him, or his Men, and then come again, and tell us what he says.

* N.B. Just at this Time we discovered the Sloop standing towards us from the East, along the Shore, at about the Distance of two Leagues, which was to our particular Satisfaction, she having been missing thirteen Days.

† Just then the Sloop fired five Guns, which was to get News of us, for they did not see us.

Dutchm. No, I will send to him, which will do as well.

Will. Do as thou wilt; but I believe thou hadst better go thy self; for if our Men fire first, I suppose he will be in a great Wrath, and it may be, at thee; for, as for his Wrath at us, we tell thee before-hand, we value it not.

Dutchm. You slight them too much, you know not what they may do.

Will. Thou makest as if those poor savage Wretches could do mighty things; prithee let us see what you can all do, we value it not; thou mayest set down thy Flag of Truce when thou pleasest, and begin.

Dutchm. I had rather make a Truce, and have you all part Friends.

Will. Thou art a deceitful Rogue thy self; for 'tis plain thou knowest these People would only perswade us on Shore, to entrap and surprize us; and yet thou that art a Christian, as thou callest thy self, would have us come on Shore, and put our Lives into their Hands who know nothing that belongs to Compassion, good Usage, or good Manners: How canst thou be such a Villain!

Dutchm. How can you call me so? What have I done to you, and what would you have me do?

Will. Not act like a Traytor, but like one that was once a Christian, and would have been so still, if you had not been a *Dutchman.*

Dutchm. I know not what to do not I, I wish I were from them, they are a bloody People.

Will. Prithee make no Difficulty of what thou shouldst do; Canst thou swim?

Dutchm. Yes, I can swim; but if I should attempt to swim off to you, I should have a Thousand Arrows and Javelins sticking in me, before I should get to your Boat.

Will. I'll bring the Boat close to thee, and take thee on board, in spite of them all. We will give them but one Volley, and I'll engage they will all run away from thee.

Dutchm. You are mistaken in them, I assure you; they would immediately come all running down to the Shore, and shoot Fire-Arrows at you, and set your Boat and Ship and all on Fire, about your Ears.

Will. We will venture that, if thou wilt come off.

Dutchm. Will you use me honourably when I am among you?

Will. I'll give thee my Word for it, if thou provest honest.

Dutchm. Will you not make me a Prisoner?

Will. I will be thy Surety Body for Body, that thou shalt be a Freeman, and go whither thou wilt, tho' I own to thee thou dost not deserve it.

Just at this time our Ship fired three Guns, to answer the Sloop, and let her know we saw her, who immediately, we perceived, understood it, and stood directly for the Place; but it is impossible to express the Confusion and filthy vile Noise, the Hurry and universal Disorder, that was among that vast Multitude of People, upon our Firing of three Guns. They immediately all repaired to their Arms, as I may call it; for, to say they put themselves into Order, would be saying nothing.

Upon the Word of Command then they advanced all in a Body to the Sea-side, and resolving to give us one Volley of their Fire Arms, for such they were, immediately they saluted us with a Hundred Thousand of their Fire-Arrows, every one carrying a little Bag of Cloath dipt in Brimstone,[222] or some such thing; which flying thro' the Air, had nothing to hinder it taking Fire as it flew, and it generally did so.

I cannot say but this Method of attacking us, by a Way we had no Notion of, might give us at first some little Surprize; for the Number was so great at first, that we were not altogether without Apprehensions that they might unluckily set our Ship on Fire; so that he resolved immediately to row on Board, and perswade us all to weigh, and stand out to Sea; but there was no time for it, for they immediately let fly a Volley at the Boat, and at the Ship from all Parts of the vast Crowd of People which stood near the Shore.

Nor did they fire, as I may call it, all at once, and so leave off; but their Arrows being soon notch'd upon their Bows, they kept continually shooting, so that the Air was full of Flame.

I could not say whether they set their Cotton Rag on Fire before they shot the Arrow, for I did not perceive they had Fire with them, which however it seems they had. The Arrow, besides the Fire it carried with it, had a Head, or a Peg, as we call it, of a Bone, and some of sharp Flint Stone; and some few of a Metal, too soft in itself for Metal, but har'd enough to cause it to enter, if it were a Plank, so as to stick where it fell.

William and his Men had Notice sufficient to lye close behind their Waste-boards,[223] which for this very Purpose they had made so high, that they could easily sink themselves behind them, so as to defend themselves from any thing that came Point blank, *as we call it*, or upon a Line; but for what might fall perpendicular out of the Air, they had no Guard, but took the Hazard of that. At first they made as if they would row away, but before they went, they gave a Volley of their small Arms, firing at those which stood with the *Dutchman*; but *William* ordered them to be sure to take their Aim at others so as to miss him, and they did so.

There was no Calling to them now, for the Noise was so great among them, that they could hear no Body; but our Men boldly row'd in nearer to them, for they were at first driven a little off, and when they came nearer, they fired a second Volley, which put the Fellows into a great Confusion, and we could see from the Ship, that several of them were killed or wounded.

We thought this was a very unequal Fight, and therefore we made a Signal to our Men, to row away, that we might have a little of the Sport as well as they; but the Arrows flew so thick upon them, being so near the Shore, that they could not sit to their Oars; so they spread a little of their Sail, thinking they might sail along the Shore, and lye behind their Waste-boards: But the Sail had not been spread six Minutes, but it had five Hundred Fire-Arrows shot into it, and thro' it, and at length set it fairly on Fire; nor were our Men quite out of the Danger of its setting the Boat on Fire, and this made them paddle and shove the Boat away as well as they could, as they lay, to get further off.

By this time they had left us a fair Mark at the whole Savage Army; and as we had sheer'd [224] the Ship as near to them as we could, we fired among the thickest of them six or seven times, five Guns at a time, which shot old Iron, Musquet Bullets &c.

We could easily see that we made Havock of them, and killed and wounded Abundance of them, and that they were in a great Surprize at it; but yet they never offered to stir, and all this while their Fire-Arrows flew as thick as before.

At last, on a sudden their Arrows stopt, and the old *Dutchman* came running down to the Water Side, all alone, with his white Flag as before, waving it as high as he could, and making Signals to our Boat to come to him again.

William did not care at first to go near him, but the Man continuing to make Signals to him to come, at last *William* went, and the *Dutchman* told him, that he had been with the General, who was much mollified by the Slaughter of his Men, and that now he could have any thing of him.

Any thing, says *William*, what have we to do with him? Let him go about his Business, and carry his Men out of Gun-Shot: Can't he?

Why, says the *Dutchman*, but he dares not stir, nor see the King's Face; unless some of your Men come on Shore, he will certainly put him to Death.

Why then, says *William*, he is a dead Man; for if it were to save his Life, and the Lives of all the Crowd that is with him, he shall never have one of us in his power.

But I'll tell thee, said *William*, how thou shalt cheat him, and gain thy own Liberty too, if thou hast any Mind to see thy own Country again, and art not turn'd Savage, and grown fond of living all thy Days among Heathens and Savages.

I would be glad to do it with all my Heart, says he; but if I should offer to swim off to you now, tho' they are so far from me, they shoot so true, that they would kill me before I got half Way.

But, says *William*, I'll tell thee how thou shalt come with his Consent; go to him, and tell him, I have offer'd to carry you on board, to try if you could perswade the Captain to come on Shore, and that I would not hinder him, if he was willing to venture.

The *Dutchman* seem'd in a Rapture at the very first Word: I'll do it, says he, I am perswaded he will give me Leave to come.

Away he runs, as if he had a glad Message to carry, and tells the General, that *William* had promised, if he would go on board the Ship with me, he would perswade the Captain to return with him. The General was Fool enough to give him Order to go, and charg'd him not to come back without the Captain, which he readily promised, and very honestly might.

So they took him in, and brought him on board, and he was as good as his Word to them, for he never went back to them any more; and the Sloop being come to the Mouth of the Inlet where we lay, we weighed, and set Sail. But as we went out, being pretty near the Shore, we fired three Guns as it were among them, but without any Shot, for it was of no Use to us, to hurt any more of them. After we had fired, we gave them a Chear, as the Seamen call it; *that is to say*, we halloo'd at them by way of Triumph, and so carried off their Ambassador; how it fared with their General, we know nothing of that.

This Passage, when I related it to a Friend of mine, after my Return from those Rambles, agreed so well with his Relation of what happened to one Mr. *Knox*, an *English* Captain, who some time ago was decoyed on Shore by those People, that it could not but be very much to my Satisfaction to think what Mischief we had all escaped; and I think it cannot but be very profitable to record the other Story, *which is but short*, with my own, to shew, whoever reads this, what it was I avoided, and prevent their falling into the like, if they have to do with the perfidious People of *Ceylon*. The Relation is as follows.

The Island of *Ceylon* being inhabited for the greatest Part by Barbarians, which will not allow any Trade or Commerce with any *European* Nation, and inaccessible by any Travellers, it will be convenient to relate the Occasion how the Author of this Story happen'd to go into this Island, and what Opportunities he had of being fully acquainted with the People, their Laws and Customs, that so we may the better depend upon the Account, and value it as it deserves, for the Rarity as well as the Truth of it; and both these the Author gives us a brief Relation of, in this Manner. His Words are as follows.[225]

In the Year 1657, the *Anne* Fregat, of *London*, Captain *Robert Knox* Commander, on the 21st of *January*, set Sail out of the *Downes*, in the Service of the Honourable the *East India* Company of *England*, bound for *Fort St. George* upon the Coast of *Coromandel*, to trade for one Year from Port to Port in *India*; which having performed, as he was lading his Goods to return for *England*, being in the Road of *Matlipatam*, on the 19th of *November* 1659, there happen'd such a mighty Storm, that in it several Ships were cast away, and he was forc'd to cut his Main Mast by the Board, which so disabled the Ship, that he could not proceed in his Voyage; whereupon, *Cotiar*, in the Island of *Ceylon* being a very commodious Bay fit for her present Distress, *Thomas Chambers*, Esq; since Sir *Thomas Chambers*, the Agent at *Fort St. George*, ordered that the Ship should take in some Cloath and *Indian* Merchants belonging to *Porta Nova*, who might trade there while she lay to set her Mast, and repair the other Damages sustained by the Storm. At her first coming thither, after the *Indian* Merchants were set on Shore, the Captain and his Men were very jealous of the People of the Place, by reason the *English* never had any Commerce or Dealing with them; but after they had been there twenty Days, going ashore and returning again at Pleasure, without any Molestation, they began to lay aside all suspicious Thoughts of the People that dwelt thereabouts, who had kindly entertained them for their Money.

By this time the King of the Country had Notice of their Arrival, and not being acquainted with their Intents, he sent down a *Dissuava*, or General, with an Army to them, who immediately sent a Messenger to the Captain on board, to desire him to come ashore to him, pretending a Letter from the King. The Captain saluted the Message with Firing of Guns, and ordered his Son *Robert Knox*, and Mr. *John Loveland*, Merchant of the Ship, to go ashore and wait on him. When they were come before him, he demanded *Who they were, and how long they should stay?* They told him, *They were* Englishmen, *and not to stay above twenty or thirty Days, and desired Permission to trade in his Majesty's Port.* His Answer was, *That the King was glad to hear that the* English *were come into his Country, and had commanded him to assist them, as they should desire, and had sent a Letter to be delivered to none but the Captain himself.* They were then twelve Miles from the Sea-Side, and therefore replied, *That the Captain could not leave his Ship to come so far; but if he pleased to go down to the Sea-Side, the Captain would wait on him to receive the Letter.* Whereupon the *Dissuava* desired them to stay that Day, and on the Morrow he would go with them; which, rather than displease him in so small a Matter, they consented to. In the Evening, the *Dissuava* sent a Present to the Captain of Cattle and Fruits, &c. which being carried all Night by the Messengers, was delivered to him in the Morning, who told him withal, that his Men were coming down with the *Dissuava*, and desired his Company on Shore against his coming, having a Letter from the King to deliver into his own Hand. The Captain mistrusting nothing, came on Shore with his Boat, and sitting under a Tamarind Tree, waited for the *Dissuava*. In the mean time, the Native Soldiers privately surrounded him and the seven Men he had with him, and seizing them, carried them to meet the *Dissuava*, bearing the Captain on a Hammock on their Shoulders.

The next Day the Long-Boat's Crew, not knowing what had happen'd, came on Shore to cut down a Tree to make Cheeks[226] for the Main-Mast, and were made Prisoners after the same Manner, tho' with more Violence, because they were more rough with them, and made Resistance, yet they were not brought to the Captain and his Company, but quarter'd in another House in the same Town.

The *Dissuava* having thus gotten two Boats, and eighteen Men, his next Care was to gain the Ship, and, to that End, telling the Captain that he and his Men were only detained because the King intended to send Letters and a Present to the *English* Nation by him, desired he would send some Men on board his Ship to order her Stay; and because the Ship was in Danger of being fired by the *Dutch*, if she stay'd long in the Bay, to bring her up the River. The Captain did not approve of the Advice, but did not dare own his Dislike; and so sent his Son with the Order, but with a solemn Conjuration to return again, which he accordingly did, bringing a Letter from the Company in the Ship, *That they would not obey the Captain, nor any other in this Matter, but were resolved to stand on their own Defence.* This Letter satisfied the *Dissuava*, who thereupon gave the Captain Leave to write for what he would have brought him from the Ship, pretending, that he had not the King's Order to release them, though it would suddenly come.

The Captain seeing he was held in Suspense, and the Season of the Year spending[227] for the Ship to proceed on her Voyage to some Place, sent Order to Mr. *John Burford* the chief Mate, to take Charge of the Ship, and set Sail to *Porta Nova*, from whence they came, and there to follow the Agent's Order.

And now began that long and sad Captivity they all along feared; the Ship being gone, the *Dissuava* was called up to the King, and they were kept under Guards a while, till a special Order came from the King to part them, and put one in a Town, for the Conveniency of their Maintenance, which the King ordered to be at the Charge of the Country. On *September*, 16, 1660, the Captain and his Son were placed in a Town called *Bonder*

Cooswat, in the Country of *Hotcurly*, distant from the City of *Candi*[228] Northward thirty Miles, and, from the rest of the *English*, a full Day's Journey. Here they had their Provisions brought them twice a Day, without Money, so much as they could eat, and as good as the Country yielded: The Situation of the Place was very pleasant and commodious; but that Year that Part of the Land was very sickly by Agues and Fevers, of which many died. The Captain and his Son, after some time, were visited with the common Distemper, and the Captain being also loaded with Grief for his deplorable Condition, languish'd more than three Months, and then died, *February* the 9th 1660.

Robert Knox his Son being now left desolate, sick, and in Captivity, having none to comfort him but God, who is the Father of the father-less, and hears the Groans of such as are in Captivity, being alone to enter upon a long Scene of Misery and Calamity, oppress'd with Weakness of Body and Grief of Soul, for the Loss of his Father, and his remediless Trouble that he was like to endure; and the first Instance of it was in the Burial of his Father: For he sent his Black Boy to the People of the Town, to desire their Assistance; because they understood not their Language; but they sent him only a Rope to drag him by the Neck into the Woods, and told him, *that they would offer him no other Help unless he would pay for it*. This barbarous Answer increased his Trouble, for his Father's Death, that now he was like to lye unburied, and be made a Prey to the wild Beasts in the Woods; for the Ground was very hard, and they had not Tools to dig with, and so it was impossible for them to bury him; but having a small Matter of Money left him, *viz.* a *Pagoda*,[229] and a Gold Ring, he hired a Man, and so buried him in as decent a Manner as their Condition would permit.

His dead Father being thus removed out of his Sight, but his Ague continuing, he was reduced very low, partly by Sorrow, and partly by his Disease; all the Comfort he had, was to go into the Wood, and Fields with a Book, either the *Practice of Piety*,[230] or Mr. *Roger's Seven Treatises*,[231] which were the only two Books he had, and meditate and read, and sometimes pray, in which, his Anguish made him often invert *Elijah's* Petition,[232] *That he might die*, because his Life was a burthen to him. God, tho' he was pleased to prolong his Life, yet he found a Way to lighten his Grief, by removing his Ague, and granting him a Desire, which above all things, was acceptable to him. He had read his two Books over so often, that he had both almost by Heart, and tho' they were both pious and good Writings, yet he long'd for the Truth from the original Fountain, and thought it his greatest Unhappiness, that he had not a Bible, and did believe, that he should never see one again: But, contrary to his Expectation, God brought him one after this Manner. As he was fishing one Day, with his Black Boy, to catch some Fish to relieve his Hunger, an old Man pass'd by them, and asked his Boy, whether his Master could read; and when the Boy had answered, *Yes*; he told him, *that he had gotten a Book from the* Portuguese *when they left* Columbo;[233] *and, if his Master pleased, he would sell it him*. The Boy told his Master, who bad him go and see what Book it was. The Boy having served the *English* some time, knew the Book, and, as soon as he had got it into his Hand, came running to him, calling out before he came to him, *'Tis the Bible*. The Words startled him, and he flung down his Angle[234] to meet him, and, finding it true, was mightily rejoyc'd to see it; but he was afraid he should not have enough to purchase it, tho' he was resolved to part with all the Money he had, which was but one *Pagoda*, to buy it; but, his Black Boy perswading him to slight it;[235] and leave it to him to buy it, he at length, obtained it for a knit Cap.

This Accident he could not but look upon as a great Miracle, that God should bestow upon him such an extraordinary Blessing, and bring him a Bible in his own native Language, in such a remote Part of the World, where his Name was not known, and where it was never heard of, that an *Englishman* had ever been before. The Enjoyment of this Mercy was a great Comfort to him in his Captivity, and tho' he wanted no bodily Convenience that the Country did afford, for the King immediately after his Father's Death had sent an express Order to the People of the Town, that they should be kind to him, and give him good Victuals; and, after he had been some time in the Country, and understood the Language, he got him good Conveniences, as, a Horse and Gardens, and falling to Husbandry, God so prospered him, that he had Plenty, not only for himself, but to lend others; which being according to the Custom of the Country, at 50 *per Cent.* a Year, much enriched him. He had also Goats, which served him for Mutton, and Hogs and Hens: Notwithstanding this, I say, for he lived as fine as any of their Noblemen, he could not so far forget his native Country, as to be contented to dwell in a strange Land, where there was to him a Famine of God's Word and Sacraments, the Want of which made all other things to be of little Value to him; therefore, as he made it his daily and fervent Prayer to God, in his good time, to restore him to both, so at length he, with one *Stephen Rutland*, who had lived with him two Years before, resolved to make their Escape, and about the Year 1673, meditated all secret Ways to compass it. They had before taken up a Way of Peddling about the Country, and buying Tobacco, Pepper, Garlick, Combs, and all forts of Iron-Ware, and carried them into those Parts of the Country where they wanted them; and now, to promote their Design, as they went with their Commodities from Place to Place, they discoursed with the Country People, *for they could now speak their Language well*, concerning the Ways and

Inhabitants where the Isle was thinnest and fullest inhabited; where and how the Watches[236] lay from one Country to another; and what Commodities were proper for them to carry into all Parts; pretending, that they would furnish themselves with such Wares as the respective Places wanted. None doubted but what they did was upon the Account of Trade because Mr. *Knox* was so well seated, and could not be supposed to leave such an Estate, was by travelling Northward, because that Part of the Land was least inhabited; and so furnishing themselves with such Wares as were vendible in those Parts, they set forth, and steered their Course towards the North Part of the Island, knowing very little of the Ways, which were generally intricate and perplexed, because they have no publick Roads, but a Multitude of little Paths from one Town to another, and those often changing; and for White Men to enquire about the Ways, was very dangerous, because the People would presently suspect their Design.

At this Time they travelled from *Canda Uda*, as far as the Country of *Neurecalava*, which is in the furthermost Parts of the King's Dominions, and about three Days Journey from their Dwelling. They were very thankful to Providence that they had passed all Difficulties so far; but yet durst not go any further, because they had no Wares left to Traffick with; and it being the first time they had been absent so long from home, they feared the Townsmen would come after them to seek for them, and so they returned home, and went eight or ten times into those Parts with their Wares, till they became well acquainted both with the People and the Paths.

In these Parts Mr. *Knox* met his black Boy, whom he had turned away divers Years before. He had now got a Wife and Children, and was very poor; but being acquainted with these Quarters, he not only took Directions of him, but agreed with him for a good Reward, to conduct him and his Companion to the *Dutch*. He gladly undertook it, and a Time was appointed between them; but Mr. *Knox* being disabled by a grievous Pain which seized him on his right Side, and held him five Days, that he could not travel, this Appointment proved in vain; for tho' he went as soon as he was well, his Guide was gone into another Country about his Business, and they durst not at that time venture to run away without him. These Attempts took up eight or nine Years, various Accidents hindring their Designs, but most commonly the dry Weather, because they fear'd, in the Woods, they should be starv'd with Thirst, all the Country being in such a Condition almost four or five Years together for Lack of Rain.

On *September* 22, 1679, they set forth again, furnished with Knives and small Axes, for their Defence, because they could carry them privately, and send all Sorts of Wares to sell, as formerly, and all necessary Provisions, the Moon being twenty seven Days old, that they might have Light to run away by, to try what Success God Almighty would now give them, in seeking their Liberty. Their first Stage was to *Anarodgburro*, in the Way to which lay a Wilderness, called *Parraoth Mocolane*, full of wild Elephants, Tygers, and Bears; and because 'tis the utmost Confines of the King's Dominions, there is always a Watch kept.

In the Middle of the Way, they heard that the Governour's Officers of these Parts were out to gather up the King's Revenues and Duties, to send them up to the City; which put them into no small Fear, lest finding them, they should send them back again: Whereupon they withdrew to the Western Parts of *Ecpoulpot*, and sat down to Knitting, till they heard they Officers were gone. As soon as they were departed, they went onwards of their Journey, having got a good Parcel of Cotton Yarn to knit Caps with, and having kept their Wares, as they pretended, to exchange for dried Fish, which was sold only in those lower Parts. Their Way lay necessarily thro' the Governour's Yard at *Collinilla*, who dwells there on Purpose to examine all that go and come. This greatly distress'd them, because he would easily suspect they were out of their Bounds, being Captives; however, they went resolutely to his House, and meeting him, presented him with a small Parcel of Tobacco and Betel;[237] and shewing him their Wares told him, they came to get dried Flesh to carry back with them. The Governour did not suspect them, but told them, he was sorry they came in so dry a Time, when no Deer could be catched, but if some Rain fell, he would soon supply them. This Answer pleased them, and they seemed contented to stay; and accordingly abiding with him two or three Days, and no Rain falling, they presented the Governour with five or six Charges of Gunpowder, which is a Rarity among them; and leaving a Bundle at his House, they desired him to shoot them some Deer, while they made a Step to *Anarodgburro*. Here also they were put in a great Fright, by the coming of certain Soldiers from the King to the Governour, to give him Orders to set a secure Guard at the Watches, that no suspicious Persons might pass; which, tho' it was only intended to prevent the Flight of the Relations of certain Nobles whom the King had clapt up; yet they feared they might wonder to see white Men here, and so send them back again. But God so ordered it, that they were very kind to them, and left them to their Business, and so they got safe to *Anarodgburro*. Their Pretence was dried Flesh, tho' they knew there was none to be had; but their real Business was to search the Way down to the *Dutch*, which they staid three Days to do: But finding, that in the Way to *Jasnapatan*, which is one of the *Dutch* Ports, there was a Watch which could hardly be pass'd, and other Inconveniencies not surmountable, they resolved to go back, and take the River *Malwatogah*, which they had before judged would be a probable Guide to lead them to the Sea; and that they might not be pursued, left *Anarodgburro* just at Night, when the People never travel for fear of wild Beasts. On *Sunday, Oct.* 12, being stored with all things needful for their Journey, *viz*. Ten Days Provision, a Basin to boil their Provision in, two Calabashes to fetch Water in, and two great Tallipat Leaves for Tents, with Jaggory, Sweet-meats, Tobacco, Betell, Tinder-Boxes, and a Deer-Skin for Shoes, to keep their Feet from Thorns, because to them they chiefly trusted. Being come to the River, they struck into the Woods, and kept by the Side of it; yet not going on the Sand, lest their Footsteps should be discerned, unless forced, and then going backwards.

Being gotten a good Way into the Wood, it began to rain, wherefore they erected their Tents, made a Fire, and refresh'd themselves against the Rising of the Moon, which was then eighteen Days old; and having tied Deer-Skins about their Feet, and eased themselves of their Wares, they proceeded in their Journey. When they had travelled three or four Hours with Difficulty, because the Moon gave but little Light among the thick Trees, they found an Elephant in their Way before them, and because they could not scare him away, they were forced to stay till Morning; and so they kindled a Fire, and took a Pipe of Tobacco. By the Light they could not discern that ever any Body had been there, nothing being to be seen but Woods, and so they were in great Hopes that they were past all Danger, being beyond all Inhabitants; but they were mistaken; for the River winding Northward, brought them into the midst of a Parcel of Towns, called *Tissea Wava*, where being in Danger of being seen, they were under a mighty Terror for had the People found them, they would have beat them, and sent them up to the King, and to avoid it, they crept into an hollow Tree, and sat there in Mud and Wet, till it began to grow dark, and then betaking themselves to their Legs, travell'd till the Darkness of Night stopt them. They heard Voices behind them, and feared 'twas somebody in Pursuit of them; but at length discerning it was only an Hallooing to keep the wild beasts out of the Corn, they pitched their Tents by the River, and having boiled Rice, and roasted Meat for their Suppers, and satisfied their Hungers, they committed themselves to God's Keeping, and laid them down to Sleep.

The next Morning, to prevent the worst, they got up early, and hasten'd on their Journey; and tho' they were now got out of all Danger of the tame *Chiangulays*,[238] they were in great Danger of the wild ones, of whom those Woods were full; and though they saw their Tents, yet they were all gone, since the Rains had fallen, from the River into the Woods; and so God kept them from that Danger, for had they met the wild Men, they had been shot.

Thus they travelled from Morning to Night several Days, thro' Bushes and Thorns, which made their Arms and Shoulders, which were naked, all of a Gore Blood. They often met with Bears, Hogs, Deer, and wild Buffloes, but they all run away as soon as they saw them. The River was exceeding full of Alligators. In the Evening they used to pitch their Tents, and make great Fires both before and behind them, to affright the wild Beasts, and tho' they heard the Voices of all sorts, they saw none.

On *Thursday* at Noon they cross'd the River *Coronda Oya*, which parts the Country of the *Malabars* from the King's, and on *Friday* about Nine or Ten in the Morning, came among the Inhabitants, of whom they were as much afraid as of the *Chiangulays* before; for tho' the *Wanniounay*, or Prince of this People, payeth Tribute to the *Dutch* out of Fear, yet he is better affected to the King of *Candi*, and if he had took them, would have sent them up to their old Master; but not knowing any Way to escape, they kept on their Journey by the River Side by Day, because the Woods were not to be travell'd by Night, for Thorns and wild Beasts, who came down then to the River to drink. In all the *Malabars* Country they met with only two Bramans,[239] who treated them civilly, and for their Money one of them conducted them till they came into the Territories of the *Dutch*, and out of all Danger from the King of *Candi*, which did not a little rejoice them; but yet they were in no small Trouble how to find the Way out of the Woods, till a *Malabar* for the Lucre of a Knife, conducted them to a *Dutch* Town, where they found Guides to conduct them from Town to Town, till they came to the Fort called *Arepa*, where they arrived *Saturday, October* 18. 1679, and there thankfully ador'd God's wonderful Providence, in thus compleating their Deliverance from a long Captivity of Nineteen Years and six Months.

I come now back to my own History, which draws near a Conclusion, as to the Travels I took in this Part of the World. We were now at Sea, and we stood away to the North for a while, to try if we could get a Market for our Spice, for we were very rich in Nutmegs, but we ill knew what to do with them; we durst not go upon the *English* Coast,[240] or, to speak more properly, among the *English* Factories to Trade; not that we were afraid to fight any two Ships they had; and besides that, we knew, that as they had no Letters of Mart[241] or of Reprisals from the Government, so it was none of their Business to act offensively, no not tho' we were Pyrates. Indeed if we had made any Attempt upon them, they might have justify'd themselves in joining together to resist, and assisting one another to defend themselves; but to go out of their Business to attack a Pyrate Ship of almost fifty Guns, as we were, it was plain, that it was none of their Business, and consequently it was none of our Concern, so we did not trouble our selves about it; but, on the other hand, it was none of our Business, to be seen among them, and to have the News of us carried from one Factory to another: So that whatever Design we might be upon at another Time, we should be sure to be prevented and discovered: Much less had we any Occasion to be seen among the *Dutch* Factories, upon the Coast of *Malabar*; for, being fully loaden with the Spices which we had in the Sense of their Trade plundered them of, it would soon have told them what we were, and all that we had been doing and they would, no doubt, have concerned themselves all manner of Ways to have fallen upon us.

The only Way we had for it was to stand away for *Goa* and Trade, if we could, for our Spices with the *Portuguese* Factory there. Accordingly we sailed almost thither, for we had made Land two Days before, and, being in the Latitude of *Goa*, were standing in fair for *Marmagoon*,[242] on the Head of *Salsat*,[243] at the going up to *Goa*, when I called to the Man at the Helm to bring the Ship to, and bid the Pilot go away N.N.W. till we came out of Sight of the Shore; when *William* and I called a Council as we used to do upon Emergences, what Course we should take to trade there, and not be discovered; and we concluded, at length, that we would not go thither at all; but that *William*, with such trusty Fellows only as could be depended upon, should go in the Sloop to *Surat*, which was still farther Northward, and trade there as Merchants, with such of the *English* Factory as they could find to be for their Turn.

To carry this with the more Caution, and so as not to be suspected, we agreed to take out all her Guns, and to put such Men into her, and no other, as would promise us not to desire or offer to go on Shore, or to enter into any Talk or Conversation with any that might come on board: And to finish the Disguise to our Mind, *William* documented two of our Men, one a Surgeon, as he himself was, and the other a ready-witted Fellow, an old Sailor, that had been a Pilot upon the Coast of *New-England*, and was an excellent Mimick; these two *William* dressed up like two Quakers, and made them talk like such. The old Pilot he made go Captain of the Sloop, and the Surgeon for Doctor, as he was, and himself Super-Cargo: In this Figure, and the Sloop all plain, no curled Work[244] upon her, indeed she had not much before, and no Guns to be seen, away he went for *Surat*.[245]

I should indeed have observed, that we went some Days before we parted, to a small sandy Island, close under the Shore, where there was a good Cove of deep Water, like a Road, and out of Sight of any of the Factories, which are here very thick upon the Coast. Here we shifted the Loading of the Sloop, and put into her such Things only as we had a mind to dispose of there, which was indeed little but Nutmegs and Cloves, but chiefly the former; and from thence *William* and his two Quakers, with about eighteen Men in the Sloop, went away to *Surat*, and came to an Anchor at a Distance from the Factory.

William used such Caution, that he found Means to go on Shore himself, and the Doctor, as he called him, in a Boat, which came on board them to sell Fish, rowed with only *Indians* of the Country, which Boat he afterwards hired to carry him on board again. It was not long that they were on Shore, but that they found Means to get Acquaintance with some *Englishmen*, who, though they lived there, and perhaps, were the Company's Servants[246] at first, yet appeared then to be Traders for themselves, in whatever Coast-Business especially came in their Way, and the Doctor was made the first to pick Acquaintance; so he recommended his Friend, the Super-Cargo, till, by Degrees, the Merchants were as fond of the Bargain as our Men were of the Merchants, only that the Cargo was a little too much for them.

However, this did not prove a Difficulty long with them; for the next Day they brought two more Merchants, *English* also, into their Bargain; and, as *William* could perceive by their Discourse, they resolved, if they bought them, to carry them to the Gulph of *Persia*, upon their own Accounts; *William* took the Hint, and, as he told me afterwards, concluded we might carry them there as well as they; but this was not *William*'s present Business; he had here no less than three and thirty Ton of Nuts, and eighteen Ton of Cloves. There was a good Quantity of Mace[247] among the Nutmegs; but we did not stand to make much Allowance. In short, they bargained, and the Merchants, who would gladly have bought Sloop and all, gave *William* Directions, and two Men for Pilots, to go to a Creek about six Leagues from the Factory, where they brought Boats, and unloaded the whole Cargo, and paid *William* very honestly for it. The whole Parcel amounting, in Money, to about thirty five thousand Pieces of Eight, besides some Goods of Value, which *William* was content to take, and two large Diamonds worth about three Hundred Pounds Sterling.

When they paid the Money, *William* invited them on board the Sloop, where they came, and the merry old Quaker diverted them exceedingly with his Talk, and *Thee'd* 'em, and *Thou'd* 'em, till he made 'em so drunk, that they could not go on Shore for that Night.

They would fain have known who our People were, and whence they came, but not a Man in the Sloop would answer them to any Question they ask'd, but in such a Manner as let them think themselves banter'd and jested with. However, in Discourse, *William* said, they were able Men for any Cargo we could have brought them, and that they would have bought twice as much Spice if we had had it. He ordered the merry Captain to tell them, that they had another Sloop that lay at *Marmagoon*, and that had a great Quantity of Spice on board also; and that if it was not sold when he went back, for that thither he was bound, he would bring her up.

Their new Chaps[248] were so eager, that they would have bargain'd with the old Captain before-hand: Nay Friend, *said he*, I will not trade with thee unsight and unseen; neither do I know whether the Master of the Sloop may not have sold his Loading already to some Merchants of *Salset*; but if he has not, when I come to him, I think to bring him up to thee.

The Doctor had his Employment all this while, as well as *William* and the old Captain; for he went on shore several Times a Day in the *Indian* Boat, and brought fresh Provisions for the Sloop, which the Men had need enough of; he brought in particularly seventeen large Casks of Arrack, as big as Buts, besides smaller Quantities, a Quantity of Rice, and Abundance of Fruits, Mangoes, Pompions, and such Things, with Fowls and Fish. He never came on board but he was deep laden; for, in short, he bought for the Ship, as well as for themselves; and particularly, they half loaded the Ship with Rice and Arrack, with some Hogs, and six or seven Cows, alive; and thus being well victualled, and having Directions for coming again, they returned to us.

William was always the lucky welcome Messenger to us, but never more welcome to us than now; for where we had thrust in the Ship we could get nothing, except a few Mangoes and Roots, being not willing to make any Steps into the Country, or make our selves known, till we had News of our Sloop; and indeed our Mens Patience was almost tired, for it was seventeen Days that *William* spent upon this Enterprize, and well bestow'd too.

When he came back, we had another Conference upon the Subject of Trade, namely, whether we should send the rest of our Spices, and other Goods we had in the Ship, to *Surat*; or, whether we should go up to the Gulph of *Persia* our selves, where it was probable we might sell them as well as the *English* Merchants of *Surat*. *William* was for going our selves, which, by the Way, was from the good frugal Merchant-like Temper of the Man, who was for the best of every Thing: But here I over-ruled *William*, which I very seldom took upon me to do; but I told him, that, considering our Circumstances, it was much better for us to sell all our Cargoe here, though we made but half Price of them, than to go with them to the Gulph of *Persia*, where we should run a greater Risque, and where People would be much more curious and inquisitive into Things than they were here, and where it would not be so easy to manage them, seeing they traded freely and openly there, not by Stealth, as those Men seemed to do; and besides, if they suspected any Thing, it would be much more difficult for us to retreat, except by meer Force, than here, where we were upon the high Sea, as it were, and could be gone whenever we pleased, without any Disguise, or indeed without the least Appearance of being pursued, none knowing where to look for us.

My Apprehensions prevailed with *William*, whether my Reasons did or no, and he submitted; and we resolved to try another Ship's Loading to the same Merchants; the main Business was to consider how to get off of that Circumstance had exposed them with the *English* Merchants; namely, that it was our other Sloop; but this the old Quaker Pilot undertook; for being, as I said, an excellent Mimick himself, it was the easier for him to dress up the Sloop in new Clothes; and first he put on all the carved Work he had taken off before; her Stern, which was painted of a dumb white, or dun Colour, before all flat, was now all lacquer'd, and blue, and I know not how many gay Figures in it; as to her Quarter,[249] the Carpenters made her a neat little Gallery on either Side; she had 12 Guns put into her, and some Patereroes upon her Gunnel,[250] none of which were there before; and to finish her new Habit or Appearance, and make her Change compleat, he ordered her Sails to be alter'd; and as she sailed before with a Half Sprit, like a Yacht, she sailed now with square Sail and Mizen Mast, like a Ketch; so that, in a Word, she was a perfect Cheat, disguised in every Thing that a Stranger could be supposed to take any Notice of, that had never had but one View; for they had been but once on board.

In this mean Figure the Sloop returned; she had a new Man put into her for Captain, one we knew how to trust; and the old Pilot appearing only as a Passenger, the Doctor and *William* acting as the Super-Cargoes, by a formal Procuration from one Captain *Singleton*, and all Things ordered in Form.

We had a compleat Loading for the Sloop; for besides a very great Quantity of Nutmegs and Cloves, Mace, and some Cinnamon, she had on board some Goods, which we took in as we lay about the *Philippine* Islands, while we waited as looking for Purchase.

William made no Difficulty of selling this Cargoe also, and in about twenty Days returned again, freighted with all necessary Provisions for our Voyage, and for a long Time; and, as I say, we had a great deal of other Goods, he brought us back about three and thirty thousand Pieces of Eight, and some Diamonds; which, tho' *William* did not pretend to much Skill in, yet he made shift to act, so as not to be imposed upon, the Merchants he had to deal with too being very fair Men.

They had no Difficulty at all with these Merchants; for the Prospect they had of Gain made them not at all inquisitive; nor did they make the least Discovery of the Sloop; and as to the Selling them Spices which were fetch'd so far from thence, it seems it was not so much a Novelty there as we believed; for the *Portugueze* had frequently Vessels which came from *Macao* in *China*, who brought Spices, which they bought of the *Chinese* Traders, who again frequently dealt among the *Dutch* Spice Islands, and received Spices in Exchange for such Goods as they carried from *China*.

This might be called indeed the only trading Voyage we had made; and now we were really very rich; and it came now naturally before us to consider whither we should go next; our proper Delivery Port, as we ought to have called it, was at *Madagascar*, in the Bay of *Mangahelly*: But *William* took me by my self into the Cabbin of the Sloop one Day, and told me, he wanted to talk seriously with me a little; so we shut our selves in, and *William* began with me.

Wilt thou give me Leave, *says William*, to talk plainly with thee upon thy present Circumstances, and the future Prospect of living, and wilt thou promise on thy Word to take nothing ill of me.

With all my Heart, *said I, William*, I have always found your Advice good, and your Designs have not only been well laid, but your Counsel has been very lucky to us; and therefore say what you will, I promise you I will not take it ill.

But that is not all my Demand, *says William*, if thou dost not like what I am going to propose to thee, thou shalt promise me not to make it publick among the Men.

I will not, *William, says I*, upon my Word, and swore to him too very heartily.

Why then, *says William*, I have but one Thing more to article with thee about, and that is that thou wilt consent, that if thou dost not approve of it for thy self, thou wilt yet consent that I shall put so much of it in Practice as relates to my self, and my new Comrade *Doctor*, so that it be in nothing to thy Detriment and Loss.

In any Thing, *says I, William*, but leaving me, I will; but I cannot part with you upon any Terms whatever.

Well, *says William*, I am not designing to part from thee, unless it is thy own Doing; but assure me in all these Points; and I will tell my Mind freely.

So I promised him every Thing he desired of me in the solemnest Manner possible, and so seriously and frankly withal, that *William* made no Scruple to open his Mind to me.

Why then, in the First Place, *says William*, shall I ask thee if thou dost not think thou and all thy Men are rich enough, and have really gotten as much Wealth together (by whatsoever Way it has been gotten, that is not the Question) as ye all know what to do with?

Why truly *William*, said I, thou art pretty right, I think we have had pretty good Luck.

Well then, *says William*, I would ask, whether, if thou hast gotten enough, thou hast any Thought of leaving off this Trade; for most People leave off Trading when they are satisfied with getting, and are rich enough; for no body trades for the sake of Trading, much less do any Men rob for the sake of Thieving.

Well, *William*, *says I*, now I perceive what it is thou art driving at; I warrant you, *says I*, you begin to hanker after Home.

Why truly, *says William*, thou hast said it, and so I hope thou dost too; it is natural for most Men that are abroad to desire to come Home again at last, especially when they are grown rich, and when they are (as thou ownest thy self to be) rich enough, and so rich, as they know not what to do with more if they had it.

Well, *William*, said I, but now you think you have laid your Preliminary at first so home, that I should have nothing to say; that is, that when I had got Money enough, it would be natural to think of going Home; but you have not explained what you mean by Home, and there you and I shall differ. Why, Man, I am at Home, here is my Habitation, I never had any other in my Life time; I was a kind of Charity School-Boy, so that I can have no Desire of going any where for being rich or poor, for I have no where to go.

Why, *says William*, looking a little confused, art not thou an *Englishman*? Yes, *says I*, I think so, you see I speak *English*; but I came out of *England* a Child, and never was in it but once since I was a Man, and then I was cheated and imposed upon, and used so ill, that I care not if I never see it more.

Why hast thou no relations or Friends there, *says he*, no Acquaintance, none that thou hast any Kindness for, or any remains of Respect for?

Not I, *William*, said I, not one, no more than I have in the Court of the Great *Mogul*.

Nor any Kindness for the Country, where thou wast born, *says William*.

Not I, any more than for the Island of *Madagascar*, nor so much neither, for that has been a fortunate Island to me more than once, as thou knowest, *William*, said I.

William was quite stunn'd at my Discourse, and held his Peace; and *I said to him*, go on, *William*, what hast thou to say farther? For I hear you have some Project in your Head, *says I*,[a] come, let's have it out.

Nay, *says William*, thou hast put me to Silence, and all I had to say is over-thrown; all my Projects are come to nothing, and gone.

Well, but *William, said I,* let me hear what they were, for tho' it is so that what I have to aim at does not look your Way; and tho' I have no Relation, no Friend, no Acquaintance in *England,* yet I do not say I like this roving, cruising Life, so well as never to give it over: Let me hear if thou canst propose to me any thing beyond it.

Certainly Friend, *says William,* very gravely, there is something beyond it, and lifting up his Hands, he seemed very much affected, and I thought I see Tears stand in his Eyes, but I, that was too hardened a Wretch to be moved with these Things, laughed at him; what, *says I,* you mean *Death,* I warrant you, don't you, that is beyond this Trade; why, when it comes, it comes, then we are all provided for.

Ay, *says William,* that is true; but it wou'd be better that some Things were thought on before that came.

Thought on, *says I,* what signifies thinking of it; to think of Death, is to dye; and to be always thinking of it, is to be all one's Life-long a dying; 'tis Time enough to think of it when it comes.

You will easily believe I was well qualified for a Pirate that could talk thus; but let me leave it upon Record for the Remark of other hardned Rogues like my self. My Conscience gave me a Pang that I had never felt before, when I said, *What signifies thinking of it,* and told me, I shou'd one Day think of these Words with a sad Heart, but the Time of my Reflection was not yet come; so I went on.

Says William, very seriously, I must tell thee, Friend, I am sorry to hear thee talk so; they that never think of dying, often dye without thinking of it.

I carried on the jesting Way a while farther, *and said,* prithee do not talk of dying; how do we know we shall ever dye, and began to laugh?

I need not answer thee to that, *says William,* it is not my Place to reprove thee who art Commander over me here, but I had rather thou wouldst talk otherwise of Death; 'tis a coarse Thing.

Say any Thing to me, *William, said I,* I will take it kindly: *I began now to be very much moved at his Discourse.*

Says William, Tears running down his Face, it is because Men live as if they were never to dye, that so many dye before they know how to live; but it was not Death that I meant, when I said, *That there was something to be thought of beyond this Way of Living.*

Why, *William, said I,* what was that?

It was *Repentance, says he.*

Why, *says I,* did you ever know a Pirate repent?

At this he started a little, and return'd, at the Gallows, I have one before, and I hope thou wilt be the second.

He spoke this very affectionately, and with an Appearance of Concern for me.

Well, *William*, says *I*, I thank you, and I am not so senseless of these Things, perhaps, as I make my self seem to be; but come, let me hear your Proposal.

My Proposal, *says William*, is for thy Good, as well as my own; we may put an End to this kind of Life, and repent; and I think the fairest Occasion offers for both at this very Time that ever did, or ever will, or indeed, can happen again.

Look you, *William*, says *I*, let me have your Proposal for putting an End to our present Way of Living first, for that is the Case before us, and you and I will talk of the other afterward. I am not so insensible, *said I*, as you may think me to be; but let us get out of this hellish Condition we are in first.

Nay, *says William*, thou art in the right there; we must never talk of repenting while we continue Pirates.

Well, *says I*, *William*, that's what I meant, for if we must not reform, as well as be sorry for what's done, I have no Notion what Repentance means; indeed, at best I know little of the Matter; but the Nature of the thing seems to tell me, that the first Step we have to take, is to break off this wretched Course, and I'll begin there with you with all my Heart.

I could see by his Countenance, that *William* was throughly pleased with the Offer; and if he had Tears in his Eyes before, he had more now, but it was from a quite differing Passion, for he was so swallow'd up with Joy, he could not speak.

Come, *William*, says *I*, thou shewest me plain enough thou hast an honest Meaning. Dost thou think 'tis practicable for us to put an End to our unhappy Way of Living here, and get off?

Yes, *says he*, I think 'tis very practicable for me, whether 'tis for thee or no, that will depend upon thy self.

Well, *says I*, I give you my Word, that as I have commanded you all along, from the Time I first took you on Board, so you shall command me from this Hour; and every thing you direct me, I'll do.

Wilt thou leave it all to me? Dost thou say this freely?

Yes, *William*, says *I*, freely, and I'll perform it faithfully.

Why then, *says William*, my Scheme is this, we are now at the Mouth of the Gulph of *Persia*, we have sold so much of our Cargo here at *Surat*, that we have Money enough; send me away for *Bassora*[251] with the Sloop, loaden with the *China* Goods we have on Board, which will make another good Cargo; and I'll warrant thee I'll find Means among the *English* and the *Dutch* Merchants there, to lodge a Quantity of Goods and Money also *as a Merchant*, so as we will be able to have Recourse to it again upon any Occasion; and when I come Home we will contrive the rest; and in the mean Time do you bring the Ship's Crew to take a Resolution to go to *Madagascar*, as soon as I return.

I told him, I thought he need not go so far as *Bassora*, but might run into *Gombaroon*,[252] or to *Ormus*, and pretend the same Business.

No, *says he*, I cannot act with the same Freedom there, because the Company's Factory are there, and I may be laid hold of there on Pretence of Interloping.

Well, but, *said I*, you may go to *Ormus* then, for I am loath to part with you so long as to go to the Bottom of the *Persian* Gulph. He return'd that I should leave it to him to do as he should see Cause.

We had taken a large Sum of Money at *Surat*; so that we had near a hundred thousand Pounds in Money at our Command; but on board the great Ship we had still a great deal more.

I ordered him publickly to keep the Money on board which he had, and to buy up with it a Quantity of Ammunition if he could get it, and so to furnish us for new Exploits; and in the mean Time I resolved to get a Quantity of Gold and some Jewels, which I had on board the great Ship, and place them so, that I might carry them off without Notice, as soon as he came back; and so according to *William*'s Directions, I left him to go the Voyage, and I went on board the great Ship, in which we had indeed an immense Treasure.

We waited no less than two Months, for *William*'s Return; and indeed I began to be very uneasy about *William*, sometimes thinking he had abandoned me, and that he might have used the same Artifice to have engaged the other Men to comply with him, and so they were gone away together; and it was but three Days before his Return, that I was just upon the Point of resolving to go away to *Madagascar*, and give him over; but the old Surgeon, who mimicked the Quaker, and passed for the Master of the Sloop at *Surat*, perswaded me against that; for which good Advice, and his apparent Faithfulness in what he had been trusted with, I made him a Party to my Design, and he proved very honest.

At length *William* came back, to our inexpressible Joy, and brought a great many necessary Things with him; as particularly, he brought sixty Barrels of Powder, some Iron Shot, and about thirty Ton of Lead; also he brought a great deal of Provisions; and in a Word, *William* gave me a public Account of his Voyage, in the Hearing of whoever happened to be upon the Quarter-Deck, that no Suspicions might be found about us.

After all was done, *William* moved, that he might go up again, and that I would go with him; named several Things which we had on board that he could not sell there, and particularly told us, he had been obliged to leave several Things there, the Caravans being not come in; and that he had ingaged to come back again with Goods.

This was what I wanted; the Men were eager for his Going, and particularly because he told them they might load the Sloop back with Rice and Provisions: But I seemed backward to going; when the old Surgeon stood up, and perswaded me to go, and with many arguments pressed me to it; as particularly, if I did not go, there would be no Order, and several of the Men might drop away, and perhaps betray all the rest; and that they should not think it safe for the Sloop to go again, if I did not go; and to urge me to it, he offered himself to go with me.

Upon these Considerations I seemed to be over perswaded to go; and all the Company seemed the better satisfied when I had consented: And accordingly we took all the Powder, Lead, and Iron out of the Sloop into the great Ship, and all the other Things that were for the Ship's Use, and put in some Bales of Spices, and Casks or Frailes²⁵³ of Cloves, in all about seven Ton, and some other Goods, among the Bales of which I had convey'd all my private Treasure, which, I assure you, was of no small Value; and away I went.

At going off, I called a Council of all the Officers in the Ship, to consider in what Place they should wait for me, and how long, where we appointed the Ship to stay eight and twenty Days, at a little island on the *Arabian* Side of the Gulph; and that if the Sloop did not come in that Time, they should sail to another Island to the West of that Place; and wait there fifteen Days more; and that then if the Sloop did not come, they should conclude some Accident must have happened, and the Rendezvous should be at *Madagascar*.

Being thus resolved, we left the Ship, which both *William*, and I, and the Surgeon never intended to see any more: We steered directly for the Gulph, and through to *Bassaro*, or *Balsara*. This City of *Balsara* lies at some Distance from the Place where our Sloop lay, and the River not being very safe, and we but ill acquainted with it, having but an ordinary Pilot, we went on Shore at a Village where some Merchants live, and which is very populous, for the sake of small Vessels riding there.

Here we stay'd, and traded three or four Days, landing all our Bales and Spices, and indeed the whole Cargoe, that was of any considerable Value; which we chose to do rather than go up immediately to *Balsara*, till the Project we had laid was put in Execution.

After we had bought several Goods, and were preparing to buy several others, the Boat being on Shore with twelve Men, my self, *William*, the Surgeon, and one Fourth Man, whom we had singled out, we contrived to send a *Turk*, just at the Dusk of the Evening, with a Letter to the Boat-swain; and giving the Fellow a Charge to run with all possible Speed, we stood at a small Distance to observe the Event. The Contents of the Letter were thus written by the old Doctor.

'Boatswain *Thomas*,

'We are all betray'd; for God's Sake make off with the Boat, and get on board, or you are all lost. The Captain, *William* the Quaker and *George* the Reformade[254] are seized and carried away; I am escaped and hid, but cannot stir out; If I do I am a dead Man. As soon as you are on board, cut or slip, and make Sail for your Lives.

'Adieu.

R. S.'

We stood undiscovered, as above, it being the Dusk of the Evening, and saw the *Turk* deliver the Letters; and in three Minutes we saw all the Men hurry into the Boat, and put off and no sooner were they on board, but they took the Hint, as we supposed; for the next Morning they were out of Sight; and we never heard Tale or Tidings of them since.

We were now in a good Place, and in very good Circumstances, for we past for Merchants of *Persia*.

It is not material to record here what Mass of ill-gotten Wealth we had got together. It will be more to the Purpose to tell you, that I began to be sensible of the Crime of getting of it in such a Manner as I had done, that I had very little Satisfaction in the Possession of it; and, as I told *William*, I had no Expectation of keeping it, nor much Desire; but as I said to him one Day walking out into the Fields near the Town at *Bassaro*, so I depended upon it, that it would be the case, which you will hear presently.

We were perfectly secured at *Bassaro*, by having frighted away the Rogues, our Comrades; and we had nothing to do but to consider how to vert[255] our Treasure in Things proper to make us look like Merchants, as we were now to be, and not like Free-booters, as we really had been.

We happened very opportunely here upon a *Dutchman*, who had travelled from *Bengal* to *Agra*, the Capital City of the *Great Mogul*, and from thence was come to the Coast of *Malabar* by Land, and got Shipping some how or other up the Gulph; and we found his Design was to go up the great River[256] to *Bagdat* or *Babylon*; and so by the Caravan to *Aleppo* and *Scanderoon*. As *William* spoke *Dutch*, and was of an agreeable insinuating Behaviour, he soon got acquainted with this *Dutchman*, and discovering our Circumstances to one another, we found he had considerable Effects with him; and that he had traded long in that Country, and was making homeward to his own Country; and that he had Servants with him, one an *Armenian*, whom he had taught to speak *Dutch*, and who had something of his own, but had a Mind to travel into *Europe*; and the other a *Dutch* Sailor, whom he had picked up by his Fancy, and reposed a great Trust in him, and a very honest Fellow he was.

This *Dutchman* was very glad of an Acquaintance, because he soon found that we directed our Thoughts to *Europe* also, and as he found we were encumber'd with Goods only, for we let him know nothing of our Money, he readily offer'd us his Assistance, to dispose of as many of them as the Place we were in would put off, and his Advice what to do with the rest.

While this was doing, *William* and I consulted what to do with our selves, and what we had; and first we resolved we would never talk seriously of any of our Measures, but in the open Fields, where we were sure no Body could hear; so every Evening, when the Sun began to decline, and the Air to be moderate, we walk'd out sometimes this Way, sometimes that, to consult of our Affairs.

I should have observed, that we had new cloathed our selves here after the *Persian* Manner in long Vests of Silk, a Gown or Robe of *English* Crimson Cloth, very fine and handsome, and had let our Beards grow so after the *Persian* Manner that we past for *Persian* Merchants, in View only, tho', *by the Way*, we could not understand or speak one Word of the Language of *Persia*, or indeed of any other but *English* and *Dutch*, and of the latter I understood very little.

However, the *Dutchman* supply'd all this for us, and as we had resolved to keep our selves as retired as we could, though there were several *English* Merchants upon the Place, yet we never acquainted our selves with one of them, or exchanged a Word with them, by which Means we prevented their Enquiry of us now, or their giving any Intelligence of us, if any News of our Landing here should happen to come, which was easy for us to know, was possible enough, if any of our Comrades fell into bad Hands, or by many Accidents which we could not foresee.

It was during my being here, for here we stay'd near two Months, that I grew very thoughtful about my Circumstances, not as to the Danger, neither indeed were we in any, but were entirely conceal'd and unsuspected; but I really began to have other Thoughts of my self, and of the World, than ever I had before.

William had struck so deep into my unthinking Temper, with hinting to me, that there was something beyond all this, that the present Time was the Time of Enjoyment, but that the Time of Account approached; that the Work that remain'd was gentler than the Labour past, *viz. Repentance*, and that it was high Time to think of it; I say these, and such Thoughts as these, engross'd my Hours, and in a Word, I grew very sad.

As to the Wealth I had, which was immensely great, it was all like Dirt under my Feet; I had no Value for it, no Peace in the Possession of it, no great Concern about me for the leaving of it.

William had perceiv'd my Thoughts to be troubled, and my Mind heavy and opprest for some Time; and one Evening, in one of our cool Walks, I began with him about the leaving our Effects. *William* was a wise and wary Man, and indeed all the Prudentials of my Conduct, had for a long Time been owing to his Advice, and so now all the Methods for preserving our Effects, and even our selves lay upon him; and he had been telling me of some of the Measures he had been taking for our making homeward, and for the Security of our Wealth, when I took him very short: *Why, William,* says I, *dost though think we shall ever be able to reach* Europe *with all this Cargo that we have about us?*

Ay, *says William,* without doubt, as well as other Merchants with theirs, as long as it is not publickly known what Quantity, or of what Value our Cargo consists.

Why, *William,* says I, smiling, do you think that if there is a *God above,* as you have so long been telling me there is, and that we must give an Account to him? I say, Do you think if he be a righteous Judge, he will let us escape thus with the Plunder, as we may call it, of so many innocent People, nay; I might say Nations, and not call us to an Account for it before we can get to *Europe,* where we pretend[257] to enjoy it?

William appeared struck and surprized at the Question, and made no Answer for a great while, and I repeated the Question, adding, that it was not to be expected.

After a little Pause, *says William,* Thou hast started a very weighty Question, and I can make no positive Answer to it, but I will state it thus; first, it is True,[a] that if we consider the Justice of God, we have no Reason to expect any Protection, but as the ordinary Ways of Providence are out of the common Road of human Affairs, so we may hope for Mercy still upon our Repentance, and we know not how good he may be to us, so we are to act as if we rather depended upon the last, I mean the merciful Part, than claimed the first, which must produce nothing but Judgment and Vengeance.

But hark ye, *William,* says I, the Nature of Repentance, as you hinted once to me, included Reformation, and we can never reform; how then can we repent?

Why, can we never reform, *says William?*

Because, *said I*, we cannot restore what we have taken away by Rapine and Spoil.

'Tis true, *says William*, we can never do that, for we can never come to the Knowledge of the Owners.

But what then must be done with our Wealth, *said I*, the Effects of Plunder and Rapine? If we keep it, we continue to be Robbers and Thieves, and if we quit it, we cannot do Justice with it, for we cannot restore it to the right Owners?

Nay, *says William*, the Answer to it is short; to quit what we have, and do it here, is to throw it away to those who have no Claim to it, and to divest our selves of it, but to do no Right with it; whereas we ought to keep it carefully together, with a Resolution to do what Right with it we are able; and who knows what Opportunity Providence may put into our Hands, to do Justice at least to some of those we have injured, so we ought at least to leave it to him, and go on, as it is, without doubt, our present Business to do, to some Place of Safety, where we may wait his Will.

This Resolution of *William* was very satisfying to me indeed, as, the Truth is, all he said, and at all Times, was solid and good; and had not *William* thus, as it were, quieted my Mind, I think verily I was so alarmed at the just Reason I had to expect Vengeance from Heaven upon me for my ill-gotten Wealth, that I should have run away from it as the Devil's Goods; that I had nothing to do with that did not belong to me, and that I had no Right to keep, and was in certain Danger of being destroy'd for.

However, *William* settled my Mind to more prudent Steps than these, and I concluded that I ought, however, to proceed to a Place of Safety, and leave the Event to God Almighty's Mercy; but this I must leave upon Record, that I had from this Time no Joy of the Wealth I had got; I look'd upon it all as a stolen, and so indeed the greatest Part of it was; I look'd upon it as a Hoard of other Mens Goods, which I had robbed the innocent Owners of, and which I ought, in a Word, to be hanged for here, and damned for hereafter; and now indeed I began sincerely to hate my self for a Dog, a Wretch that had been a Thief, and a Murtherer; a Wretch, that was in a Condition which no Body was ever in; for I had robb'd, and tho' I had the Wealth by me, yet it was impossible I should ever make any Restitution; and upon this Account it run in my Head, that I could never repent, for that Repentance could not be sincere without Restitution, and therefore I must of Necessity be damned, there was no room for me to escape: I went about with my Heart full of these Thoughts, little better than a distracted Fellow; in short, running headlong into the dreadfullest Despair, and premeditated nothing but how to rid my self out of the World; and indeed the Devil, if such Things are of the Devil's immediate doing, followed his Work very close with me, and nothing lay upon my Mind for several Days, but to shoot my self into the Head with my Pistol.

I was all this while in a vagrant Life, among Infidels, Turks, Pagans, and such Sort of People; I had no Minister, no Christian, to converse with, but poor *William*, he was my Ghostly Father, or Confessor, and he was all the Comfort I had. As for my Knowledge of Religion, you have heard my History; you may suppose I had not much, and as for the Word of God, I don't remember that I ever read a Chapter in the *Bible* in my Life-time since I[a] was *little Bob* at *Busselton*, and went to School to learn my *Testament*.

However, it pleased God to make *William* the Quaker every thing to me; upon this Occasion I took him out one Evening as usual, and hurried him away into the Fields with me, in more Haste than ordinary, and there, in short, I told him the Perplexity of my Mind, and under what terrible Temptations of the Devil I had been, that I must shoot my self, for I could not support the Weight and Terror that was upon me.

Shoot your self, *says William*, why, what will that do for you?

Why, *says I*, 'twill put an End to a miserable Life.

Well, *says William*, are you satisfied the next will be better?

No, no, *says I*, much worse to be sure.

Why then, *says he*, shoot your self is the Devil's Notion, no doubt, for 'tis the Devil of a Reason, that because thou art in an ill Case, that therefore thou must put thy self into a worse.

This shock'd my Reason indeed: Well, but *says I*, there is no bearing the miserable Condition I am in.

Very well, *says William*, but it seems there is some bearing a worse Condition, and so you will shoot your self, that you may be past Remedy.

I am past Remedy already, *says I*.

How do you know that, *says he*?

I am satisfied of it, *said I*.

Well, *says he*, but you are not sure, so you will shoot your self to make it certain; for tho' on this side Death you can't be sure you will be damned at all, yet the Moment you step on the other side of Time, you are sure of it; for when 'tis done, 'tis not to be said then that you will, but that you are damned.

Well, but, says William, *as if he had been between Jest and Earnest*, pray, what didst thou dream of last Night?

Why, *said I*, I had frightful Dreams all Night, and particularly I dreamt that the Devil came for me, and asked me what my Name was? and I told him, then he askt me what Trade I was? Trade, *says I*, I am a Thief, a Rogue, by my Calling; I am a Pirate, and a Murtherer, and ought to be hanged; ay, ay, says the Devil, so you do and you are the Man I look'd for, and therefore come along with me, at which I was most horribly frighted, and cried out, so that it waked me, and I have been in a horrible Agony ever since.

Very well, *says William*, come, give me the Pistol thou talk'st of just now.

Why, *says I*, what will you do with it?

Do with it, *says William*, why, thou needst not shoot thy self, I shall be obliged to do it for thee, why, thou wilt destroy us all.

What do you mean, *William*, said I?

Mean, *said he*, nay, what dist thou mean? to cry out aloud in thy Sleep, *I am a Thief, a Pirate, a Murtherer, and ought to be hanged*; why, thou wilt ruine us all, 'twas well the *Dutchman* did not understand *English*: In short, I must shoot thee to save my own Life; come, come, *says he*, give me thy Pistol.

I confess, this terrified me again another Way and I began to be sensible, that if any Body had been near me to understand *English*, I had been undone, and the Thought of shooting my self forsook me from that Time, and I turned to *William*; you disorder me extremely, *William, said I*, why, I am never safe, nor is it safe to keep me Company, what shall I do? I shall betray you all.

Come, come, Friend *Bob*, *says he*, I'll put an End to it all, if you will take my Advice.

How's that, *said I*?

Why only, *says he*, that *the next Time thou talkest with the Devil, thou wilt talk a little softlier*, or we shall be all undone, and you too.

This frighted me, I must confess, and allay'd a great deal of the Trouble of Mind I was in; but *William*, after he had done jesting with me, entered upon a very long and serious Discourse with me about the Nature of my Circumstances, and about Repentance, that it ought to be attended indeed with a deep Abhorrence of the Crime that I had to charge my self with, but that to despair of God's Mercy was no Part of Repentance, but putting my self into the Condition of the Devil; indeed, that I must apply my self with a sincere humble Confession of my Crime, to ask Pardon of God whom I had offended, and cast my self upon his Mercy, resolving to be willing to make Restitution, if ever it should please God to put it into my Power, even to the utmost of what I had in the World; and this he told me was the Method which he had resolved upon himself, and in this he told me he had found Comfort.

I had a great deal of Satisfaction in *William's* Discourse, and it quieted me very much; but *William* was very anxious ever after about my talking in my Sleep, and took care to lye with me always himself, and to keep me from Lodging in any House, where so much as a Word of *English* was understood.

However, there was not the like Occasion afterward, for I was much more composed in my Mind, and resolved for the future to live a quite differing Life from what I had done: As to the Wealth I had, I look'd upon it as nothing; I resolved to set it apart to any such Opportunity of doing Justice, that God should put into my Hand, and the miraculous Opportunity I had afterwards of applying some Parts of it to preserve a ruined Family, whom I had plunder'd, may be worth reading, if I have Room for it in this Account.

With these Resolutions I began to be restored to some Degrees of Quiet in my Mind, and having after almost three Months Stay at *Bassora* disposed of some Goods; but having a great Quantity left, we hired Boats according to the *Dutchman*'s Direction, and went up to *Bugdat*, or *Babylon*, on the River *Tygris*, or rather *Euphrates*; we had a very considerable Cargo of Goods with us, and therefore made a great Figure there, and were receiv'd with Respect; we had in Particular, two and Forty Bales of *Indian* Stuffs of sundry Sorts, Silk, Muslins, and fine Chints; we had Fifteen Bales of very fine *China* Silks, and Seventy Packs or Bales of Spices, particularly Cloves and Nutmegs, with other Goods; we were bid Money here for our Cloves, but the *Dutchman* advised us not to part with them, and told us, we should get a better Price at *Aleppo*, or in the *Levant*, so we prepared for the Caravan.

We concealed our having any Gold, or Pearls, as much as we could, and therefore sold Three or Four Bales of *China* Silks, and *Indian* Callicoes, to raise Money to buy Camels, and to pay the Customs, which are taken at several Places, and for our Provisions over the Desarts.

I travelled this Journey careless to the last Degree of my Goods or Wealth, believing, that as I came by it all by Rapine and Violence, God would direct, that it should be taken from me again in the same Manner; and indeed, I think I might say, I was very willing it should be so; but as I had a merciful Protector above me, so I had a most faithful Steward, Counsellor, Partner, or whatever I might call him, who was my Guide, my Pilot, my Governor, my every thing, and took care both of me, and of all we had; and tho' he had never been in any of these Parts of the World, yet he took the Care of all upon him; and in about Nine and Fifty Days we arriv'd from *Bassora*, at the Mouth of the River *Tygris* and *Euphrates*, thro' the Desart, and thro' *Aleppo* to *Alexandria*, or as we call it, *Scanderoon*,[258] in the *Levant*.

Here *William* and I, and the other two, our faithful Comrades, debated what we should do; and here *William* and I resolved to separate from the other Two, they resolving to go with the *Dutchman* into *Holland*, and by the Means of some *Dutch* Ship which lay then in the Road: *William* and I told them, we resolved to go and settle in the *Morea*, which then belonged to the *Venetians*.

It is true, we acted wisely in it not to let them know whither we went, seeing we had resolved to separate, but we took our old Doctor's Directions how to write to him in *Holland*, and in *England*, that we might have Intelligence from him on Occasion, and promised to give him an Account how to write to us, which we afterwards did, as may in Time be made out.

We stay'd here some Time after they were gone, till at length not being thoroughly resolved whither to go till then, a *Venetian* Ship touch'd at *Cyprus*, and put in at *Scanderoon* to look for Freight Home: We took the Hint, and bargaining for our Passage, and the Freight of our Goods, we embark'd for *Venice*, where in two and Twenty Days we arrived safe with all our Treasure, and with such a Cargo, take our Goods, and our Money, and our Jewels together, as I believe was never brought into the City by Two single Men, since the State of *Venice* had a Being.

We kept our selves here *incognito* for a great while, passing for Two *Armenian* Merchants still, as we had done before; and by this Time we had gotten so much of the *Persian* and *Armenian* Jargon, which they talk'd at *Bassora*, and *Bagdat*, and every where that we came in the Country, as was sufficient to make us able to talk to one another, so as not to be understood by any Body, though sometimes hardly by our selves.

Here we converted all our Effects into Money, settled our Abode as for a considerable Time, and *William* and I maintaining an inviolable Friendship and Fidelity to one another, lived like two Brothers; we neither had or sought any separate Interest; we convers'd seriously and gravely, and upon the Subject of our Repentance continually; we never changed, that is to say, so as to leave off our *Armenian* Garbs, and we were called at *Venice* the two *Grecians*.[259]

I have been two or three times going to give a Detail of our Wealth, but it will appear incredible, and we had the greatest Difficulty in the World how to conceal it, being justly apprehensive lest we might be assassinated in that Country for our Treasure; at length *William* told me, he began to think now that he must never see *England* any more, and that indeed he did not much concern himself about it; but seeing we had gained so great a Wealth, and he had some poor Relations in *England*, and, if I was willing, he would write to know if they were living, and to know what Condition they were in; and if he found such of them were alive, as he had some Thoughts about, he would, with my Consent, send them something to better their Condition.

I consented most willingly, and accordingly *William* wrote to a Sister, and an Uncle, and in about five Weeks Time receiv'd an Answer from them both, directed to himself, under Cover of a hard *Armenian* Name that he had given himself, *viz.* Seignior *Constantine Alexion of Ispahan* at *Venice*.

It was a very moving Letter he receiv'd from his Sister, who after the most passionate Expressions of Joy to hear he was alive, seeing she had long ago had an Account that he was murthered by the Pirates in the *West-Indies*; she intreats him to let her know what Circumstances he was in; tells him, she was not in any Capacity to do any thing considerable for him, but that he should be welcome to her with all her Heart; that she was left a Widow with Four Children, but kept a little Shop in the *Minories*, by which she made shift to maintain her Family; and that she had sent him Five Pound, lest he should want Money in a strange Country, to bring him Home.

I could see the Letter brought Tears out of his Eyes, as he read it, and indeed when he shewed it me, and the little Bill for Five Pounds upon an *English* Merchant in *Venice*, it brought Tears out of my Eyes too.

After we had been both affected sufficiently with the Tenderness and Kindness of this Letter, he turns to me, *says he*, what shall I do for this poor Woman? I mused a while, at last, *says I*, I will tell you what you shall do for her; she has sent you Five Pounds, and she has Four Children, and her self, that's Five; such a Sum from a poor Woman in her Circumstances, is as much as Five Thousand Pounds is to us: You shall send her a Bill of Exchange for Five Thousand Pounds *English* Money, and bid her conceal her Surprize at it, till she hears from you again, but bid her leave off her Shop, and go and take a House some where in the Country, not far off from *London*, and stay there in a moderate Figure, till she hears from you again.

Now, says *William*, I perceive by it that you have some Thoughts of venturing into *England*.

Indeed *William*, said I, you mistake me, but it presently occurred to me that you should venture; for what have you done that you may not be seen there? Why should I desire to keep you from your Relations purely to keep me Company?

William look'd very affectionately upon me; nay, *says he*, we have embarked together so long, and come together so far, I am resolved I'll never part with thee as long as I live, go where thou wilt, or stay where thou wilt; and as for my Sister, said *William*, I cannot send her such a Sum of Money; for whose is all this Money we have? 'tis most of it thine.

No, *William*, *said I*, there is not a Penny of it mine but what is yours too, and I won't have any thing but an equal Share with you, and therefore you shall send it to her, if not, I will send it.

Why, *says William*, it will make the poor Woman distracted, she will be so surprized, she will go out of her Wits; well, *said William*, you may do it prudently; send her a Bill back'd[260] of a Hundred Pounds, and bid her expect more in a Post or two; and that you will send her enough to live on without keeping Shop, and then send her more.

Accordingly *William* sent her a very kind Letter, with a Bill upon a Merchant in *London* for a Hundred and Sixty Pound, and bid her comfort her self with the Hope, that he should be able in a little Time to send her more. About ten Days after he sent her another Bill of Five Hundred and Forty Pound, and a Post or two after another for Three Hundred Pound, making in all a Thousand Pound; and told her he would send her sufficient to leave off her Shop, and directed her to take a House, as above.

He waited then till he received an Answer to all the Three Letters, with an Account, that she had received the Money, and which I did not expect, that she had not let any other Acquaintance know that she had received a Shilling from any Body, or so much as that he was alive, and would not till she heard again.

When he shewed me this Letter, well, *William said I*, this Woman is fit to be trusted with Life or any thing, send her the rest of the Five Thousand Pound; and I'll venture to *England* with you, to this Woman's House, whenever you will.

In a Word, we sent her Five Thousand Pound in good Bills, and she receiv'd them punctually, and in a little Time sent her Brother Word, that she had pretended to her Uncle that she was sickly, and could not carry on the Trade any longer, and that she had taken a large House about Four Miles from *London*, under Pretence of letting Lodgings for her Livelihood; and, in short, intimated as if she understood that he intended to come over to be *Incognito*, assuring him he should be as retired as he pleased.

This was opening the very Door for us, that we thought had been effectually shut for this Life; and in a Word, we resolved to venture, but to keep our selves entirely concealed, both as to Name, and every other Circumstance; and accordingly *William* sent his Sister Word, how kindly he took her prudent Steps, and that she had guessed right, that he desired to be retired, and that he obliged her not to increase her Figure,[261] but live private, till she might perhaps see him.

He was going to send the Letter away; come, *William*, said I, you shan't send her an empty Letter, tell her, you have a Friend coming with you, that must be as retired as your self, and I'll send her Five Thousand Pound more.

So in short we made this poor Woman's Family rich, and yet when it came to the Point, my Heart failed me, and I durst not venture, and for *William*, he would not stir without me, and so we stayed about two Year after this, considering what we should do.

You may think, perhaps, that I was very prodigal of my ill-gotten Goods, thus to load a Stranger with my Bounty, and give a Gift like a Prince to one that had been able to merit nothing of me, or indeed know me: But my Condition ought to be considered in this Case; though I had Money to Profusion, yet I was perfectly destitute of a Friend in the World to have the least Obligation or Assistance from, or knew not either where to dispose or trust any Thing I had while I lived, or whom to give it to, if I died.

When I had reflected upon the Manner of my Getting of it, I was some-times for giving of it all to charitable Uses, as a Debt due to Mankind, though I was no^a Roman-Catholick, and not at all of the Opinion, that it would purchase me any Repose to my Soul; but I thought, as it was got by a general Plunder, and which I could make no Satisfaction for, it was due to the Community, and I ought to distribute it for the general Good. But still I was at a Loss how, and where, and by whom to settle this Charity, not daring to go Home to my own Country, lest some of my Comrades stroled[262] Home should see and detect me; and, for the very Spoil of my Money, or the Purchase of his own Pardon, betray and expose me to an untimely End.

Being thus destitute, I say, of a Friend, I pitch'd thus upon *William*'s Sis-ter; the kind Step of her's to her Brother, who she thought to be in Distress, signifying a generous Mind, and a charitable Disposition; and having resolved to make her the Object of my first Bounty, I did not doubt but I should purchase something of a Refuge for my self, and a kind of a Centre, to which I should tend in my future Actions; for really a Man that has a Subsistance, and no Residence, no Place that has a Magnetick Influ-ence upon his Affections, is in one of the most odd uneasy Conditions in the World; nor is it in the Power of all his Money to make it up to him.

It was, as I told you, two Year and upwards, that we remained at *Venice*, and thereabout, in the greatest Hesitation imaginable, irresolute and unfixed to the last Degree. *William*'s Sister importuned us daily to come to *England*, and wondered we should not dare to trust her, whom we had to such a Degree obliged to be faithful; and in a Manner lamented her being suspected by us.

At last I began to incline; and I said to *William*, Come; Brother *William*, *said I, for ever since our Discourse at* Balsara, *I called him Brother*, if you will agree to two or three Things with me, I'll go Home to *England* with all my Heart.

Says William, let me know what they are.

Why first, *Says I*, you shall not disclose your self to any of your Relations in *England*, but your Sister, no not to one.

Secondly, we will not shave off our Mustachoes or Beards, (for we had all along worn our Beards after the *Grecian* Manner) nor leave off our long Vests, that we may pass for *Grecians* and Foreigners.

Thirdly, That we shall never speak *English* in publick before any body, your Sister excepted.

Fourthly, That we will always live together, and pass for Brothers.

William said, he would agree to them all with all his Heart; but that the not speaking *English* would be the hardest; but he would do his best for that too: So, in a Word, we agreed to go from *Venice* to *Naples*, where we verted a large Sum of Money in Bales of Silk, left a large Sum in a Merchant's Hands at *Venice*, and another considerable Sum at *Naples*, and took Bills of Exchange for a great deal too; and yet we came with such a Cargoe to *London*, as few *American* Merchants had done for some Years; for we loaded in two Ships seventy three Bales of thrown Silk, besides thirteen Bales of wrought Silks from the Dutchy of *Milan*, shipt at *Genoa*; with all which I arrived safely, and some time after married my faithful Protectress, *William*'s Sister, with whom I am much more happy than I deserve.

And now, having so plainly told you, that I am come to *England*, after I have so boldly own'd what Life I have led abroad, 'tis Time to leave off, and say no more for the present, lest some should be willing to inquire too nicely after

Your Old Friend,

CAPTAIN BOB.

APPENDIX

The Naked White Man

There is an admirable discussion of the 'naked white man' episode in *Captain Singleton* in chapter 3 of Peter Knox-Shaw's *The Explorer in English Fiction* (London, 1987), and also of the real-life figure it was based on, a factor of the Royal African Company named John Freeman who was dismissed in 1706 for failing to prevent the capture of the Company's fort at Sherbro (in Sierra Leone) by the French. Knox-Shaw draws on numerous items in the registers of the Company now available in the National Archives, and I will quote a paragraph or two of his account.

> John Freeman's dismissal and recrimination for arbitrary conduct is mentioned in a history of the Royal African Company by K. G. Davies; and the archives of this infamous institution contain not only the correspondence over his period of service at Sherbro (1702–6) but several reports of subsequent adventure up to his death in Sierra Leone five years later ...
>
> Quite apart from the complaints that he abandoned an island to the French or often cursed the Company, vowing 'he came not over to defend or Fight for [its] Interest', the testimony to Freeman's misconduct certainly mounts up. At different times he is accused of embezzling diet-money by keeping his men on short commons, of dealing – against prescription – with freelance traders or the Dutch, of underhand hoarding and downright theft. More tellingly perhaps, a junior member seconded to his station instantly returned, alluding darkly to the manager's 'unlawful ways'. After his dismissal and year in London, Freeman resumed trade at Sherbro in opposition to the Crown, but despite his boast that no one enjoyed such an 'Interest among the Natives as himself', blurted out in the course of a pathetic appeal for re-employment, he seems to have met with little success. There can be no reason to doubt the sober asides that now sparsely punctuate the flow of company business. We hear of 'Mr. Freeman and his gang' preparing to convert ships, or 'reflecting scandalously' on their rivals in an attempt to win

over former colleagues. One defects; but Freeman is forced to shift the scene of his ambitions.

> He dares not be seen in Sherbro River – he is gone to Serraleon and builds houses tho' Ready dayly to be murdered by ye Country people for his base behaviour.

No details are supplied, but there is mention later of Freeman's setting fire to a tribal settlement. The rest of his life is covered in three sentences, each separated by over a year:

> Mr. Freeman has lost his interest in the river ...
>
> Mr. Freeman has several small vessels going to decay ...
>
> Mr. Freeman died ye 3rd of December.

As mentioned in the Introduction (p. 5), there is a striking passage about Freeman in the *Atlas Maritimus & Commercialis* of 1728 (pp. 251–2), which runs as follows:

> There was an *English* Gentleman in the Service of the *Guinea* Company whom I personally knew, who being put out of his employ by the Company, and afterwards entertain'd in Opposition to them by some separate Traders, presum'd so much upon his Interest with the Country *Negroes*, as to put himself a little too far into their Power; here they did not think fit to let him return, but kept him Prisoner many Months, us'd him very ill, and upon every Occasion of dislike threatned to sacrifice him.
>
> Tired with this Usage, tho not able to get away from them, yet he so well manag'd them, that they did not kill him; and after some time he made his Escape farther into the Country from the People he was at first among, and so farther and farther till he was got near 500 miles from the shore. And as he said afterwards, he might have gone as far upwards as he would, but found no possibility to come down towards the Sea side: Till at length seeing no hope of ever returning, he took up in a little *Indian* village or Town, where he found the People kind, and willing to let him live among them: And there he resolv'd to end his Days.
>
> Here he lived near eight Years, tho he knew not but by the returns of the Sun to the Zenith, how to reckon his Time. Having worn out all his clothes, and being in no condition to receive more, he gradually accustom'd himself to go naked, without any regret at all; the People where he then was, both Men and Women, doing the same; And here he employ'd himself as well as he could, in planting such Roots as the Country produced, and hunting to procure himself Food, tho he could never arrive to such Dexterity, by shooting with Bow and Arrow, as to kill anything either Bird or Beast; but he found means by some ingenious Turns, to do such things for his *Negro* Neighbours, that they in return gave him Shares with them in their Booty.
>
> At other times he pick'd up Gold Dust among the small Brooks, which issued out of the Mountains upon the Winter Rains, till he had laid up about the quantity of eight Pound weight, but knew not how to convey it to the

Sea side, where he might have dispos'd of it for Clothes and necessary Things: Nor had he anything so much as to put it in, to keep it together, but some large Shells, like the Scollop Fish Shell, which he found in the Waters: And in these he preserved it, tho without so much as hope of ever conversing with Christians again, or of disposing it to his Advantage.

After eight Years living in this disconsolate Condition, and almost grown stupid and senseless with the Misery he was in, he was one Morning surpriz'd with the Noise of a Gun, a thing which he had not heard for some Years before: for the *Negroes* had no such thing among them, at least not at that remote distance from the Sea. At this Noise he started out of his Hut to see what it should be; but hearing no more of it, he stoop'd down to do something to his Garden Stuff in his little Plantation near his Hut; presently after which he thought he heard the Voices of Men at a distance, which did not talk the *Negro* Language: upon which turning himself a little about, he saw thirteen Men clothed, and white, so that he presently knew them to be *Europeans* and Christians. They had every Man a Fuzee or Musket, with some Baggage in Skins, like Knapsacks, hanging over their Shoulders; They had no Shoes, but had their Feet wrapt in Skins like Deer Skins; and it was apparent they had travell'd a great way, but from whence or which way going he could not imagine.

As he was so inexpressibly surpriz'd with the Sight, he was not able to speak for some time, but spread out his hands by way of admiration, as if questioning whether they really were Men, or whether it was a Vision.

If he was surpriz'd on the one hand, they were astonish'd on the other, being over-glad to see a white Man in that remote part of the World: in that naked and despicable Condition he appear'd strangely almost red, yet was so discolour'd by being expos'd to the excessive Heats of the Climate, that it was tann'd like Leather, scaly and scrophulous, being blister'd with the Sun, and dried again to a hardness like the Callus of a heal'd wound: His Beard was grown to a frightful length, and being of no form, was ugly not graceful: his Body all very hairy, and the Hair of his Head hung down almost for a Covering to him.

In a word, not the fable of *Orson*, the Brother of *Valentine*,[1] could represent a wild Man more to the purpose, than Mr. *Freeman* appear'd to them, (for that was his Name).

After the first Transports on both sides were over, let any one judge what an addition it was to his Joy, when all the Men speaking *Portuguese*, he found one of them also speak in *English*, and another in *Latin*, which he likewise understood very well.

---

1 The story of the twin brothers Valentine and Orson, nephews of King Pepin, first appeared in a medieval French romance. The brothers are separated in childhood, Orson being carried off by a bear and brought up as a wild man. Valentine, however, having become a knight, finds him, conquers him, and tames him.

How accurate a Description both of the Country and the People could this Person have given, had he lived to come to *England*. But Providence disposed otherwise of him; for after conducting the Strangers not only thro' the several Nations of *Negroes* which he had been among, but others, and whom those Men, being well arm'd, were able to deal with, and to preserve themselves and him; I say, after he had guided them, and they guarded him to one of the Portuguese Settlements, he died there.

From this Man's Story it was that I gave the Account above, how the Elephants Teeth, which are brought over in so great Quantities, are procured, and describ'd to you the Place where they are found: It was about three Days Journey from the Spot where this unhappy Man had taken up his Stand, and where they found him, that the vast great Place I there mention'd is situated; it should not be called a Desart, he said, because it was not a sandy or barren Soil; but yet it might seem to be so, as it was uninhabited. There were some Woods and Coppices, or wild Places, upon it, but not many; and the Surface yielded good Grass in many places, having several small Rivulets of Water runnng, some one way, some another: Which I take notice of again here, to intimate that the Elephants are chiefly found in such open Places, where good Pasture and good Water is to be had, and not among thick Woods and cover'd Places, as some have weakly suggested: Their Bulk naturally intimating that the Woods must be cumbersome and uneasy to them, and that they rather covet the open Country, provided they have grass to eat, for the Grass, not Boughs of Trees is their stated Food. And this is the Plain where, according to my former Account, those Travellers pass'd over, and the Description of which this poor unhappy Exile confirm'd. He told them he very seldom saw any Elephants there, no not on the Plain it self; yet he confirm'd that the Teeth were always found scatter'd about over the whole Plain, in so much that he thought the Number was prodigious. He added that to this Plain the *Negroes* often travell'd to fetch large Teeth, and that he had been with them there, and had help'd to carry them, when four or five *Negroes* would set their Shoulders to one Tooth, till they gall'd themelves so as not to able to carry it at all, and then throw it down and leave it, and get more help, being a Fortnight or better dragging it down to the Sea side; till at length he taught them how to make Rafts of Wood in the Winter or rainy Seasons, and so, when the Waters were high enough, to carry 10 or 20 large Teeth at a time, bringing to a place where they had Canoes upon the *Rio Cobre*, and another River which he named to them; but we find no name of that kind in use: And then they paddled them down in their Canoes one or two at a time.

What a Treasure must be upon that Desart! and what prodigious Numbers of Elephants must be found upon those wild abandon'd Plains! After this it seems he carried the men to his Hut, gave them what little Provisions he had; and they gave him some spare Clothes to cover him, and in particular an old chequer'd Linen Shirt and a pair of Drawers, which was almost as much clothing as he desir'd.

He then entertain'd them so, as that he kept them till the rainy Season was over; they also assisting him with their Fire Arms, so that they killed Provisions sufficient for them all during the wet months. And then leading them among the Rivers under the Mountains and Water-falls, after the Rains and Floods were ceas'd, he brought them to some Places, where they pick'd up in about two Months more, so much Gold, that they divided at last above 23 Pound weight a Man; For they made a solemn Covenant to divide it equally.

Thus far the Account is suitable to our present Description of the Country, and may I believe be depended upon for fact, I mean so far as it relates to the Product and Customs of the Place, and of the People. There is a larger Account of the Journey of the Thirteen *Portuguese* before they met with this white Man; which as it is too long for this place, so not relating to the Description of this part of the Country, I omit it.

The *Atlas Maritimus & Commercialis* is a lengthy and admirably organised verbal account, country by country, of the world's coasts and trading systems, accompanied by a collection of sailing charts (by Nathaniel Cutler). Its information is drawn from many published and unpublished sources, and since the work contains lengthy quotations from several of Defoe's published writings it is sometimes claimed that he was the editor – or even the author – of the whole vast compilation. (For a discussion of this possibility, see the entry in P. N. Furbank and W. R. Owens, *A Critical Bibliography of Daniel Defoe* (London, 1998), pp. 276–9.)

In the present extract there is nothing in the context to indicate who the 'I', in the words 'whom I personally knew', is; but the 'larger Account of the Journey of the Thirteen *Portuguese*' mentioned in the final sentence could well be a reference to *Captain Singleton*. The account of Freeman in the *Atlas Maritimus* is evidently well informed and will be seen to correspond at various points with the references to him in the Royal African Company's registers (quoted by Knox-Shaw, above, pp. 227–8). On the other hand, unlike those, it gives no suggestion that Freeman was a scoundrel. Thus it must be regarded as a work of fiction, a 'retelling with a difference' of the incident in Defoe's *Captain Singleton*, whether by Defoe himself or by another writer.

EXPLANATORY NOTES

The following abbreviation is used throughout the explanatory notes:

OCCS   *The Oxford Companion to Ships and the Sea*, ed. I. C. Dear and
            P. Kemp (2nd edn, Oxford, 2005)

The Life, Adventures, and Pyracies, of the Famous Captain Singleton was adver-
tised as published 'this day' in the *St. James's Post* for 3–6 June 1720.

page
17   1   *Paraguay*: canoe.
20   2   *the Strolling Trade*: One of the meanings of to 'stroll' is to rove, like a
            beggar or gipsy, or a pirate.
        3   *minded my Book*: became proficient in reading.
        4   *shifted by Passes*: moved from one parish to another by means of an offi-
            cial licence.
        5   *Busselton*: Busselton (or Buselton) was the site of an important naval
            shipyard.
        6   *Turks*: The commanders and fighting men, as distinct from the crew, of
            the privateeering ships of Algiers, Tripoli and Tunis would have been
            Turkish-appointed janissaries. Otherwise these three 'regencies' were
            only loosely associated with the Turkish empire, though the sobriquet
            'Turks' was widely used both for praise and blame. In the *Atlas Mariti-
            mus & Commercialis* of 1728, p. 242, we read: 'The Algerines, Tuniseens
            and Tripolins are fond of being call'd *Turks* or *Mussulmans*, not *Moors*,
            and take it very ill to be call'd *Moors*.'
21   7   *dull*: downcast.
        8   *Gallion*: a large, heavily armed vessel, usually with four decks, used by
            the Spanish and Portugese to transport treasure.
        9   *Carrack*: a large ship of burden used by the Portugese for their trade
            with the East Indies.
        10 *Succades*: candied fruit.
22   11 *Bays*: i.e. baize.
        12 *Artist*: man of skill.

page
22   13 *Moydores*: A moidore was a gold coin of Portugal current in the earlier eighteenth century, being the equivalent of 4,000 *reis*.

        14 *Adventure*: financial venture.

        15 *Cape de Bona Speranza*: Cape of Good Hope.

24   16 *it passed but a little, but*: It came near to it that.

        17 *simply*: ignorantly, foolishly.

25   18 *soon satisfied*: i.e. that he was not circumcised (which would be the sign of a Muslim).

        19 *Ormus*: (now Hormuz) a great market for pearls and gems, in the Persian Gulf.

        20 *Chains*: forced service.

27   21 *Part*: career, situation.

        22 *Dollars*: The dollar was the English name for the Spanish *peso* or 'piece of eight'.

28   23 *stand in*: make for the shore.

29   24 *Road*: a sheltered piece of water near the shore.

        25 *tho' they hanged him*: even if they were to hang him.

30   26 *Capstern*: capstan, a rotating cylinder or barrel pushed by men walking round it, for weighing anchor. It was evidently a place dedicated to punishment.

        27 *Barricado*: railings.

        28 *Juncto's and Cabals*: private alliances and conspiracies.

31   29 *Fire-lock*: a musket fitted with a gunlock in which sparks were produced to ignite the priming.

32   30 *Arrack*: 'In Eastern countries any spirituous liquor of native manufacture; *esp.* that distilled from the fermented sap of the coco-palm' (*OED*).

        31 *Pinnace*: a ship's boat rowed with eight (later sixteen) oars.

35   32 *Go together by the ears*: fight one another.

        33 *chaffering*: bargaining.

        34 *whether*: whither.

36   35 *Pay*: smear or cover with pitch or tar to make them waterproof.

        36 *Bark or Sloop, or Shalloup*: the smaller types of sailing vessel.

        37 *Coast of Malabar*: the southern portion of the west coast of India, from Goa to Cape Comerin.

37   38 *Perspective Glass*: pocket telescope.

38   39 *giving her fresh Way*: enabling her to sail more freely.

        40 *Tossel*: tuft or tassel.

40   41 *cruize*: To 'cruise' had the specific meaning of cruising for plunder.

        42 *broiled*: grilled.

41   43 *Hogshead*: a large cask (of varying capacity).

        44 *Main*: mainland.

42   45 *Flags*: reeds.

        46 *the Tropick*: i.e. of Capricorn.

page

43   47   *Frigates*: a playful name for their canoes.

44   48   *Withes*: bands of tough willow twigs.

          49   *Zanquebar*: Zanzibar.

45   50   *lye close upon a Wind*: keep to a straight course in relation to a wind.

46   51   *carrying two long Poles in their Hands*: There is a more elaborate account of such a practice in *The Farther Adventures of Robinson Crusoe* (*The Novels*, Vol. 2, p. 128). Defoe's source for this may have been an account of a meeting and exchange of gifts with local dignitaries in Madagascar, in *The Voyages & Travels of J. Albert de Mandelslo*, in *The Voyages & Travels of the Ambassadors sent by Frederick Duke of Holstein*, trans. John Davies (London, 1662), p. 254.

47   52   *Plantanes*: The plantain here referred to is 'a tree-like herbaceous plant (*Musa paradisiaca*) closely allied to the Banana' (*OED*).

48   53   *Ketch*: a strongly built two-masted vessel.

          54   *Galliot*: a small galley or boat used for swift navigation.

          55   *Mizen Mast:* the aftermost mast of a three-masted ship.

49   56   *Craddles*: perhaps an alternative spelling of 'cradles'.

51   57   *fair Cast*: hopeful prospect (literally, hopeful throw of the dice).

52   58   *More*: i.e. moor.

53   59   *Nova Zembla*: Novaya Zemlya, an arctic archipelago off the coast of European Russia.

54   60   *Civet Cats*: The civet cat produces a secretion in the anal pouch which is a valuable ingredient in perfumery.

56   61   *great Lake*: see Introduction, p. 4.

57   62   *Chapman*: salesman.

          63   *huff'd him*: treated him with arrogance.

          64   *Fuzee*: a light flintlock musket.

58   65   *the Law of Arms*: It was a generally accepted custom that an enemy who surrendered might save his life by becoming a slave,

63   66   *Ce Seignior*: The Portuguese for 'yes' is, in fact, *sim*.

64   67   *antick*: grotesque.

65   68   *Quilloa*: an earlier name for the River Rufifi, in present-day Tanzania.

67   69   *Flags*: see note 45 above.

69   70   *People behind who came from the Sun*: We may compare this passage about native sun-worshippers with one in Hakluyt, *Principal Navigations* (12 vols, Glasgow, 1903–5), vol. 9.

70   71   *Aesop's Basket of Bread*: In the fable, Aesop's master has ordered him and other servants to go on a journey, and when they are dividing up their burdens Aesop says he wants the lightest, but puzzles his fellow-servants by choosing the bread-basket, which is the heaviest. Or at least, it is so until dinner-time, when it grows distinctly lighter, and by the time they have had supper it weighs nothing.

71   72   *flash in the Pan*: 'an explosion of gunpowder without any communication beyond the touch-hole' (*OED*).

page

77   73 *a vast howling Wilderness*: cf. Deuteronomy 32:10: 'He found him in a desert land, and in the waste howling wilderness.'

80   74 *Bass*: flexible fibrous bark.

82   75 *a great Lake*: This lake appeared in seventeenth-century maps as Lake Zaffran.

84   76 *to his Trumps*: to his last expedient.

86   77 *Wild-fire*: a highly inflammable composition used in warfare.

87   78 *Carts*: i.e. charts.

89   79 *Makebait*: a breeder of strife.

       80 *upon one Bottom*: partners in the same concern.

90   81 *Spar*: one of a number of crystalline minerals admitting of easy cleavage.

93   82 *Clutter*: confusion, hubbub.

94   83 *Andronicus*: (or rather, Androcles.) As a runaway slave, he did a lion a good service by extracting a thorn from his paw, and when later he is forced to fight a lion in the Roman arena his adversary proves to be the same one and treats him with love and gratitude. The story is related in Aulus Gellius's *Noctes Atticae*.

97   84 *the sons of Noah*: After the building of the Tower of Babel, the sons of Noah, Shem, Ham and Japeth, supposedly spread over the whole earth, founding the various divisions of humankind.

       85 *Forestaff*: instrument for taking the altitude of the sun (also known as a 'cross-staff').

99   86 *the Rio Grande*: the Niger.

100   87 *Indians*: Defoe sometimes uses the name 'Indians' as a generic term for natives of whatever country. Cf. *Robinson Crusoe* in *The Novels*, Vol. 1, p. 118: 'we carried the Hatchets for Traffick with the *Indians*'.

101   88 *Bait*: food, refreshment.

       89 *to make that salt Water fresh*: This desalination technique was employed by the buccaneers.

102   90 *ferine*: a synonym for 'wild'.

104   91 *Meridian*: longitudinal.

105   92 *spreading*: spreading through.

108   93 *a White Man*: see Introduction, pp. 4–5, and Appendix, pp. 227–31.

110   94 *politick*: hard-headed, cunning.

       95 *Cowries*: the shell of *Cypraea moneta*, used as currency in Asia and Africa.

       96 *artificially*: expertly.

       97 *English Guiney Company*: another name for the Royal African Company.

       98 *Separate Traders*: traders not belonging to the Royal African Company.

114   99 *Pompions*: pumpkins.

115 100 *spangled*: i.e. glittering like spangles.

116 101 *Pistole*: a Spanish gold coin, equivalent to the French *louis*.

page

117 102 *Proveditor*: purveyor, steward.

120 103 *find us in*: supply us with.

104 *Dutch Factory*: a 'factory' was the name for a trading station.

121 105 *Cape Coast Castle*: This was a fortified building on the coast of present-day Ghana, serving as (in the words of one of its governors) 'the grand emporium of the British slave-trade'. It was erected in 1664 and belonged to the Royal African Company. See William St Clair, *The Grand Slave Emporium* (London, 2006).

106 *the Groyn*: another name for Corunna.

123 107 *call'd young Captain Kid*: i.e. after the notorious pirate William Kid, executed in 1701.

108 *Barco Longo's*: longboats.

109 *Runlets*: casks.

110 *Puncheons*: A puncheon is 'a large cask for liquids, fish, etc.' (*OED*).

111 *Cartagena*: in present-day Colombia.

124 112 *Brigantine*: a two-masted vessel, equipped both for sail and oar, enlarged for purposes of piracy and espionage, etc.

113 *Frigat-built ship*: A frigate was 'a light and swift vessel, originally built rowing, afterwards for sailing' (*OED*).

114 *Bay of Campeachy*: i.e. Campeachy Bay, on the coast of Yucatan in the Gulf of Mexico, where, according to the *Atlas Maritimus* (p. 301), 'our *English* Sailors (Rogues I should say) cut Logwood, and from which Trade they often turn *Buccaneers*, and of late Pirates and High Sea Robbers'.

115 *Culverdine*: a sea gun of large bore and long range.

125 116 *Birth*: i.e. berth.

117 *a Dram*: a drink.

126 118 *embay'd*: shut in.

119 *St. Martha*: Santa Marta, on the northern coast of Colombia.

127 120 *Jury Fore-Top-Mast*: a makeshift foretop-mast.

121 *unmore*: unmoor.

122 *Island of Si—*: unidentified.

123 *in the Brails*: Brails are the small ropes fastened to the edges of sails to truss them up before furling (*OED*).

128 124 *clewed them up*: drew them up to the yard, in preparation for furling.

125 *crowd*: press.

126 *Larboard tacks*: Larboard is the side of a vessel to the left hand of someone looking from the stern to the bows. (It is nowadays called the 'port' side, to distinguish it more clearly from its opposite, 'starboard'.) 'Tacks are the ropes or chains securing to the ship's side the windward clews' (*OED*).

127 *Top-gallant Sails*: The topgallant sail was the sail set from the topgallant yard of a square-rigger (*OCSS*).

237

page

128   128   *Rope-Yarns*: 'A rope-yarn is a single yarn forming part of a strand in a rope' (*OED*).

129   129   *Main and Fore-Yards*: the yards on which the mainsail is extended and the lowest yards on the foremast.

       130   *Geers*: rigging.

       131   *struck* surrendered.

       132   *Top-Mast*: a smaller mast fixed on the top of a lower one.

130   133   *Calenture*: a species of fever, inducing hallucinations, suffered by sailors in tropical seas.

131   134   *luffed up*: sailed nearer to the wind.

       135   *under our Lee*: under the side of their ship away from the wind.

       136   *hard a Weather*: 'Hard', in a nautical sense, means 'to the extreme limit'.

       137   *Lee Braces*: Braces are the ropes rove to the end of the yards in a square-rigged ship, to brace or swing them.

       138   *Hawse*: the part of a ship's bows in which the hawse-holes are cut for the cables to pass through (*OED*).

       139   *Boltsprit*: obsolete spelling of 'bowsprit'.

       140   *Shrouds*: 'a set of ropes, usually in pairs, leading from the head of a mast and serving to relieve the latter of lateral strain' (*OED*).

       141   *steerage*: a large living space below the quarterdeck and immediately before the bulkhead of the great cabin.

132   142   *Forecastle*: a short raised deck forward.

       143   *Grenadoes*: grenades.

       144   *their Ancient struck*: their ensign hauled down.

133   145   *Captain Avery*: Henry Avery the famous pirate (known also as Bridgeman and as 'Long Ben') was born in Devonshire and sailed as mate in several trading voyages in the early 1690s. He served as first mate aboard the *Duke*, a ship built at Bristol for the Spanish service, and while this vessel was anchored at Corunna waiting to take on passengers, he concerted a mutiny, tempting his fellow-conspirators with the wealth they might lay hands on off the coast of India, and they succeeded in seizing the ship and putting to sea while the captain was still asleep. This was the first episode of his piratical career. His second, and very famous, achievement was, in 1695, to capture one of the Great Mogul's ships in the Arabian Sea, loaded with treasure and carrying persons from the Mogul's court, among them the Mogul's own daughter. For this purpose Avery had joined forces with two sloops, near Madagascar, but he managed to trick them out of their share of the treasure, and he and his own crew made their way to New England, where they exchanged their great ship for a smaller one to divert suspicion. They were intending to find buyers for the Mogul's diamonds and settle peaceably on the proceeds for the rest of their life. However, the project proved more difficult and dangerous than they had foreseen,

and Avery escaped with a few companions to Ireland. Here he attempted, again unsuccessfully, to dispose of their loot by covert negotiations with some merchants, who defrauded him, and he appears to have died in poverty, 'not being worth as much as would buy his Coffin', though it is not certain when or where.

Some of Avery's crew were tried *in absentia* for theft in 1696, amid great publicity, and as a result the events of his brief career were exaggerated into the myth of a fabulous pirate commonwealth in a tropical paradise on Madagascar, negotiating as an equal with the English crown. (See *A General History of the Pyrates* (1724), ed. Manuel Schonhorn (London, 1972), pp. xviii–xix and 49–62.) Singleton several times alludes to this, e.g. on p. 133: 'I had heard some flaming Stories of Captain Avery, and the fine things he had done in the *Indies*, which were doubled and doubled even Ten Thousand-fold'.

133 146 *hankered*: lingered.

134 147 *chopt about*: veered.

148 *Pareil*: obsolete spelling of 'parrel' or 'parral', a device to attach a yard to the masts of a square-rigger.

149 *flown*: lying loose.

150 *with the wind quartering*: with the wind steady behind it.

151 *Fore-chains*: Chains (or chain-wales) were wooden projections used to carry the lower shrouds of a mast clear of a ship's side.

152 *enter her Men in the Waste*: The 'waste' or waist was the part of the upper deck between the fore- and mainmasts (*OCSS*).

135 153 *lay'd her abroad*: boarded her.

136 154 *Round-house*: 'a name give to square or rectangular cabins built on the quarter-deck of passenger ships and East Indiamen … They were called round because one could walk round them' (*OCSS*).

139 155 *Crows*: crowbars.

140 156 *at a Dead-lift*: when extreme effort was called for.

141 157 *Cape de St. Thomas*: Cape Sao Tomé, a headland on the Atlantic in Rio de Janeiro State, Brazil.

158 *Isles de Tuberon*: the name is perhaps a variant of Tubarao.

142 159 *obliged to use great Caution*: Unlicensed trade in slaves was illegal.

160 *weigh*: raise his anchor and leave.

143 161 *would not command her as a Fregat*: i.e. as a Quaker, he would not take charge of her as a fighting vessel.

162 *Purchase*: plunder.

163 *Paterero's*: cannonades, or small mortars.

144 164 *upon the Account*: Halliday Sparling, in his edition of the novel (London, 1887), explains this phrase as deriving 'From the men agreeing not for wages, but for shares in the proceeds'.

145 165 *Brewes*: brewis, or broth.

page

146 166 *Fort St. George*: Madras.

167 *Streight of Babelmandel*: The Strait of Bab El Mandel joins the Red Sea to the Gulf of Aden.

147 168 *Port Dauphin*: Now Port Louis, north of Tamatave.

148 169 *Jonk*: i.e. junk, a type of vessel common in the China seas.

170 *Saffra's*: couches.

171 *Dofar in Arabia*: Defoe is perhaps referring to Doha, now known as Qatar.

172 *Mocha*: port on the Red Sea, 85 km north-west of the Strait of Bab El Mandel.

149 173 *Cape Guarde Foy*: Guardafuy, on the coast of Somalia.

174 *chopp'd*: stumbled.

175 *great Bay of Mangahelly*: in the northern part of Madagascar.

152 176 *Captain Avery*: see note 145 above.

177 *Launch*: launching platform or slide.

155 178 *Judda*: Jedda.

179 *Buccanier Words*: abusive language.

180 *sorted with*: joined.

181 *minded our Hits*: made the most of our opportunities.

156 182 *simple*: foolish.

183 *Trade*: trade wind.

184 *Ancient and Pendant*: ensign and pennant.

185 *black Flag with two cross Daggers*: perhaps a predecessor of the classic pirate flag of a skull and crossbones.

157 186 *Batavia*: city and province in the Dutch East Indies, on the north-west coast of Java.

187 *Sundy*: the Sunda strait between Java and Sumatra.

159 188 *Tack at the Cat-head*: The *OCSS* defines 'cathead' as 'a heavy piece of curved timber projecting from each bow of a ship for the purpose of holding anchors'.

189 *Fort St. David*: Cuddalore.

190 *Romalls*: a romal is a silk or cotton handkerchief.

191 *river Hugely*: (Hugli Hooghly or Hoogly) the most important of the mouths of the Ganges.

160 192 *Guams*: perhaps an alternative spelling of yams.

193 *Amboyna*: an island and town in the Moluccas in which Portuguese, English and Dutch forts were established in the sixteenth and seventeenth centuries. It was the scene of a notorious massacre of some Englishmen by the Dutch in 1623, here alluded to.

194 *Banda Island or Islands*: The Banda islands are a group in the southern Moluccas.

161 195 *Ternate*: town and island in the Moluccas, an exporter of spices.

196 *Hand*: furl.

page
162 197 *unbent*: untied.

198 *Tallow'd*: i.e. its keel greased.

199 *Jealousy*: suspicion.

200 *Island of Dumas*: an island in the Moluccas.

201 *stood away large*: Halliday Sparling explains this in his edition (London, 1887) as 'Going with the wind free when the studding sails will draw'.

163 202 *Fore-sheet*: The rope by which the lee corner of the foresail is kept in place (*OED*).

203 *Child of Shadwell, or Francis Spira*: John Child (d. 1684) and Francesco Spira (d. 1548) became famous as examples of the horrors of religious despair. Spira, a lawyer from Padua, renounced his Protestant faith under threat of torture and returned to Catholicism. His feelings of guilt led to severe depression, which lasted for seven years before his death (possibly by his own hand). Nathaniel Bacon's *Relation of the Fearfull Estate of Francis Spira*, first published in 1638, ran through eleven editions before the end of the seventeenth century. Child, a former Baptist and colleague of John Bunyan, conformed to the Church of England after the Restoration and moved to London, where he published pamphlets attacking Dissenters. In the early 1680s he fell into a state of despondency, believing that he had committed the unpardonable sin, and hanged himself. The story of his suicide was often published along with that of Spira's.

164 204 *Head*: the bows.

205 *Island of Gilolo*: This perhaps refers to the island now known as Waiego.

206 *Formosa*: the present-day Taiwan.

165 207 *Laconia*: i.e. Luzon.

167 208 *Poop*: stern.

169 209 *Straits of Sundy*: the Sunda strait between Java and Sumatra.

173 210 *Clutter*: clatter.

175 211 *Medium*: expedient.

179 212 *black Flag ... bloody Flag*: The black flag signified a pirate ship and the red flag the warning that no 'quarter' would be given.

213 *made a clear Ship*: disentangled cables and cordage.

214 *struck*: surrendered.

215 *Bantam*: seaport of Japan.

182 216 *came home*: were dislodged.

217 *Sheet Anchor*: an additional anchor carried on large ships for security in case the bower anchors fail to hold.

184 218 *Knox*: see p. 184 above and note 225 below.

219 *touched*: persuaded.

220 *turned short with*: spoke irritably to.

185 221 *stubbs*: short, thick nails.

193 222 *Brimstone*: sulphur.

241

page
193 223 *Waste-boards*: boards protecting the 'waist' of the boat.

194 224 *sheer'd*: approached obliquely to.

196 225 *His Words are as follows*: Pages 196–203 are condensed from pages 117–65 of Robert Knox's *An Historical Relation of the Island Ceylon, in the East-Indies* (London, 1681). A great proportion is given in Knox's own words, though here and there Defoe adds a linking passage. I have not thought it necessary to annotate all of the Ceylonese place names mentioned by Knox, since the information does not come directly from Defoe.

197 226 *Cheeks*: pieces of timber to be bolted to the mast below the masthead to support the trestle trees.

227 *spending*: passing.

198 228 *Candi*: (or Kandy) formerly the capital of Ceylon.

229 *Pagoda*: A pagoda was a gold or silver coin current in South India.

230 *The Practice of Piety*: by Lewis Bayley (d. 1631), a Puritan clergyman and later Bishop of Bangor. The date of the first edition is unknown; a third edition appeared in 1631. It became one of the most popular works of the seventeenth century and was translated into several other languages.

231 *Mr. Rogers's Seven Treatises*: Richard Rogers, *Seven Treatises Leading and Guiding to True Happiness* (1603).

232 *Elijah's Petition*: see 1 Kings 19:4: 'But he himself went a day's journey into the wilderness, and came and sat down under a juniper tree; and he requested for himself that he might die; and said, It is enough; now, O LORD, take away my life; for I am not better than my fathers'.

199 233 *Columbo*: Colombo.

234 *Angle*: fishing rod.

235 *slight it*: show no interest in it.

200 236 *Watches*: surveillance stations.

201 237 *Betel*: the leaf of a plant wrapped round parings of the areca nut, used as a masticatory.

202 238 *Chiangulays*: wild men of Ceylon.

203 239 *Bramans*: Brahmins.

240 *English Coast*: the Coromandel coast of India, i.e. the east coast, between Cape Calimore and the mouth of the Kistna river.

241 *Letters of Mart*: see Introduction, p. 6.

204 242 *Marmagoon*: Marmagoa, a seaport town in the Portuguese territory of Goa.

243 *Salsat*: This perhaps refers to Salsette, one of the islands on which Mumbai stands.

244 *curled Work*: elaborate ornamentation.

245 *Surat*: a port near Mumbai. It was an important trading centre for the East India Company.

page

205   246   *Company's Servants*: employees of the East India Company.

           247   *Mace*: a spice consisting of the dried outer covering of the nutmeg (*OED*).

206   248   *Chaps*: traders.

207   249   *Quarter*: one of the two after-parts of the ship.

           250   *Gunnel*: gunwale.

211   251   *Bassora*: Basra.

212   252   *Gombaroon*: a great entrepôt for trade with India and China, near the mouth of the Persian Gulf. In the *Atlas Maritimus* it is spelt Gomberoon.

213   253   *Frailes*: baskets made of rushes.

214   254   *George the Reformade*: A 'reformade' was a Christian recreant.

           255   *vert*: convert or invest.

           256   *the great River*: the Tigris, one of the two large rivers of Iraq. It rises in the Taurus mountains in Turkey, flows through Baghdad and is joined by the Euphrates 80 km north-west of Basra to form the Shatt-al-Arab.

216   257   *pretend*: lay claim.

220   258   *Scanderoon*: This name seems, rather, to apply to Iskenderun, the main port of Aleppo, in the gulf of the same name.

221   259   *passing for Two Armenian Merchants … Grecians*: We may compare Defoe's *The Conduct of Christians Made the Sport of Infidels* (1717) in *Satire, Fantasy and Writings on the Supernatural* (London, 2005), Vol. 5, ed. David Blewett, p. 25, describing how Kara Selym Oglan 'took his first Tour thro' *France* and *Germany*, going in the Habit of an *Armenian Merchant*, or as we vulgarly stile them, a *Grecian*'.

222   260   *back'd*: in legal terms, 'accepted'.

223   261   *increase her Figure*: live a more ostentatious life.

224   262   *stroled*: see note 2 above.

TEXTUAL NOTES

The textual policy for *The Novels of Daniel Defoe* is described in the General Editors' Preface printed in Vol. 1, pp. 3–4. As is explained there, the normal practice throughout the edition is to adopt as copy-text the earliest available edition, emending this only in the case of obvious corrections, or where readings in later editions may be judged to be authorial.

Jonathan Hill, in an article 'Defoe's *Singleton?*', *Papers of the Bibliographical Society of America*, 84 (1990), pp. 285–96, records forty-four manuscript emendations in a copy of the first edition, which, he says, 'on the basis of both stylistic and handwriting evidence seem to be those of Defoe himself'. Quite a few of these emendations strike one as distinct, if slight, improvements to the sense of the original, though none of them absolutely imperative. However, the theory that they were made by Defoe himself runs up against a serious objection. For the emender on four occasions emends 'to', in the expression 'bring to', to 'too' giving the impression that he does not realise that 'bring to' (i.e. bring to a standstill) – especially in a nautical context – is perfectly good English. (See *OED*, s.v. 'bring'.) This argues strongly against the emendations being authorial; and, as for the handwriting evidence, experience teaches one that, as regards Defoe's period, it is difficult conclusively to identify short pieces of handwriting.

The copy-text for the present edition is the first edition of 1720, the only one (other than the serial version in the Exeter *Post-Master*, 4 November 1720 to 10 November 1721) to appear in Defoe's lifetime. Emendations are as follows (the numbers in the left-hand column refer to the Pickering & Chatto page-numbers).

115a full of Sand,] full Sand,
115b of] off
119a their] there
138a tell what, if] tell. What if
151a so that it] that

245

177a me] CAPT. WILMOT
209a *I,*] *he,*
216a True] Time
218a Life-time since I] Life-time; I
224a no] a